Please remember that this is a library and that it belongs only temporarily to each person who uses it. Be considerate. Do not write in this, or any, library book.

P9-CEN-560

The Female Offender

The Female Offender

Edited by

Laura Crites

Lexington Books

D.C. Heath and Company
Lexington, Massachusetts
Toronto

Grateful acknowledgment is made for permission to reprint the following:

"Hustling for Rights," Marilyn Haft, *The Civil Liberties Review,* © 1974 by the American Civil Liberties Union; "Discriminatory Sentencing of Women Offenders: The Argument for ERA in a Nutshell," Carolyn Engel Temin, *The American Criminal Law Review,* vol. 11:355–372, 1973; "The Etiology of Female Crime: A Review of the Literature," Dorie Klein, *Issues in Criminology,* vol. 8, no. 2, Fall, 1973, pp. 3–30; "Women's Prisons: Laboratories for Penal Reform," Helen Gibson, *Wisconsin Law Review,* 1973, pp. 210–33, © University of Wisconsin; "Women in Southern Jails," Patsy Sims, 1975. Southern Regional Council, Inc., Atlanta.

Library of Congress Cataloging in Publication Data

Main entry under title:
The Female offender.

    Includes index.
    1. Female offenders–United States–Addresses, essays, lectures. 2. Women prisoners–United States–Addresses, essays, lectures. 3. Criminal justice, Administration of–United States–Addresses, essays, lectures. I. Crites, Laura.
HV6046.F373   364.3'74'0973   76-2933
ISBN 0-669-00635-1

Copyright © 1976 by D.C. Heath and Company

All rights reserved. No part of this publication may be reproduced or transmitted in any form or by any means, electronic or mechanical, including photocopy, recording, or any information storage or retrieval system, without permission in writing from the publisher.

Third printing, November 1979.

Published simultaneously in Canada

Printed in the United States of America

International Standard Book Number: 0-669-00635-1

Library of Congress Catalog Card Number: 76-2933

364.374
F329

Contents

34655

Foreword

About ten years ago, with the help of Quakers in eastern Pennsylvania and southern New Jersey, I became acutely aware of the terrible conditions under which women were held in county jails. Sometimes they were incarcerated on second floors with no possibility of ever getting outside; often the quarters were so cramped (women having been an afterthought in the construction of the jail) that they had to be locked in their cells 24 hours a day. In larger jails the women wandered around the cell blocks having nothing to do but play cards and smoke cigarettes. Sometimes they got into fights simply to break the tension and boredom.

The isolation of women from the community (and even from other women in the rural jails) was extreme because they were alloted fewer visiting days than men and could not see their children even then. The few volunteers coming in (teachers, ministers) spent their time with the men, although occasionally women's groups would teach handicrafts and bring food baskets at Christmas.

Work "programs" primarily consisted of scrubbing floors and washing underwear. There were no educational programs because (even if someone had thought of it) traditional education courses were not feasible for eight to ten women, most of whom were there for less than two months.

Equally difficult to obtain were the services of the legal profession. Many women approached their trial without ever having seen a public defender. Since their charges were less serious and since there were fewer women, lawyers went to the men's section of the jail. Because most women were in jail for lack of bail money they obviously could not hire private counsel. Many also had been sentenced to 60 or 90 days by justices of the peace who often had little or no legal training. The jail sentence was given because the women had no money to pay a fine; no defendants were represented by counsel in this kind of proceeding.

Even in the Pennsylvania state prison whose population then averaged 105 women, the only program relevant to their needs was that of the General Equivalency Degree, which certified that they had completed high school. This was only offered from November until May, the rest of the year being devoted to farming and canning of food. Maintenance of the institution — laundry, cooking, scrubbing — doubled as work details and vocational training. Although some women completed several hundred hours of a cosmetology course, they could not become beauticians upon their release since the state licensing board issued licenses only to "women of good moral character."

Large amounts of medication were dispensed by matrons with no medical training. Although the original prescriptions were written by a part-time doctor who made hurried visits to the institution, the purpose of the drugs was

control rather than cure. The minimal psychiatric service available was devoted
to diagnosis, not therapy.

The staff of the state prison was totally absorbed in enforcing rules designed
to prevent or punish homosexual behavior estimated to involve 80 percent of the
population. Institutional records, however, showed that only 5 percent of the
women were classified as homosexual upon admission.

Altogether, prison or jail was a very unhealthy place for women to enter.

What had the women done that made it worth the disruption of families,
the decrease in health, the general demoralization and degradation that incarceration brings? The Pennsylvania Program for Women and Girl Offenders, with
volunteers from the American Association of University Women in Pennsylvania,
conducted the first county jail survey in the country in order to answer this
question.

Although the numbers would differ from state to state, subsequent studies
showed that the findings were generally applicable throughout the United States.

Judges and wardens alike agreed that the women were not particularly
dangerous and we could only agree when we found that about 80 percent were
in jail on disorderly conduct, drunkenness, prostitution, or minor larceny
charges. Of the remaining 20 percent who were charged with felonies, over
40 percent of those were first offenders. Less than 6 percent had long criminal
records. These were not histories building up to more and more serious
offenses, but instead, the criminal records showed multiple arrests for prostitution, drunkenness, drug use, and disorderly conduct — evidence to us of a
deteriorating life rather than a criminal career.

A statewide task force made up of citizens and state and local officials
issued a report to the state attorney general and recommended that drastic
changes be made at the state institution. It also recommended that regional
residential facilities be established for women to substitute for the use of county
jails. Legislation was passed and an additional appropriation for the state Bureau
of Correction's budget was obtained to establish such facilities. Many humanizing,
and a few programmatic changes were made at the state prison, but the intent
of the legislation has not been carried out.

A Release on Recognizance project for women in Philadelphia sensitized
judges to the problems of applying standard guidelines for the pretrial release of
women. Information on the results of court actions helped some judges to re-
think their practices; and today in Philadelphia few women are in jail for prostitution or disorderly conduct. The average daily female population in the
Philadelphia prisons has dropped from 120 to about 65 although the number of
arrests is about the same. In view of the supposed increase in the number of
crimes committed by women, particularly in the urban areas, one might say
that the effort to educate and sensitize the bench in Philadelphia has been successful. That is not true throughout the state, however.

Judges in other counties, having learned of the dreadful county jail facilities, are now sentencing more women to the state prison, which is located in rural, north-central Pennsylvania. The prison population has risen from 105 to about 185 per day. This change means that women are much further from home and now suffer a different kind of isolation. The space available at this minimum-security, cottage-type institution is much greater than that in any county jail but the increase in programs in the state prison has been meager and there still is no meaningful vocational training. Women there are still asking to be provided with better training and job placement. Since the legislation providing regional substitutes for county jails was not carried out, the education of the judges was a mixed success.

It is obvious that political leadership changes as do prison personnel. What appears to be a success one day becomes utter failure the next. New laws do not in and of themselves bring solutions. Laws may not be implemented at all or they may be implemented in weak and meaningless ways.

A new attitude toward women based on heightened consciousness and an understanding of women as human beings is needed before any lasting change will be made. Myths about women in general must be destroyed so that sentences will realistically help the women offenders cope with problems that led to their criminal behavior. The problems that confront all women, but especially those who live in poverty have to be more widely understood. The criminal justice system merely reflects and distills the attitudes of the public, granted that it uses the most authoritarian and punitive filter available.

Ten years ago the available studies of women who had committed crimes generally reflected a male orientation to women and showed little personal experience with the women who were subjects of those books. Even female researches in institutions spent little time with the women themselves except in artificial research situations. Often the research was designed by men, and the women researchers saw little connection between themselves and the women they studied. Today that is changing as evidenced by this book.

Women themselves need to play a leading role in bringing about a change in attitude based on a new awareness. They can help judges reevaluate their expectations for the outcome of prison sentences. Women will have to assume responsibility for monitoring the implementation of legislation and expensive new programs intended to reduce crime. They should share in defining public policy, which must surely include reexamination of our policy on drugs and the crime industry that surrounds drugs. A close scrutiny of the medical profession is in order since that profession has demonstrated a total lack of concern for the physical and mental health of incarcerated women.

Finally, legislators, criminal justice officials, and women must work together to reduce the overuse of the court and correctional system in handling society's deviants. A similar cooperative effort should be used in developing different approaches toward dealing with the problems of troubled human beings. Books such as this, which bring together new viewpoints of women on these problems, are a necessary part of that complex process.

Margery L. Velimesis
Executive Director
Pennsylvania Program for
Women & Girl Offenders

Preface

Although once ignored by studies, glossed over in textbooks, and forgotten by corrections officials, the female offender is now a subject of increasing interest. Much of this new concern stems from statistics indicating a growing female participation in crime. It is also influenced in several respects by the women's movement. For example, popular theorists attribute the increased arrests of women during the last decade to the women's liberation movement, explaining that increased female assertiveness is resulting in more aggressive and violent crimes and that expanded employment of women is leading to increased embezzlement by females.

On the other hand, members of the women's movement are in many respects orchestrating this new concern over female offenders. In the process of descending from the pedestal, women are becoming increasingly aware of the extent to which the "pedestal factor" acted to control their behavior and thwart their protests. They now recognize that the same "factor" is controlling the budding protestations of women offenders, a subpopulation group of females. Just as women in general were discouraged from decrying their limited role out of the belief that they were, after all, advantaged, so, too, were female offenders who, in spite of their exclusion from rehabilitation programs, were assured that they were the favored clients of the criminal justice system.

This book presents a realistic picture of female offenders. Although recognizing that, in some respects, they have been treated more leniently within the system, the articles conclude that, as with women at large, the "pedestal factor" has seldom operated to the advantage of women in the criminal justice system.

Just as significant individuals and groups are credited with the growing success of the women's rights movement, acknowledgment should be made to those who have played and continue to play an important role in the "woman offender movement." A primary force in that movement continues to be Laurel Rans, chairperson of the National Association of Women in Criminal Justice. The Women's Bureau of the Department of Labor for several years patiently pushed the cause of the female offender and continues to contribute in sharing information. Dr. Rosemary Sarri has spoken on many occasions about the discriminatory treatment of juvenile female offenders, sharing her research findings with others. Margery Velimesis, in her landmark study of women offenders in Pennsylvania, influenced many of us to become concerned about these "forgotten offenders." A personal note of gratitude to Laurie Robinson of the American Bar Association and to Catherine Pierce, my very special assistant, in their support of my efforts while director of the American Bar Association's National Resource Center on Women Offenders.

For supporting my efforts in preparation of this anthology, a final word of appreciation to my favorite feminist, my husband, Dr. Timothy Keck, whose concern for the rights and treatment of women in this society occasionally surpasses my own.

Part I

Female Offenders, Past and Present

Introduction to Part I

The female offender—atavism or demented woman? Criminologists searched their repertoires to discover a cause for the criminality of women. The wide range of causal theories and the heavy male bias behind them is surfaced in chapter 1. According to Dorie Klein, Otto Pollak saw the female offender as deceptive and conniving. Freud viewed her as driven by her inferior sexual nature—avenging her lack of penis on men. Cesare Lombroso saw her as a biological atavism, closest to lower forms of nature in her behavior. All theorists discounted possible social or economic motivations for female criminality.

Current theories regarding female deviancy see it as increasingly influenced by social change, specifically, that change bringing women out of the kitchen and into society at large. The stimulus is reputed to be the women's rights movement, and its effect on females is seen in part as increased and more serious criminality. This theory is examined in chapter 2 by Laura Crites, who tests the validity of three popular beliefs: that the women's movement is contributing to increased female criminality; that this criminality is more violent and aggressive in nature; and that female offenders continue to be treated with paternalism by the criminal justice system.

1

The Etiology of Female Crime: A Review of the Literature

Dorie Klein

The criminality of women has long been a neglected subject area of criminology. Many explanations have been advanced for this, such as women's low official rate of crime and delinquency and the preponderance of male theorists in the field. Female criminality has often ended up as a footnote to works on men that purport to be works on criminality in general.

There has been, however, a small group of writings specifically concerned with women and crime. This paper will explore those works concerned with the etiology of female crime and delinquency, beginning with the turn-of-the-century writing of Lombroso and extending to the present. Writers selected to be included have been chosen either for their influence on the field, such as Lombroso, Thomas, Freud, Davis and Pollak, or because they are representative of the kinds of work being published, such as Konopka, Vedder and Somerville, and Cowie, Cowie and Slater. The emphasis is on the continuity between these works, because it is clear that, despite recognizable differences in analytical approaches and specific theories, the authors represent a tradition to a great extent. It is important to understand, therefore, the shared assumptions made by the writers that are used in laying the groundwork for their theories.

The writers see criminality as the result of *individual* characteristics that are only peripherally affected by economic, social and political forces. These characteristics are of a *physiological* or *psychological* nature and are uniformly based on implicit or explicit assumptions about the *inherent nature of women*. This nature is *universal*, rather than existing within a specific historical framework.

Since criminality is seen as an individual activity, rather than as a condition built into existing structures, the focus is on biological, psychological and social factors that would turn a woman toward criminal activity. To do this, the writers create two distinct classes of women: good women who are "normal" noncriminals, and bad women who are criminals, thus taking a moral position that often masquerades as a scientific distinction. The writers, although they may be biological or social determinists to varying degrees, assume that individuals have *choices* between criminal and noncriminal activity. They see persons as

I wish to acknowledge the major contributions made by the Women's Caucus of the School of Criminology, University of California, Berkeley.

Reprinted with permission from "The Etiology of Female Crime: A Review of the Literature," by Dorie Klein, published in *Issues in Criminology*, Vol. 8, No. 2 (Fall, 1973), pp. 3-30, by the graduate students of the School of Criminology at the University of California, Berkeley.

atomistically moving about in a social and political vacuum; many writers use marketplace models for human interaction.

Although the theorists may differ on specific remedies for individual criminality, ranging from sterilization to psychoanalysis (but always stopping far short of social change), the basic thrust is toward *individual adjustment*, whether it be physical or mental, and the frequent model is rehabilitative therapy. Widespread environmental alterations are usually included as casual footnotes to specific plans for individual therapy. Most of the writers are concerned with *social harmony* and the welfare of the existing social structure rather than with the women involved or with women's position in general. None of the writers come from anything near a "feminist" or "radical" perspective.

In *The Female Offender,* originally published in 1903, Lombroso described female criminality as an inherent tendency produced in individuals that could be regarded as biological atavisms, similar to cranial and facial features, and one could expect a withering away of crime if the atavistic people were prohibited from breeding. At this time criminality was widely regarded as a physical ailment, like epilepsy. Today, Cowie, Cowie and Slater (1968) have identified physical traits in girls who have been classified as delinquent, and have concluded that certain traits, such as bigness, may lead to aggressiveness. This theme of physiological characteristics has been developed by a good number of writers in the last seventy years, such as the Gluecks (1934). One sees at the present time a new surge of "biological" theories of criminality; for example, a study involving "violence-prone" women and menstrual cycles has recently been proposed at UCLA.[1]

Thomas, to a certain degree, and Freud extend the physiological explanation of criminality to propose a psychological theory. However, it is critical to understand that these psychological notions are based on assumptions of universal *physiological* traits of women, such as their reproductive instinct and passivity, that are seen as invariably producing certain psychological reactions. Women may be viewed as turning to crime as a *perversion of* or *rebellion against* their *natural feminine roles.* Whether their problems are biological, psychological or social-environmental, the point is always to return them to their roles. Thomas (1907; 1923), for example, points out that poverty might prevent a woman from marrying, whereby she would turn to prostitution as an alternative to carry on her feminine service role. In fact, Davis (1961) discusses prostitution as a parallel illegal institution to marriage. Pollak (1950) discusses how women extend their service roles into criminal activity due to inherent tendencies such as deceitfulness. Freud (1933; Jones, 1961) sees any kind of rebellion as the result of a failure to develop healthy feminine attitudes, such as narcissism, and Konopka (1966) and Vedder and Somerville (1970) apply Freudian thought to the problem of female delinquency.

The specific characteristics ascribed to women's nature and those critical to theories of female criminality are uniformly *sexual* in their nature. Sexuality is seen as the root of female behavior and the problem of crime. Women are defined as sexual beings, as sexual capital in many cases, physiologically, psychologically and socially. This definition *reflects* and *reinforces* the economic position of women as reproductive and domestic workers. It is mirrored in the laws themselves and in their enforcement, which penalize sexual deviations for women and may be more lenient with economic offenses committed by them, in contrast to the treatment given men. The theorists accept the sexual double standard inherent in the law, often noting that "chivalry" protects women, and many of them build notions of the universality of *sex repression* into their explanations of women's position. Women are thus the sexual backbone of civilization.

In setting hegemonic standards of conduct for all women, the theorists define *femininity*, which they equate with healthy femaleness, in classist, racist and sexist terms, using their assumptions of women's nature, specifically their sexuality, to justify what is often in reality merely a defense of the existing order. Lombroso, Thomas and Freud consider the upper-class white woman to be the highest expression of femininity, although she is inferior to the upper-class white man. These standards are adopted by later writers in discussing femininity. To most theorists, women are inherently inferior to men at masculine tasks such as thought and production, and therefore it is logical that their sphere should be reproductive.

Specific characteristics are proposed to bolster this sexual ideology, expressed for example by Freud, such as passivity, emotionalism, narcissism and deceitfulness. In the discussions of criminality, certain theorists, such as Pollak, link female criminality to these traits. Others see criminality as an attempt away from femininity into masculinity, such as Lombroso, although the specifics are often confused. Contradictions can be clearly seen, which are explained by the dual nature of "good" and "bad" women and by the fact that this is a mythology attempting to explain real behavior. Many explanations of what are obviously economically motivated offenses, such as prostitution and shoplifting, are explained in sexual terms, such as prostitution being promiscuity, and shoplifting being "kleptomania" caused by women's inexplicable mental cycles tied to menstruation. Different explanations have to be made for "masculine" crimes, *e.g.*, burglary, and for "feminine" crimes, *e.g.*, shoplifting. Although this distinction crops up consistently, the specifics differ wildly.

The problem is complicated by the lack of knowledge of the epidemiology of female crime, which allows such ideas as "hidden crime," first expressed by Pollak (1950), to take root. The problem must be considered on two levels: women, having been confined to certain tasks and socialized in certain ways, are *in fact* more likely to commit crime related to their lives which are sexually oriented; yet even nonsexual offenses are *explained* in sexual terms by the theorists. The writers ignore the problems of poor and Third World women,

concentrating on affluent white standards of femininity. The experiences of these
overlooked women, who *in fact* constitute a good percentage of women caught
up in the criminal justice system, negate the notions of sexually motivated crime.
These women have real economic needs which are not being met, and in many
cases engage in illegal activities as a viable economic alternative. Furthermore,
chivalry has never been extended to them.

The writers largely ignore the problems of sexism, racism and class, thus
their work is sexist, racist and classist in its implications. Their concern is adjustment of the woman to society, not social change. Hence, they represent a tradition in criminology and carry along a host of assumptions about women and
humanity in general. It is important to explore these assumptions and traditions
in depth in order to understand what kinds of myths have been propagated around
women and crime. The discussions of each writer or writers will focus on these
assumptions and their relevance to criminological theories. These assumptions
of universal, biological/psychological characteristics, of individual responsibility
for crime, of the necessity for maintaining social harmony, and of the benevo-
lence of the state link different theories along a continuum, transcending political labels and minor divergences. The road from Lombroso to the present is
surprisingly straight.

II. Lombroso: "There Must Be Some Anomaly...."

Lombroso's work on female criminality (1920) is important to consider today
despite the fact that his methodology and conclusions have long been successfully
discredited. Later writings on female crime by Thomas, Davis, Pollak and others
use more sophisticated methodologies and may proffer more palatable liberal
theories. However, to varying degrees they rely on those sexual ideologies based
on *implicit* assumptions about the physiological and psychological nature of
women that are *explicit* in Lombroso's work. Reading the work helps to
achieve a better understanding of what kinds of myths have been developed for
women in general and for female crime and deviance in particular.

One specific notion of women offered by Lombroso is women's physiological immobility and psychological passivity, later elaborated by Thomas, Freud
and other writers. Another ascribed characteristic is the Lombrosian notion of
women's adaptability to surroundings and their capacity for survival as being
superior to that of men. A third idea discussed by Lombroso is women's amor-
ality: they are cold and calculating. This is developed by Thomas (1923), who
describes women's manipulation of the male sex urge for ulterior purposes; by
Freud (1933), who sees women as avenging their lack of a penis on men; and
by Pollak (1950), who depicts women as inherently deceitful.

When one looks at these specific traits, one sees contradictions. The myth
of compassionate women clashes with their reputed coldness; their frailness

belies their capacity to survive. One possible explanation for these contradictions
is the duality of sexual ideology with regard to "good" and "bad" women.[2] Bad
women are whores, driven by lust for money or for men, often essentially
"masculine" in their orientation, and perhaps afflicted with a touch of penis
envy. Good women are chaste, "feminine," and usually not prone to criminal
activity. But when they are, they commit crime in a most *ladylike* way such as
poisoning. In more sophisticated theory, all women are seen as having a bit of
both tendencies in them. Therefore, women can be compassionate *and* cold,
frail *and* sturdy, pious *and* amoral, depending on which path they choose to
follow. They are seen as rational (although they are irrational, too!), atomistic
individuals making choices in a vacuum, prompted only by personal, physiologi-
cal/psychological factors. These choices relate only to the *sexual* sphere.
Women have no place in any other sphere. Men, on the other hand, are not held
sexually accountable, although, as Thomas notes (1907), they are held responsible in *economic* matters. Men's sexual freedom is justified by the myth of
masculine, irresistible sex urges. This myth, still worshipped today, is frequently
offered as a rationalization for the existence of prostitution and the double
standard. As Davis maintains, this necessitates the parallel existence of classes
of "good" and "bad" women.

   These dual moralities for the sexes are outgrowths of the economic, political
and social *realities* for men and women. Women are primarily workers within
the family, a critical institution of reproduction and socialization that services
such basic needs as food and shelter. Laws and codes of behavior for women
thus attempt to maintain the smooth functioning of women in that role, which
requires that women act as a conservative force in the continuation of the nuclear
family. Women's main tasks are sexual, and the law embodies sexual limitations
for women, which do not exist for men, such as the prohibition of promiscuity
for girls. This explains why theorists of female criminality are not only concerned
with sexual violations by female offenders, but attempt to account for even
nonsexual offenses, such as prostitution, in sexual terms, *e.g.*, women enter prostitution for sex rather than for money. Such women are not only economic
offenders but are sexual deviants, falling neatly into the category of "bad"
women.

   The works of Lombroso, particularly *The Female Offender* (1920), are a
foremost example of the biological explanation of crime. Lombroso deals
with crime as an atavism, or survival of "primitive" traits in individuals, particularly those of the female and nonwhite races. He theorizes that individuals
develop differentially within sexual and racial limitations which differ hierarch-
ically from the most highly developed, the white men, to the most primitive,
the nonwhite women. Beginning with the assumption that criminals must be
atavistic, he spends a good deal of time comparing the crania, moles, heights,
etc. of convicted criminals and prostitutes with those of normal women. Any
trait that he finds to be more common in the "criminal" group is pronounced

an atavistic trait, such as moles, dark hair, etc., and women with a number of these telltale traits could be regarded as potentially criminal, since they are of the atavistic type. He specifically rejects the idea that some of these traits, for example obesity in prostitutes, could be the *result* of their activities rather than an indicator of their propensity to them. Many of the traits depicted as "anomalies," such as darkness and shortness, and characteristic of certain racial groups, such as the Sicilians, who undoubtedly comprise an oppressed group within Italy and form a large part of the imprisoned population.

Lombroso traces an overall pattern of evolution in the human species that accounts for the uneven development of groups: the white and nonwhite races, males and females, adults and children. Women, children and nonwhites share many traits in common. There are fewer variations in their mental capacities: "even the female criminal is monotonous and uniform compared with her male companion, just as in general woman is inferior to man" (*Ibid.*:122), due to her being "atavistically nearer to her origin than the male" (*Ibid.*:107). The notion of women's mediocrity, or limited range of mental possibilities, is a recurrent one in the writings of the twentieth century. Thomas and others note that women comprise "fewer geniuses, fewer lunatics and fewer morons" (Thomas 1907:45); lacking the imagination to be at either end of the spectrum, they are conformist and dull . . . not due to social, political or economic constraints on their activities, but because of their innate physiological limitations as a sex. Lombroso attributes the lower female rate of criminality to their having fewer anomalies, which is one aspect of their closeness to the lower forms of less differentiated life.

Related characteristics of women are their passivity and conservatism. Lombroso admits that women's traditional sex roles in the family bind them to a more sedentary life. However, he insists that women's passivity can be directly traced to the "immobility of the ovule compared with the zoosperm" (1920:109), falling back on the sexual act in an interesting anticipation of Freud.

Women, like the lower races, have greater powers of endurance and resistance to mental and physical pain than men. Lombroso states: "denizens of female prisoners . . . have reached the age of 90, having lived within those walls since they were 29 without any grave injury to health" (*Ibid.*:125). Denying the humanity of women by denying their capability for suffering justifies exploitation of women's energies by arguing for their suitability to hardship. Lombroso remarks that "a duchess can adapt herself to new surroundings and become a washerwoman much more easily than a man can transform himself under analogous conditions" (*Ibid.*:272). The theme of women's adaptability to physical and social surroundings, which are male initiated, male controlled, and often expressed by saying that women are actually the "stronger" sex, is a persistent thread in writings on women.

Lombroso explains that because women are unable to feel pain, they are

insensitive to the pain of others and lack moral refinement. His blunt denial of
the age-old myth of women's compassion and sensitivity is modified, however,
to take into account women's low crime rate:

Women have many traits in common with children; that their moral sense is
deficient; that they are revengeful, jealous . . . In ordinary cases these defects
are neutralized by piety, maternity, want of passion, sexual coldness, weakness
and an undeveloped intelligence (*Ibid.*:151).

Although women lack the higher sensibilities of men, they are thus restrained
from criminal activity in most cases by lack of intelligence and passion, qualities
which *criminal* women possess as well as all *men*. Within this framework of biological limits of women's nature, the female offender is characterized as *masculine* whereas the normal woman is *feminine*. The anomalies of skull, physiogno-
my and brain capacity of female criminals, according to Lombroso, more
closely approximate that of the man, normal or criminal, than they do those of
the normal woman; the female offender often has a "virile cranium" and
considerable body hair. Masculinity in women is an anomaly itself, rather than
a sign of development, however. A related notion is developed by Thomas,
who notes that in "civilized" nations the sexes are more physically different.

What we look for most in the female is femininity, and when we find the
opposite in her, we must conclude as a rule that there must be some anomaly
. . . Virility was one of the special features of the savage woman . . . In the
portraits of Red Indian and Negro beauties, whom it is difficult to recognize
for women, so huge are their jaws and cheekbones, so hard and coarse their
features, and the same is often the case in their crania and brains (*Ibid.*:112).

The more highly developed races would therefore have the most feminized
women with the requisite passivity, lack of passion, etc. This is a *racist* and
classist definition of femininity—just as are almost all theories of *femininity*
and as, indeed, is the thing itself. The ideal of the lady can only exist in a
society built on the exploitation of labor to maintain the woman of leisure who
can *be* that ideal lady.
   Finally, Lombroso notes women's lack of *property sense*, which contributes
to their criminality.

In their eyes theft is . . . an audacity for which account compensation is due to
the owner . . . as an individual rather than a social crime, just as it was regarded
in the primitive periods of human evolution and is still regarded by many un-
civilized nations (*Ibid.*:217).

One may question this statement on several levels. Can it be assumed to have any
validity at all, or is it false that women have a different sense of property than

men? If it is valid to a degree, is it related to women's lack of property ownership and nonparticipation in the accumulation of capitalist wealth? Indeed, as
Thomas (1907) points out, women are considered property themselves. At any
rate, it is an interesting point in Lombroso's book that has only been touched
on by later writers, and always in a manner supportive of the institution of
private property.

III. Thomas: "The Stimulation She Craves"

The works of W. I. Thomas are critical in that they mark a transition from
purely physiological explanations such as Lombroso's to more sophisticated
theories that embrace physiological, psychological and social-structural factors.
However, even the most sophisticated explanations of female crime rely on
implicit assumptions about the *biological* nature of women. In Thomas' *Sex
and Society* (1907) and *The Unadjusted Girl* (1923), there are important contradictions in the two approaches that are representative of the movements
during that period between publication dates: a departure from biological
Social-Darwinian theories to complex analyses of the interaction between
society and the individual, *i.e.,* societal repression and manipulation of the
"natural" wishes of persons.

In *Sex and Society* (1907), Thomas poses basic biological differences
between the sexes as his starting point. Maleness is "katabolic," the animal
force which is destructive of energy and allows men the possibility of creative
work through this outward flow. Femaleness is "anabolic," analogous to a
plant which stores energy, and is motionless and conservative. Here Thomas
is offering his own version of the age-old male/female dichotomy expressed
by Lombroso and elaborated on in Freud's paradigm, in the structural-
functionalist "instrumental-expressive" duality, and in other analyses of the
status quo. According to Thomas, the dichotomy is most highly developed
in the more civilized races, due to the greater differentiation of sex roles.
This statement ignores the hard physical work done by poor *white* women at
home and in the factories and offices in "civilized" countries, and accepts a
ruling-class definition of femininity.

The cause of women's relative decline in stature in more "civilized"
countries is a subject on which Thomas is ambivalent. At one point he
attributes it to the lack of "a superior fitness on the motor side" in women
(*Ibid.*:94); at another point, he regards her loss of *sexual freedom* as critical,
with the coming of monogamy and her confinement to sexual tasks such as
wifehood and motherhood. He perceptively notes:

Women were still further degraded by the development of property and its
control by man, together with the habit of treating her as a piece of property,
whose value was enhanced if its purity was assured (*Ibid.*:297).

However, Thomas' underlying assumptions in his explanations of the inferior
status of women are *physiological* ones. He attributes to men high amounts
of sexual energy, which lead them to pursue women for their sex, and he attributes to women maternal feelings devoid of sexuality, which lead *them* to exchange sex for domesticity. Thus monogamy, with chastity for women, is the
accommodation of these basic urges, and women are domesticated while men
assume leadership, in a true market exchange.

Why, then, does Thomas see problems in the position of women? It is
because modern women are plagued by "irregularity, pettiness, ill health
and inserviceableness" (*Ibid.*:245). Change is required to maintain *social
harmony,* apart from considerations of women's needs, and women must be
educated to make them better wives, a theme reiterated throughout this
century by "liberals" on the subject. Correctly anticipating a threat, Thomas
urges that change be made to stabilize the family, and warns that "no civilization can remain the highest if another civilization adds to the intelligence of
its men the intelligence of its women" (*Ibid.*:314). Thomas is motivated by
considerations of social integration. Of course, one might question how women
are to be able to contribute much if they are indeed anabolic. However, due to
the transitional nature of Thomas' work, there are immense contradictions in
his writing.

Many of Thomas' specific assertions about the nature of women are indis-
tinguishable from Lombroso's; they both delineate a biological hierarchy along
race and sex lines.

Man has, in short, become more somatically specialized an animal than women,
and feels more keenly any disturbance of normal conditions with which he has
not the same physiological surplus as woman with which to meet the disturbance . . . It is a logical fact, however, that the lower human races, the lower
classes of society, women and children show something of the same quality in
their superior tolerance of surgical disease (*Ibid.*:36).

Like Lombroso, Thomas is crediting women with superior capabilities of
survival because they are further down the scale in terms of evolution. It is
significant that Thomas includes the lower classes in his observation; is he
implying that the lower classes are in their position *because* of their natural
unfitness, or perhaps that their *situation* renders them less sensitive to pain?
At different times, Thomas implies both. Furthermore, he agrees with
Lombroso that women are more nearly uniform than men, and says that they
have a smaller percentage of "genius, insanity and idiocy" (*Ibid.*:45) than men,
as well as fewer creative outbursts of energy.

Dealing with female criminality in *Sex and Society* (1907), Thomas begins
to address the issue of morality, which he closely links to legality from a standpoint of maintaining social order. He discriminates between male and female
morality:

Morality as applied to men has a larger element of the contractual, representing the adjustment of his activities to those of society at large, or more particularly to the activities of the male members of society; while the morality which we think of in connection with women shows less of the contractual and more of the personal, representing her adjustment to men, more particularly the adjustment of her person to men (*Ibid.*:172).

Whereas Lombroso barely observes women's lack of participation in the institution of private property, Thomas' perception is more profound. He points out that women *are* property of men and that their conduct is subject to different codes.

Morality, in the most general sense, represents the code under which activities are best carried on and is worked out in the school of experience. It is preeminently an adult and male system, and men are intelligent enough to realize that neither women nor children have passed through this school. It is on this account that man is merciless to woman from the standpoint of personal behavior, yet he exempts her from anything in the way of contractual morality, or views her defections in this regard with allowance and even with amusement (*Ibid.*:234).

Disregarding his remarks about intelligence, one confronts the critical point about women with respect to the law: because they occupy a *marginal* position in the productive sphere of exchange commodities outside the home, they in turn occupy a marginal position in regard to "contractual" law which regulates relations of property and production. The argument of differential treatment of men and women by the law is developed in later works by Pollak and others, who attribute it to the "chivalry" of the system which is lenient to women committing offenses. As Thomas notes, however, women are simply not a serious *threat* to property, and are treated more "leniently" because of this. Certain women do become threats by transcending (or by being denied) their traditional role, particularly many Third World women and political rebels, and they are *not* afforded chivalrous treatment! In fact, chivalry is reserved for the women who are least likely to ever come in contact with the criminal justice system: the ladies, or white middle-class women. In matters of *sexual* conduct, however, which embody the double standard, women are rigorously prosecuted by the law. As Thomas understands, this is the sphere in which women's functions *are* critical. Thus it is not a matter of "chivalry" how one is handled, but of different forms and thrusts of social control applied to men and women. Men are engaged in productive tasks and their activities in this area *are* strictly curtailed.

In *The Unadjusted Girl* (1923), Thomas deals with female delinquency as a "normal" response under certain social conditions, using assumptions about the nature of women which he leaves unarticulated in this work. Driven by basic "wishes," an individual is controlled by society in her activities through institutional transmission of codes and mores. Depending on how they are manipulated, wishes can be made to serve social or antisocial ends. Thomas stresses the institutions that socialize, such as the family, giving people certain "definitions of the situation." He confidently—and defiantly—asserts:

There is no individual energy, no unrest, no type of wish, which cannot be sublimated and made socially useful. From this standpoint, the problem is not the right of society to protect itself from the disorderly and antisocial person, but the right of the disorderly and antisocial person to be made orderly and socially valuable . . . The problem of society is to produce the right attitudes in its members (*Ibid.*:232-233).

This is an important shift in perspective, from the traditional libertarian view of protecting society by punishing transgressors, to the *rehabilitative* and *preventive* perspective of crime control that seeks to control *minds* through socialization rather than to merely control behavior through punishment. The autonomy of the individual to choose is seen as the product of his environment which the state can alter. This is an important refutation of the Lombrosian biological perspective, which maintains that there are crime-prone individuals who must be locked up, sterilized or otherwise incapacitated. Today, one can see an amalgamation of the two perspectives in new theories of "behavior control" that use tactics such as conditioning and brain surgery, combining biological and environmental viewpoints.[3]

Thomas proposes the manipulation of individuals through institutions to prevent antisocial attitudes, and maintains that there is no such person as the "crime prone" individual. A hegemonic system of belief can be imposed by sublimating natural urges and by correcting the poor socialization of slum families. In this perspective, the *definition* of the situation rather than the situation *itself* is what should be changed; a situation is what someone *thinks* it is. The response to a criminal woman who is dissatisfied with her conventional sexual roles is to change not the roles, which would mean widespread social transformations, but to change her attitudes. This concept of civilization as repressive and the need to adjust is later refined by Freud.

Middle class women, according to Thomas, commit little crime because they are socialized to sublimate their natural desires and to behave well, treasuring their chastity as an investment. The poor woman, however, "is not immoral, because this implies a loss of morality, but amoral" (*Ibid.*:98). Poor women are not objectively driven to crime; they long for it. Delinquent girls are motivated by the desire for excitement or "new experience," and forget the repressive urge of "security." However, these desires are well within Thomas' conception of *femininity*: delinquents are not rebelling against womanhood, as Lombroso suggests, but merely acting it out illegally. Davis and Pollak agree with this notion that delinquent women are not "different" from nondelinquent women.

Thomas maintains that it is not sexual desire that motivates delinquent girls, for they are no more passionate than other women, but they are *manipulating* male desires for sex to achieve their own ulterior ends.

The beginning of delinquency in girls is usually an impulse to get amusement, adventure, pretty clothes, favorable notice, distinction, freedom in the larger world . . . The girls have usually become 'wild' before the development of sexual desire, and their casual sex relations do not usually awaken sex feeling. Their sex is used as a condition of the realization of other wishes. It is their capital (*Ibid.*:109).

Here Thomas is expanding on the myth of the manipulative woman, who is cold and scheming and vain. To him, good female sexual behavior is a protective measure—"instinctive, of course" (1907:241), whereas male behavior is uncontrollable as men are caught by helpless desires. This is the common Victorian notion of the woman as seductress which in turn perpetuates the myth of a lack of real sexuality to justify her responsibility for upholding sexual mores. Thomas uses a market analogy to female virtue: good women *keep* their bodies as capital to sell in matrimony for marriage and security, whereas bad women *trade* their bodies for excitement. One notes, of course, the familiar dichotomy. It is difficult, in this framework, to see how Thomas can make *any* moral distinctions, since morality seems to be merely good business sense. In fact, Thomas' yardstick is social harmony, necessitating *control*.

Thomas shows an insensitivity to real human relationships and needs. He also shows ignorance of economic hardships in his denial of economic factors in delinquency.

An unattached woman has a tendency to become an adventuress not so much on economic as on psychological grounds. Life is rarely so hard that a young woman cannot earn her bread; but she cannot always live and have the stimulation she craves (*Ibid.*:241).

This is an amazing statement in an era of mass starvation and illness! He rejects economic causes as a possibility at all, denying its importance in criminal activity with as much certainty as Lombroso, Freud, Davis, Pollak and most other writers.

IV. Freud: "Beauty, Charm and Sweetness"

The Freudian theory of the position of women is grounded in explicit biological assumptions about their nature, expressed by the famous "Anatomy is Destiny." Built upon this foundation is a construction incorporating psychological and social-structural factors.

Freud himself sees women as anatomically inferior; they are destined to be wives and mothers, and this admittedly an inferior destiny as befits the inferior sex. The root of this inferiority is that women's *sex organs* are inferior to those of men, a fact *universally* recognized by children in the Freudian scheme. The girl assumes that she has lost a penis as punishment, is traumatized, and grows up envious and revengeful. The boy also sees the girl as having lost a penis, fears a similar punishment himself, and dreads the girl's envy and vengeance. Feminine traits can be traced to the inferior genitals themselves, or to women's inferiority complex arising from their response to them: women are exhibition-istic, narcissistic, and attempt to compensate for their lack of a penis by being well dressed and physically beautiful. Women become mothers trying to replace the lost penis with a baby. Women are also masochistic, as Lombroso and Thomas have noted, because their *sexual* role is one of receptor, and their sexual pleasure consists of pain. This woman, Freud notes, is the *healthy* woman. In the familiar dichotomy, the men are aggressive and pain inflicting. Freud comments:

The male pursues the female for the purposes of sexual union, seizes hold of her, and penetrates into her . . . by this you have precisely reduced the characteristic of masculinity to the factor of aggressiveness (Millett, 1970:189).

Freud, like Lombroso and Thomas, takes the notion of men's activity and women's inactivity and *reduces* it to the sexual level, seeing the sexual union itself through Victorian eyes: ladies don't move.

Women are also inferior in the sense that they are concerned with personal matters and have little social sense. Freud sees civilization as based on repression of the sex drive, where it is the duty of men to repress their strong instincts in order to get on with the worldly business of civilization. Women, on the other hand,

have little sense of justice, and this is no doubt connected with the preponder-ance of envy in their mental life; for the demands of justice are a modification of envy; they lay down the conditions under which one is willing to part with it. We also say of women that their social interests are weaker than those of men and that their capacity for the sublimation of their instincts is less (1933: 183).

Men are capable of sublimating their individual needs because they rationally perceive the Hobbesian conflict between those urges and social needs. Women are emotional and incapable of such an adjustment because of their innate inability to make such rational judgments. It is only fair then that they should have a marginal relation to production and property.

In this framework, the deviant woman is one who is attempting to be a *man.* She is aggressively rebellious, and her drive to accomplishment is the expression of her longing for a penis; this is a hopeless pursuit, of course, and she will only end up "neurotic." Thus the deviant woman should be treated and helped to *adjust* to her sex role. Here again, as in Thomas' writing, is the notion of individual accommodation that repudiates the possibility of social change.

In a Victorian fashion, Freud rationalizes women's oppression by glorifying their duties as wives and mothers:

It is really a stillborn thought to send women into the struggle for existence exactly the same as men. If, for instance, I imagined my sweet gentle girl as a competitor, it would only end in my telling her, as I did seventeen months ago, that I am fond of her, and I implore her to withdraw from the strife into the calm, uncompetitive activity of my home . . . Nature has determined woman's destiny through beauty, charm and sweetness . . . in youth an adored darling, in mature years a loved wife (Jones 1961:117-118).

In speaking of femininity, Freud, like his forebearers, is speaking along racist and classist lines. Only upper and middle class women could possibly enjoy lives as sheltered darlings. Freud sets hegemonic standards of femininity for poor and Third World women.

It is important to understand Freudianism because it reduces categories of sexual ideology to explicit sexuality and makes these categories *scientific*. For the last fifty years, Freudianism has been a mainstay of sexist social theory. Kate Millett notes that Freud himself saw his work as stemming the tide of feminist revolution, which he constantly ridiculed:

Coming as it did, at the peak of the sexual revolution, Freud's doctrine of penis envy is in fact a superbly timed accusation, enabling masculine sentiment to take the offensive again as it had not since the disappearance of overt misogyny when the pose of chivalry became fashionable (Millet 1970:189).

Freudian notions of the repression of sexual instincts, the sexual passivity of women, and the sanctity of the nuclear family are conservative not only in their contemporary context, but in the context of their own time. Hitler writes:

For her [woman's] world is her husband, her family, her children and her home . . . The man upholds the nation as the woman upholds the family. The equal rights of women consist in the fact that in the realm of life determined for her by nature, she experience the high esteem that is her due. Woman and man represent quite different types of being. Reason is dominant in man . . . Feeling, in contrast, is much more stable than reason, and woman is the feeling, and therefore the stable, element (*Ibid.*:170).

One can mark the decline in the position of women after the 1920's through the use of various indices: by noting the progressively earlier age of marriage of women in the United States and the steady rise in the number of children born to them, culminating in the birth explosion of the late forties and fifties; by looking at the relative decline in the number of women scholars; and by seeing the failure to liberate women in the Soviet Union and the rise of fascist sexual ideology. Freudianism has had an unparalleled influence in the United States (and came at a key point to help swing the tide against the women's movement) to facilitate the return of women during the depression and postwar years to the home, out of an economy which had no room for them. Freud affected such writers on female deviance as Davis, Pollak and Konopka, who turn to concepts of sexual maladjustment and neurosis to explain women's criminality. Healthy women would now be seen as masochistic, passive and sexually indifferent. Criminal women would be seen as *sexual* misfits. Most importantly, *psychological* factors would be used to explain criminal activity, and social, economic and political factors would be ignored. Explanations would seek to be *universal,* and historical possibilities of change would be refuted.

V. Davis: "The Most Convenient Sexual Outlet for Armies . . ."

Kingsley Davis' work on prostitution (1961) is still considered a classical analysis on the subject with a structural-functionalist perspective. It employs assumptions about "the organic nature of man" and woman, many of which can be traced to ideas proffered by Thomas and Freud.

Davis sees prostitution as a structural necessity whose roots lie in the *sexual* nature of men and women; for example, female humans, unlike primates, are sexually available year-round. He asserts that prostitution is *universal* in time and place, eliminating the possibilities of historical change and ignoring critical differences in the quality and quantity of prostitution in different societies. He maintains that there will always be a class of women who will be prostitutes, the familiar class of "bad" women. The reason for the universality of prostitution is that sexual *repression,* a concept stressed by Thomas and Freud, is essential to the functioning of society. Once again there is the notion of sublimating "natural" sex urges to the overall needs of society, namely social order. Davis notes that in our society sexuality is permitted only within the structure of the nuclear family, which is an institution of stability. He does not, however, analyze in depth the economic and social functions of the family, other than to say it is a bulwark of morality.

The norms of every society tend to harness and control the sexual appetite, and one of the ways of doing this is to link the sexual act to some stable or potentially stable social relationship . . . Men dominate women in economic, sexual and familial relationships and consider them to some extent as sexual property, to be prohibited to other males. They therefore find promiscuity on the part of women repugnant (*Ibid.*:264).

Davis is linking the concept of prostitution to promiscuity, defining it as a *sexual* crime, and calling prostitutes sexual transgressors. Its origins, he claims, lie not in economic hardship, but in the marital restraints on sexuality. As long as men seek women, prostitutes will be in demand. One wonders why sex-seeking women have not created a class of male prostitutes.

Davis sees the only possibility of eliminating prostitution in the liberalization of sexual mores, although he is pessimistic about the likelihood of total elimination. In light of the contemporary American "sexual revolution" of commercial sex, which has surely created more prostitutes and semi-prostitutes rather than eliminating the phenomenon, and in considering the revolution in China where, despite a "puritanical" outlook on sexuality, prostitution has largely been eliminated through major economic and social change, the superficiality of Davis' approach becomes evident. Without dealing with root economic, social and political factors, one cannot analyze prostitution.

Davis shows Freudian pessimism about the nature of sexual repression:

We can imagine a social system in which the motive for prostitution would be completely absent, but we cannot imagine that the system will ever come to pass. It would be a regime of absolute sexual freedom with intercourse practiced solely for pleasure by both parties. There would be no institutional control of sexual expression . . . All sexual desire would have to be mutually complementary . . . Since the basic causes of prostitution—the institutional control of sex, the unequal scale of attractiveness, and the presence of economic and social inequalities between classes and between males and females—are not likely to disappear, prostitution is not likely to disappear either (*Ibid.*:286).

By talking about "complementary desire," Davis is using a marketplace notion of sex: two attractive or unattractive people are drawn to each other and exchange sexual favors; people are placed on a scale of attractiveness and may be rejected by people above them on the scale; hence they (*men*) become frustrated and demand prostitutes. Women who become prostitutes do so for good pay *and* sexual pleasure. Thus one has a neat little system in which everyone benefits.

Enabling a small number of women to take care of the needs of a large number of men, it is the most convenient sexual outlet for armies, for the legions of strangers, perverts and physically repulsive in our midst (*Ibid.*:288).

Prostitution "functions," therefore it must be good. Davis, like Thomas, is motivated by concerns of social order rather than by concerns of what the needs and desires of the women involved might be. He denies that the women involved are economically oppressed; they are on the streets through autonomous, *individual* choice.

Some women physically enjoy the intercourse they sell. From a purely economic point of view, prostitution comes near the situation of getting something
for nothing . . . Women's wages could scarcely be raised significantly without
also raising men's. Men would then have more to spend on prostitution (*Ibid.*:
277).

It is important to understand that, given a *sexual* interpretation of what is an
economic crime, and given a refusal to consider widespread change (even equal-
ization of wages, hardly a revolutionary act), Davis' conclusion is the logical
technocratic solution.

In this framework, the deviant women are merely adjusting to their
feminine role in an illegitimate fashion, as Thomas has theorized. They are *not*
attempting to be rebels or to be "men," as Lombroso's and Freud's positions
suggest. Although Davis sees the main difference between wives and prostitutes
in a macrosocial sense as the difference merely between legal and illegal roles,
in a personal sense he sees the women who *choose* prostitution as maladjusted
and neurotic. However, given the universal necessity for prostitution, this
analysis implies the necessity of having a perpetually ill and maladjusted class
of women. Thus oppression is *built into* the system, and a healthy *system* makes
for a sick *individual*. Here Davis is integrating Thomas' notions of social integration with Freudian perspectives on neurosis and maladjustment.

VI. Pollak: "A Different Attitude Toward Veracity"

Otto Pollak's *The Criminality of Women* (1950) has had an outstanding influence
on the field of women and crime, being the major work on the subject in the
postwar years. Pollak advances the theory of "hidden" female crime to account
for what he considers unreasonably low official rates for women.

A major reason for the existence of hidden crime, as he sees it, lies in the
nature of women themselves. They are instigators rather than perpetrators of
criminal activity. While Pollak admits that this role is partly a socially enforced
one, he insists that women are inherently deceitful for *physiological* reasons.

Man must achieve an erection in order to perform the sex act and will not be
able to hide his failure. His lack of positive emotion in the sexual sphere must
become overt to the partner, and pretense of sexual response is impossible for
him, if it is lacking. Woman's body, however, permits such pretense to a certain
degree and lack of orgasm does not prevent her ability to participate in the sex
act (*Ibid.*:10).

Pollak *reduces* women's nature to the *sex act*, as Freud has done, and finds
women inherently more capable of manipulation, accustomed to being sly, passive and passionless. As Thomas suggests, women can use sex for ulterior

purposes. Furthermore, Pollak suggests that women are innately deceitful on yet another level:

Our sex mores force women to conceal every four weeks the period of menstruation . . . They thus make concealment and misrepresentation in the eyes of women socially required and must condition them to a different attitude toward veracity than men (*Ibid.*:11).

Women's abilities at concealment thus allow them to successfully commit crimes in stealth.

Women are also vengeful. Menstruation, in the classic Freudian sense, seals their doomed hopes to become men and arouses women's desire for vengeance, especially during that time of the month. Thus Pollak offers new rationalizations to bolster old myths.

A second factor in hidden crime is the roles played by women which furnish them with opportunities as domestics, nurses, teachers and housewives to commit undetectable crimes. The *kinds* of crimes women commit reflect their nature: false accusation, for example, is an outgrowth of women's treachery, spite or fear and is a sign of neurosis; shoplifting can be traced in many cases to a special mental disease—kleptomania. Economic factors play a minor role; *sexual-psychological* factors account for female criminality. Crime in women is *personalized* and often accounted for by mental illness.

Pollak notes:

Robbery and burglary . . . are considered specifically male offenses since they represent the pursuit of monetary gain by overt action . . . Those cases of female robbery which seem to express a tendency toward masculinization comes from . . . [areas] where social conditions have favored the assumptions of male pursuits by women . . . The female offenders usually retain some trace of femininity, however, and even so glaring an example of masculinization as the 'Michigan Babes,' an all woman gang of robbers in Chicago, shows a typically feminine trait in the modus operandi (*Ibid.*:29).

Pollak is defining crimes with economic motives that employ overt action as *masculine,* and defining as *feminine* those crimes for *sexual* activity, such as luring men as baits. Thus he is using circular reasoning by saying that feminine crime is feminine. To fit women into the scheme and justify the statistics, he must invent the notion of hidden crime.

It is important to recognize that, to some extent, women *do* adapt to their enforced sexual roles and may be more likely to instigate, to use sexual traps, and to conform to all the other feminine role expectations. However, it is not accidental that theorists label women as conforming even when they are *not*; for example, by inventing sexual motives for what are clearly crimes of economic necessity, or by invoking "mental illness" such as kleptomania for shoplifting.

It is difficult to separate the *theory* from the *reality*, since the reality of female crime is largely unknown. But it is not difficult to see that Pollak is using sexist terms and making sexist assumptions to advance theories of hidden female crime.

Pollak, then, sees criminal women as extending their sexual role, like Davis and Thomas, by using sexuality for ulterior purposes. He suggests that the condemnation of extramarital sex has "delivered men who engage in such conduct as practically helpless victims" (*Ibid.*:152) into the hands of women blackmailers, overlooking completely the possibility of men blackmailing women, which would seem more likely, given the greater taboo on sex for women and their greater risks of being punished.

The final factor that Pollak advances as a root cause of hidden crime is that of "chivalry" in the criminal justice system. Pollak uses Thomas' observation that women are differntially treated by the law, and carries it to a sweeping conclusion based on *cultural* analyses of men's feelings toward women.

One of the outstanding concomitants of the existing inequality . . . is chivalry, and the general protective attitude of man toward woman . . . Men hate to accuse women and thus indirectly to send them to their punishment, police officers dislike to arrest them, district attorneys to prosecute them, judges and juries to find them guilty, and so on (*Ibid.*:151).

Pollak rejects the possibility of an actual discrepancy between crime rates for men and women; therefore, he must look for factors to expand the scope of female crime. He assumes that there is chivalry in the criminal justice system that is extended to the women who come in contact with it. Yet the women involved are likely to be poor and Third World women or white middle-class women who have stepped *outside* the definitions of femininity to become hippies or political rebels, and chivalry is *not* likely to be extended to them. Chivalry is a racist and classist concept founded on the notion of women as "ladies" which applies only to wealthy white women and ignores the double sexual standard. These "ladies," however, are the least likely women to ever come in contact with the criminal justice system in the first place.[4]

VII. The Legacy of Sexism

A major purpose in tracing the development and interaction of ideas pertaining to sexual ideology based on implicit assumptions of the inherent nature of women throughout the works of Lombroso, Thomas, Freud, Davis and Pollak, is to clarify their positions in relation to writers in the field today. One can see the influence their ideas still have by looking at a number of contemporary theorists on female criminality. Illuminating examples can be found in

Gisela Konopka's *Adolescent Girl in Conflict* (1966), Vedder and Somerville's
The Delinquent Girl (1970) and Cowie, Cowie and Slater's *Delinquency in Girls*
(1968). The ideas in these minor works have direct roots in those already traced
in this paper.

Konopka justifies her decision to study delinquency in girls rather than in
boys by noting girls' *influence* on boys in gang fights and on future generations
as mothers. This is the notion of women as instigators of men and influencers
on children.

Konopka's main point is that delinquency in girls can be traced to a specific
emotional response: loneliness.

What I found in the girl in conflict was . . . loneliness accompanied by despair.
Adolescent boys too often feel lonely and search for understanding and friends.
Yet in general this does not seem to be the central core of their problems, not
their most outspoken ache. While these girls also strive for independence, their
need for dependence is unusually great (1966:40).

In this perspective, girls are driven to delinquency by an emotional problem—
loneliness and dependency. There are *inherent* emotional differences between
the sexes.

Almost invariably her [the girl's] problems are deeply personalized. Whatever
her offense—whether shoplifting, truancy or running away from home—it is
usually accompanied by some disturbance or unfavorable behavior in the
sexual area (*Ibid.*:4).

Here is the familiar resurrection of female personalism, emotionalism, and above
all, *sexuality*—characteristics already described by Lombroso, Thomas and
Freud. Konopka maintains:

The delinquent girl suffers, like many boys, from lack of success, lack of opportunity. But her drive to success is never separated from her need for people,
for interpersonal involvement (*Ibid.*:41).

Boys are "instrumental" and become delinquent if they are deprived of the
chance for creative success. However, girls are "expressive" and happiest dealing
with people as wives, mothers, teachers, nurses or psychologists. This perspective is drawn from the theory of delinquency as a result of blocked opportunity
and from the instrumental/expressive sexual dualism developed by structural-
functionalists. Thus female delinquency must be dealt with on this *psychological* level, using therapy geared to their needs as future wives and mothers. They
should be *adjusted* and given *opportunities* to be pretty, sociable women.

The important point is to understand how Konopka analyzes the roots of
girls' feelings. It is very possible that, given women's position, girls may be in
fact more concerned with dependence and sociability. One's understanding of

this, however, is based on an understanding of the historical position of women and the nature of their oppression. Konopka says:

What are the reasons for this essential loneliness in girls? Some will be found in the nature of being an adolescent girl, in her biological makeup and her particular position in her culture and time (*Ibid.*).

Coming from a Freudian perspective, Konopka's emphasis on female emotions as cause for delinquency, which ignores economic and social factors, is questionable. She employs assumptions about the *physiological* and *psychological* nature of women that very well may have led her to see only those feelings in the first place. For example, she cites menstruation as a significant event in a girl's development. Thus Konopka is rooted firmly in the tradition of Freud and, apart from sympathy, contributes little that is new to the field.[5]

Vedder and Somerville (1970) account for female delinquency in a manner similar to that of Konopka. They also feel the need to justify their attention to girls by remarking that (while female delinquency may not pose as much of a problem as that of boys) because women raise families and are critical agents of socialization, it is worth taking the time to study and control them. Vedder and Somerville also stress the dependence of girls on boys and the instigatory role girls play in boys' activities.

Like Freud and Konopka, the authors view delinquency as blocked access or maladjustment to the normal feminine role. In a blatant statement that ignores the economic and social factors that result from racism and poverty, they attribute the high rates of delinquency among black girls to their lack of "healthy" feminine narcissism, *reducing* racism to a psychological problem in totally sexist and racist terms.

The black girl is, in fact, the antithesis of the American beauty. However loved she may be by her mother, family and community, she has no real basis of female attractiveness on which to build a sound feminine narcissism . . . Perhaps the 'black is beautiful' movement will help the Negro girl to increase her femininity and personal satisfaction as a black woman (*Ibid.*:159-160).

Again the focus is on a lack of *sexual* opportunities for women, *i.e.*, the Black woman is not Miss America. *Economic* offenses such as shoplifting are explained as outlets for *sexual* frustration. Since healthy women conform, the individual delinquents should be helped to adjust; the emphasis is on the "definition of the situation" rather than on the situation.

The answer lies in *therapy*, and racism and sexism become merely psychological problems.

Special attention should be given to girls, taking into consideration their

constitutional biological and psychological differences, and their social position
in our male dominated culture. The female offender's goal, as any woman's, is
a happy and successful marriage; therefore her self-image is dependent on the
establishment of satisfactory relationships with the opposite sex. The double
standard for sexual behavior on the part of the male and female must be recognized (*Ibid.*:153).

Like Konopka, and to some extent drawing on Thomas, the authors see female
delinquents as extending femininity in an illegitimate fashion rather than
rebelling against it. The assumptions made about women's goals and needs,
including *biological* assumptions, lock women into a system from which there
is no escape, whereby any behavior will be sexually interpreted and dealt with.

   The resurgence of biological or physiological explanations of criminality
in general has been noteworthy in the last several years, exemplified by the
XYY chromosome controversy and the interest in brain wave in "violent"
individuals.[6] In the case of women, biological explanations have *always* been
prevalent; every writer has made assumptions about anatomy as destiny.
Women are prey, in the literature, to cycles of reproduction, including menstruation, pregnancy, maternity and menopause; they experience emotional responses
to these cycles that make them inclined to irrationality and potentially violent
activity.

   Cowie, Cowie and Slater (1968) propose a *chromosomal* explanation of
female delinquency that hearkens back to the works of Lombroso and others
such as Healy (1926), Edith Spaulding (1923) and the Gluecks (1934). They
write:

The chromosomal difference between the sexes starts the individual on a divergent
path, leading either in a masculine or feminine direction . . . It is possible that
the methods of upbringing, differing somewhat for the two sexes, may play some
part in increasing the angle of this divergence (*Ibid.*:171).

This is the healthy, normal divergence for the sexes. The authors equate *masculinity* and *femininity* with *maleness* and *femaleness,* although contemporary
feminists point out that the first categories are *social* and the latter ones *physical.*[7] What relationship exists between the two—how femaleness determines
femininity—is dependent on the larger social structure. There is no question that
a wide range of possibilities exist historically, and in a non-sexist society it is
possible that "masculinity" and "femininity" would disappear, and that the
sexes would differ only biologically, specifically by their sex organs. The authors,
however, lack this understanding and assume an ahistorical sexist view of women,
stressing the *universality* of femininity in the Freudian tradition, and of women's
inferior role in the nuclear family.[8]

   In this perspective, the female offender is *different* physiologically and
psychologically from the "normal" girl.

The authors conclude, in the tradition of Lombroso, that female delinquents are *masculine*. Examining girls for physical characteristics, they note:

Markedly masculine traits in girl delinquents have been commented on . . . [as well as] the frequency of homosexual tendencies . . . Energy, aggressiveness, enterprise and the rebelliousness that drives the individual to break through conformist habits are thought of as being masculine . . . We can be sure that they have some physical basis (*Ibid.*:172).

The authors see crime as a *rebellion* against sex roles rather than as a maladjusted expression of them. By defining rebellion as *masculine,* they are ascribing characteristics of masculinity to any female rebel. Like Lombroso, they spend time measuring heights, weights, and other *biological* features of female delinquents with other girls.

Crime defined as masculine seems to mean violent, overt crime, whereas "ladylike" crime usually refers to sexual violations and shoplifting. Women are neatly categorized no matter *which* kind of crime they commit: if they are violent, they are "masculine" and suffering from chromosomal deficiencies, penis envy, or atavisms. If they conform, they are manipulative, sexually maladjusted and promiscuous. The *economic* and *social* realities of crime—the fact that poor women commit crimes, and that most crimes for women are property offenses —are overlooked. Women's behavior must be *sexually* defined before it will be considered, for women count only in the sexual sphere. The theme of sexuality is a unifying thread in the various, often contradictory theories.

VIII. Conclusion

A good deal of the writing on women and crime being done at the present time is squarely in the tradition of the writers that have been discussed. The basic assumptions and technocratic concerns of these writers have produced work that is sexist, racist and classist; assumptions that have served to maintain a repressive ideology with its extensive apparatus of control. To do a new kind of research on women and crime—one that has feminist roots and a radical orientation—it is necessary to understand the assumptions made by the traditional writers and to break away from them. Work that focuses on human needs, rather than those of the state, will require new definitions of criminality, women, the individual and her/his relation to the state. It is beyond the scope of this paper to develop possible areas of study, but is is nonetheless imperative that this work be made a priority by women *and* men in the future.

Notes

1. Quoted from the 1973 proposal for the Center for the Study and

Reduction of violence prepared by Dr. Louis J. West, Director, Neuropsychiatric Institute, UCLA: "The question of violence in females will be examined from the point of view that females are more likely to commit acts of violence during the pre-menstrual and menstrual periods" (1973:43).

2. I am indebted to Marion Goldman for introducing me to the notion of the dual morality based on assumptions of different sexuality for men and women.

3. For a discussion of the possibilities of psychosurgery in behavior modification for violence-prone" individuals, see Frank Ervin and Vernon Mark, *Violence and the Brain* (1970). For an eclectic view of this perspective on crime, see the proposal for the Center for the Study and Reduction of Violence (footnote #1).

4. The concept of hidden crime is reiterated in Reckless and Kay's report to the President's Commission on Law Enforcement and the Administration of Justice. They note:

A large part of the infrequent officially acted upon involvement of women in crime can be traced to the masking effect of women's roles, effective practice on the part of women of deceit and indirection, their instigation of men to commit their crimes (the Lady MacBeth factor), and the unwillingness on the part of the public and law enforcement officials to hold women accountable for their deeds (the chivalry factor) (1967:13).

5. Bertha Payak in "Understanding the Female Offender" (1963) stresses that women offenders have poor self-concepts, feelings of insecurity and dependency, are emotionally selfish and prey to irrationality during menstruation, pregnancy, and menopause (a good deal of their life!).

6. See Theodore R. Sarbin and Jeffrey E. Miller, "Demonism Revisited: The XYY Cromosomal Anomaly." *Issues in Criminology* 5(2)(Summer 1970).

7. Kate Millett (1970) notes that "sex is biological, gender psychological and therefore cultural . . . if the proper terms for sex are male and female, the corresponding terms for gender are masculine and feminine; these latter may be quite independent of biological sex" (*Ibid.*:30).

8. Zelditch (1960), a structural-functionalist, writes that the nuclear family is an inevitability and that within it, women, the "expressive" sex, will inevitably be the domestics.

References

Bishop, Cecil
    1931   Women and Crime. London: Chatto and Windus.

Cowie, John, Valerie Cowie and Eliot Slater
    1968   Delinquency in Girls. London: Heinemann.

Davis, Kingsley
    1961   "Prostitution." Comtemporary Social Problems. Edited by
            Robert K. Merton and Robert A. Nisbet. New York: Harcourt
            Brace and Jovanovich. Originally published as "The Sociology of
            Prostitution." American Sociological Review 2(5) (October 1937).

Ervin, Frank and Vernon Mark
    1970   Violence and the Brain. New York: Harper and Row.

Fernald, Mabel, Mary Hayes and Almena Dawley
    1920   A Study of Women Delinquents in New York State. New York:
            Century Company.

Freud, Sigmund
    1933   New Introductory Lectures on Psychoanalysis. New York:
            W. W. Norton.

Glueck, Eleanor and Sheldon
    1934   Four Hundred Delinquent Women. New York: Alfred A. Knopf.

Healy, William and Augusta Bronner
    1926   Delinquents and Criminals: Their Making and Unmaking. New York:
            Macmillan and Company.

Hemming, James
    1960   Problems of Adolescent Girls. London: Heinemann.

Jones, Ernest
    1961   The Life and Works of Sigmund Freud. New York: Basic Books

Konopka, Gisela
    1966   The Adolescent Girl in Conflict. Englewood Cliffs, New Jersey:
            Prentice-Hall.

Lombroso, Cesare
    1920   The Female Offender. (translation). New York: Appleton. Orig-
            inally published in 1903.

Millet, Kate
    1970   Sexual Politics. New York: Doubleday and Company.

Monahan, Florence
    1941   Women in Crime. New York: I. Washburn.

Parsons, Talcott
    1942   "Age and Sex in the Social Structure." American Sociological
            Review 7 (October).

Parsons, Talcott and Renee Fox
    1960   "Illness, Therapy and the Modern 'Urban' American Family." The
            Family. Edited by Normal Bell and Ezra Vogel. Glencoe, Illinois:
            The Free Press.

Payak, Bertha
    1963   "Understanding the Female Offender." Federal Probation XXVII.

Pollak, Otto
    1950   The Criminality of Women. Philadelphia: University of Pennsylvania
            Press.

Reckless, Walter and Barbara Kay
    1967   The Female Offender. Report to the President's Commission on Law
            Enforcement and the Administration of Justice. Washington, D.C.:
            Government Printing Office.

Sarbin, Theodore R. and Jeffrey E. Miller
    1970   "Demonism Revisited: The XYY Chromosomal Anomaly." Issues in
            Criminology 5(2) (Summer).

Schwendinger, Herman and Julia.
    1973   "The Founding Fathers: Sexists to a Man." Sociologists of the Chair.
            New York: Basic Books

Spaulding, Edith
    1923   An Experimental Study of Psychopathic Delinquent Women. New
            York: Rand McNally.

Thomas, W. I.
    1907   Sex and Society. Boston: Little, Brown and Company.
    1923   The Unadjusted Girl. New York: Harper and Row.

Vedder, Clyde and Dora Somerville
    1970   The Delinquent Girl. Springfield, Illinois: Charles C. Thomas.

West, Dr. Louis J.
    1973   Proposal for the Center for the Study and Reduction of Violence.
            Neuropsychiatric Institute, UCLA (April 10).

Zelditch, Morris, Jr.
1960   "Role Differentiation in the Nuclear Family: A Comparative Study."
        The Family. Edited by Norman Bell and Ezra Vogel. Glencoe,
        Illinois: The Free Press.

2

Women Offenders: Myth vs. Reality

Laura Crites

Women offenders have been variously described as childlike, manipulative, mentally deficient, and morally depraved. As their numbers increase on arrest rolls, however, they are now more frequently viewed as violent and aggressive, incited by the women's rights movement to new dimensions in crime (Adler 1975). Although the feminist movement is reputed to be moving women closer to men in their crime patterns, many argue that it has had little effect on the chivalrous approach taken toward women by the criminal justice system.

This chapter examines the veracity of these three popular beliefs, namely, that increased criminality of females is trending toward more violent and aggressive crimes; that their increased criminality is influenced by the women's rights movement; and that in spite of the movement's reputed effect on female deviant behavior, it has had little influence within the criminal justice system where women continue to be treated with chivalry and paternalism.

Rise of the Aggressive and Violent Female

With the rise in feminist consciousness, many theorists see a corresponding involvement of women in crime, specifically in more aggressive and violent crimes. They offer yearly FBI *Uniform Crime Reports* as supporting evidence, quoting an alarming 108 percent increase in arrests of females between 1960 and 1974 compared with a 23 percent increase for males. As table 2-1 illustrates, arrests of females have increased more than male arrests over the last 14 years.

It is important to view these statistics in their proper perspective. Without examining the base figures, quotations of such rates of increase in female criminality are truly alarming. They are also misleading. An impressive rate of increase can be achieved relatively quickly with a small base figure. For example, 1974 statistics show a 450 percent increase in arrests of adolescent females for negligent manslaughter compared with a 36 percent drop for young males. This figure is much less sensational, however, when one sees that it results from an increase from 2 females arrested in 1960 to 11 arrested throughout the United States in 1974. One would not point to these 11 as proof of a trend toward violence on the part of young females.

Although the rate of arrests for women in all offenses has increased 108 percent in the last 14 years, actual figures show that only 281,949 more

Table 2-1
Arrest Trends by Sex, 1960-74

Arrests for	Total Arrests (1960)	Total Arrests (1974)	Percent Arrest Change (Rate of)	Female Percent of Total (1960)	Female Percent of Total (1974)	Female Net Change
All offenses						
Females	259,038	540,987	108.0	10.7	16.9	6.2
Males	2,155,159	2,665,339	23.6			
Index crimes[a]						
Females	36,957	159,011	330.0	10.6	19.4	8.8
Males	311,855	660,351	111.7			
Violent index[b]						
Females	7,563	19.720	160.7	10.3	10.9	0.6
Males	66,220	161,803	144.0			
Property index[c]						
Females	29,292	139,159	375.0	10.6	22.5	11.9
Males	244,562	479,676	96.0			

Source: Adapted from FBI *Uniform Crime Reports* (Washington, D.C.: Federal Bureau of Investigation, U.S. Department of Justice, 1975), p. 184.

[a]Includes criminal homicide, rape, robbery, aggravated assault, burglary, larceny, auto theft.
[b]Includes criminal homicide, rape, robbery, aggravated assault.
[c]Includes larceny, burglary, auto theft.

women were arrested in 1974 than in 1960 in all categories of crimes. To achieve that same rate of increase for males, it would have been necessary to arrest over 2 million more men in 1974 than in 1960. The implication is clear: because traditionally fewer women have been arrested than men, any increase in female arrests is likely to result in a higher percentage "rate of increase."

Setting aside, then, the "rate of increase" as a valuable measure for determining upward trends in serious female criminality, we can more appropriately examine the issue by analyzing changes in the female percentage of total arrests. This means of viewing the statistics places any increased criminality of women in a more realistic perspective. The FBI *Uniform Crime Reports* for 1975 (table 2-1) shows that arrests of women for all offenses in 1960 constituted 10.7 percent of total arrests; females in 1974 made up 16.9 percent of all arrests, a 6.2 percent increase.

It is important to determine whether these increased arrests also indicate a new trend in more aggressive and violent female criminality. According to table 2-1, women are committing more index crimes, which include homicide, rape, robbery, aggravated assault, burglary, larceny, and auto theft, and are generally considered to be the most serious. In dividing these serious crimes into "property" and "violent," however, it is clear that the bulk of the increase in serious female criminality lies within the property crime category. For example, women are being arrested for the property crime of larceny at a much greater rate now than they were two decades ago. In 1953 about 1 out of every 20 women were arrested for larceny. In 1972 the ratio had dropped to 1 out of 5 (Simon 1975:42).

The violent nature of female crime has not increased, however. Females constituted 10 percent of the arrests for violent crimes in 1960 and that figure has remained constant.

In the same report, the rank ordering of arrests for females in 1960 and 1974 shows that the crimes for which women are most frequently arrested are distinctly nonviolent and nonaggressive.

According to table 2-2, larceny-theft is the most common offense for which women are now arrested, up from 3rd in 1960. Women continue, apparently, to be drunk and disorderly at approximately the same rate in 1974 as their sisters 14 years ago. They are involved more heavily, however, in narcotics violations, an escapist crime that may have implications for interpreting the nature of today's female criminality.

Combining information from tables 2-1 and 2-2, there appears to be little validity to the myth of the new, violent, and aggressive female criminal. Women are evidently becoming more hungry and/or greedy; witness the increase in thefts. They may also be more unhappy, escaping through use of drugs. But the most frequent crimes for which they are arrested are distinctly nonviolent and nonaggressive.

Table 2-2
Rank Ordering of Most Frequent Arrests for Females,
1960 and 1974

1960	*1974*
Drunkenness	Larceny-theft
Disorderly conduct	Disorderly conduct
Larceny-theft	Drunkenness
Prostitution	Narcotic drug laws
Other assaults	Prostitution
Liquor laws	Other assaults

Source: FBI *Uniform Crime Reports* (Washington, D.C.:
Federal Bureau of Investigation, U.S. Department of Justice,
1975), p. 184.

Note: Excludes "all other offenses" category, which accounts
for a high percentage of misdemeanant female arrests.

Women's Liberation and Women's Crime

Although there seems to be little statistical evidence to support the contention
that increased assertive behavior among women is being expressed in increased
aggressive and violent female criminality, it is the case that women are being
arrested more frequently now than in 1960. Criminologists and sociologists
have posited a correlation between this rise in female crime and the women's
liberation movement (Simon 1975; Adler 1975). They theorize that the nascent
economic independence and increased psychological liberation of women is
contributing to a new and more serious form of criminality. Advocates of this
theory see female offenders moving into aggressive, violent offenses (aggravated
assault, robbery, murder) as a reflection of their psychological independence
and into more sophisticated white-collar crimes such as embezzling as a result
of increased employment in positions of responsibility.

Although there appears to be little support for advocates of the violent-
aggressive theory, it is worth examining what, if any, effect the women's rights
movement may have on an acknowledged increase in female crime.

Leading proponents of this theory use Labor Department statistics to
establish a significant rise of women in the labor force over the last 70 years.
Specifically, women's participation rose from 18 percent in 1900 to 37 percent
in 1972. The value of these statistics in support of a correlation between
feminism and crime, however, falters when examined more closely and in conjunction with a demographic profile of the female offender. Such an examination reveals that employment benefits derived from the feminist push for equal
employment opportunities accrue predominantly to white, middle-class females. The women's rights movement has largely swept over the subpopulation

group of poor, minority females, into which the female offender falls. These women, rather than being recipients of expanded rights and opportunities gained by the women's movement, are, instead, witnessing declining survival options.

Demographic information shows that women offenders are most frequently from minority groups. A recent national study of female offenders found that 64 percent of the institutionalized women are minorities. In one state where the black female population is approximately 10 percent, 51 percent of the women in prison are black (Glick 1976).

Women offenders are predominantly poor. One-third of the women in federal institutions had earned less than $240 a month and one-half had earned less than $280 a month during their working careers (Hovey 1971). Moreover, female offenders are most frequently responsible for their own support. Approximately 90 percent of the women in federal institutions expected to support themselves and possibly others upon release. Their work experience had been in low-wage, low-status occupations, and well over half had not graduated from high school, thus, further limiting their employment potential (Ibid).

Finally, most female offenders also have children for whom they are responsible. Figures on the percentage of female offenders responsible for children vary from less than 50 percent (Glick 1976) to approximately 80 percent (Velemesis 1969). In sum, the woman offender is poor, uneducated, a racial minority, responsible for her own support and often the support of her children. And according to statistics her situation is not improving.

For this woman, the phenomena of the women's rights movement has been almost totally meaningless. In 1969 the median annual income of white and nonwhite males and females was as follows: white male, $7,610; nonwhite $5,194; white female, $3,649; nonwhite female, $3,008 (U.S. Bureau of the Census 1975). In general, women's earnings relative to men's have decreased from 64 percent of male earnings in 1955 to 57 percent in 1973.

Further, a higher percentage of minority women are unemployed and seeking work. In 1973 minority women had a 10.5 percent unemployment rate compared with a 5.3 percent rate for white women (Women's Bureau 1975:70). This figure carries more significance when one sees that many minority women are heads of households, and they are finding themselves in that position with greater frequency. According to 1974 statistics from the Women's Bureau, 34 percent of the black families are headed by women, up from 23.7 percent in 1965. This compares with a current 9.9 percent for white women. Black female heads are more likely than their white sisters to have children to support, and these families are more likely to be below the legal poverty level—33 percent of the minority female heads versus 20 percent of the white female heads of families earn less than the poverty minimum (Ibid:5).

These figures confirm that, in spite of the women's rights movement, unemployment, underemployment, and poverty are visited mostly on women and disproportionately on minority women. They also show that although some women may be moving at an accelerated rate into managerial and professional positions under the stimulus of equal employment rights for women, this is essentially a white, middle-class phenomenon. Although it may be "good times" for some women as a result of the movement, for the women described above— and they constitute the majority of women involved in crime—the existence of the feminist movement has hardly produced a leap into prosperity. Life for these women can be described as follows:

The black woman is the head of the family, but the family is in disarray; she may work at any job but there are few good ones for which she is qualified; she has freedom of movement but there is no place to go. (Adler 1975:152)

These women have not only derived little benefit from the expanded labor market with which the feminist movement is credited, but they have also not adopted the consciousness-related aspects of the women's rights movement. For these women, more and more of whom are self-supportive, survival in an inflation economy without skills, education, or training leaves little time for identity crises and exercises in assertiveness training. They neither feel part of the women's movement nor support its principles (Bruck 1975). Many vocally oppose any association with the movement (Adler 1975). They come from the lower socioeconomic stratas of society that traditionally recognize male dominance and superiority. Their psychological dependency on males may even contribute to their delinquency. (Ward 1968)

To sum up: if the two primary contributions of the women's rights movement are increased psychological independence and expanded economic opportunities, the movement appears to have had little effect on female offenders and their peers. Their crimes continue to mirror their traditional role in society. They are predominantly small-scale property and victimless offenses reflecting both the female status as a minor consumer and her tendency to inflict self-directed rather than outward-directed injury. These women's infrequent participation in burglary and robbery is normally as a supportive female in the company of a male. The cases of assaults and homicides reflect their sex roles in so far as they are most often against persons with whom they have had affectional relationships such as husbands, lovers, and children (Ward 1968). There are exceptions—Freda Adler has noted them—but there is insufficient evidence to interpret these exceptions as a trend toward more serious criminality on the part of women. Nor can one conclude from them that they represent the "darker side" of the women's rights movement.

There are alternative hypotheses for increased female arrests. Laurel Rans looks to the nature of the economy, data gathering, and law enforcement as possible explanations. She points out that inflation has increased the cost of many items women steal, thus placing them in the felony-serious crime category. The result is that a woman may be a felon for stealing the same item that would have made her a misdemeanant 14 years ago.

Rans also contends that FBI figures do not control for increased arrests due to improved and expanded policing, nor do they consider increases in population. Finally, she points out that the practice of separating arrest statistics by sex was frequently not observed in the 1960s with the result that women's arrests were categorized with those of men. Now, with more refined data gathering, these "hidden women" are emerging (Rans 1975:2-3).

Another possible reason for increased arrests of females relates to the labor, income, and unemployment statistics discussed earlier. Black females have the highest unemployment rate of any group and, for those who are working, the lowest median income. Studies have shown a correlation between economic need and crime. In Colorado, the director of research for corrections found a three-month lag between an increase in unemployment and an increase in crime in that state (Philips 1976). A more extensive study, with possible application here, was done of crime in war and postwar Germany. This study showed a decided increase in crime during postwar depression, particularly among women and juveniles. "The number of women and children convicted of crime, particularly of property crime, rose tremendously" (Wickersham Commission 1968:112). Although we are not now in a depression, the situation of many black females relative to rising inflation in this country may resemble that state. These women may simply have surveyed their options, found them limited, and turned to theft as a rational means of survival.

Women and a Paternalistic Criminal Justice System

Increase in female arrests may also be due to a changing attitude within the criminal justice system toward females. While female offenders may not have benefited positively from the women's rights movement, they may be experiencing a negative residual effect of the movement. Although they treated women leniently in the past, criminal justice personnel may be prompted by the movement's rhetoric and activities to view female offenders now with less paternalism. Police officers who state, in effect, "If it's equality these women want, we'll see that they get it," lend credence to this speculation (Simon 1975:18).

It is not possible to quantify the effect of police attitude on offender arrests but existing statistics indicate that women continue to receive differential treatment at various stages within the criminal justice process. This treatment is, in some cases, preferential.

The most valuable and complete judicial statistics for the purpose of examining possible differential treatment of women are from California and will, therefore, be relied on for that purpose. Conviction rates in California for 1972 indicate evenhanded treatment of male and female offenders for both property and violent offenses. Women experience a slightly higher rate of conviction for drunken driving, embezzlement, fraud and petty theft than do men but the

difference is not significant. Statistics do show that women are more likely to
be acquitted than men if they plead not quilty (Simon 1975:57).

According to further data from California, however, women do appear to
receive preferential treatment at the sentencing stage. For all serious offenses,
convicted men are twice as likely to be sentenced to prison than are women.
Women charged with violent crimes, however, have a higher rate of commitment to prison than those convicted of property crimes. Although women are
treated most leniently when convicted of theft and narcotics, they are less likely
than men to be sentenced to prison regardless of the crime (California Bureau
of Criminal Statistics 1972).

A different story typically prevails, however, for female adolescents.

... while females constituted only about seventeen to twenty percent of the
(Honolulu) court's total population between 1954 and 1964, they accounted
for almost thirty percent of the admissions to the detention home for this
period. Additionally, adolescent females generally comprised about half of
those confined in the detention home at any given time due to the fact that
they spent, on the average, three times as long in these facilities as did their
male counterparts." (Chesney-Lind 1973:57)

Thus, evidence indicates that female juvenile offenders appear to be more
likely than males to be sent to detention and to remain there longer.

For women in prison seeking parole, their sex appears to make little difference. Women sentenced for forgery, fraud, and willful manslaughter are
slightly more likely to be paroled than their male counterparts. Those in
prison for burglary and armed robbery are less likely than men to be paroled.
With these exceptions, parole hearing outcomes are relatively the same for
men and women (Simon 1975:89-90).

Again, treatment differs for adolescent females who typically remain for
longer periods in institutions than do their male peers. For example, the
average length of stay for girls at a Texas juvenile institution is 12.4 months.
For boys, it is 10.1 months (Wooden 1976:119). In Connecticut juvenile
institutions, the average length of stay for females is seven months, compared
to five months for boys (Rogers 1972:226-7).

In reviewing the figures on female involvement with crime and the criminal
justice system, it is evident that (1) females are arrested at a greater rate than
before; (2) their crimes are predominantly economically motivated and nonviolent; (3) women receive little or no preferential treatment at the trial stage;
(4) when convicted, adult women are less frequently sentenced to prison than
men, but female adolescents appear more likely to be incarcerated than males;
and (5) while in prison, a woman's chance of parole is relatively equal to that
of a man, but girls tend to be detailed longer in juvenile institutions than do
boys. In sum, female offenders are occasionally treated differentially, but often
to their disadvantage.

The greatest discrepancy in treatment of males and females appears to be the sentencing stage. In the case of women, judges seem clearly less inclined to send them to prison than a man. This could be due to several factors. Women's crimes are generally less violent than men's and they, therefore, pose less of a threat to the community. Also, violent crimes women do commit are most frequently tied to their sex roles; that is, their victims are family members or lovers rather than strangers or fellow travelers in a bar. A 1968 study of violent women and crime found that 51.9 percent of the victims of female violence were family members, compared with 16.5 percent for male offenders. An additional 20.9 percent of the women's victims were lovers (Ward 1968:868). Few of these crimes by women were premeditated—most were the outcome of frustration and abuse, two motives that judges and society may be inclined to view more leniently.

Another factor influencing judges may be the secondary role played by women in the more serious crimes. The same 1968 study found that women charged with robbery were either accessories or partners in 80 percent of the cases (Ibid.:867). A recent survey of 30 judges and states' attorneys confirmed that most women are neither the planners nor the managers of crimes for which they are arrested (Simon 1975:109).

Judges may also be affected by the impact a decision to send a woman to prison will have on her family. As a superintendent of the California Institution for Women pointed out:

If a man goes to prison, the wife stays home and he usually has the family to return to and the household is there when he gets out. But women generally don't have family support from the outside. Very few men are going to sit around and take care of the children and be there when she gets back. So—to send a woman to prison means you are virtually going to disrupt her family." (Ibid:77)

Although these factors appear to influence judicial leniency for women, other factors have a reverse effect for girls. Judicial practices reveal a strong concern over guarding the sexual virtue of these girls. A study of Connecticut juvenile institutions showed that 31 percent of the girls were institutionalized for sexually related behavior such as sexual misconduct and pregnancy but no boys were sentenced for similar behavior. An additional 36 percent of the girls were incarcerated for noncriminal offenses such as runaway and incorrigibility but only 0.05 percent of the boys were (Rogers 1972:225).

In Honolulu, juvenile judges consistently, over a 26-year period, ordered physical examinations of female juvenile offenders in order to determine the virtue of the girls. Examination reports informed the judges whether the hymen was intact, ruptured, or torn, and whether the girl admitted having intercourse (Chesney-Lind 1973:56).

The overriding concern regarding girls appears to be their relative likelihood of pregnancy. As one juvenile counselor explained, "girls can get pregnant and boys can't."

Several studies show that judicial chivalry not only differs according to the age of the offender but also may differ according to the race. Racial bias is supported by a study of juvenile institutions reported in chapter 8. This study consisted of a self-reporting survey of delinquents in institutions across the country. It revealed that white youth of both sexes had committed more frequent and serious delinquent acts prior to incarceration than black youth. The study also found that, in spite of less frequent and serious delinquent behavior, black youth experienced more correctional handling prior to institutionalization. Both black and white females, however, reported more contact with the juvenile justice system than their male counterparts, regardless of the offense.

Although the women's liberation movement appears to have had little, if any, effect on the rise in female crime, the nature of female criminality, or the treatment of women as they move through the criminal justice process, there is a final area the movement does appear to have touched. That is the treatment of women in jails and prisons.

Deviant, incarcerated women in this country have always been treated as disgraced stepchildren and they have responded with appropriate contrition. While inmates of male prisons conducted demonstrations, riots, and press conferences demanding better jobs, shorter working hours, and longer visiting hours, women prisoners quietly continued to launder and mend institutional clothes and scrub institutional floors.

Although several strides behind the male-dominated prisoners' rights movement, the woman offender movement has begun. Assisted by members of the feminist movement, women offenders are beginning to make themselves heard. Quiet, but determined demonstrations have been conducted in several female institutions including those in New York and Colorado. A violent demonstration by female inmates at the North Carolina institution in the summer of 1975 brought the plight of the women to state, if not national, attention.

Women offenders are also beginning to recognize the potential value in law suits. Often helped by their liberated sisters, these women are taking to the courts to remedy their situation. A legal training class at the New York state institution for women is conducted by law students from New York University, providing fundamental information on the legal rights of the women prisoners. A successful law suit brought by the women at Bedford Hills, New York abolished that institution's practice of sending women inmates to the state mental institution as punishment for infractions.

Another law suit brought by the women inmates in the New Mexico penitentiary was successful in demanding equal vocational training and access to legal materials. Women in the North Carolina prison filed a class action against the method of administering vaginal and rectal examinations to female inmates.

In Mississippi, by threatening suit, women won the right to conjugal visits, which had been given to male offenders for many years. The list goes on.

Other changes are occurring through legislation, much of which is due in part to the efforts of women's rights advocates. The California prohibition on coed county jail programs was abolished by legislation in 1975. New York state has passed legislation calling for equal rehabilitation programs for male and female inmates. Legislation is pending, or has been passed, in several states authorizing expenditures for improved facilities and programming for female offenders.

Although most female offenders verbally dissociate themselves from the women's rights movement, they are increasingly beneficiaries of that movement. It is difficult to forecast where this will take them. Some women complain that the leniency they once enjoyed within the criminal justice system is now passing as a result of feminist activities. Others quickly sign up for carpentry and welding classes now offered at several institutions in response to feminist influence. One can hope that the trend toward equal opportunity for males and females in society will result in the best of both worlds for male and female offenders.

References

Adler, Freda. 1975. *Sisters in Crime,* New York, McGraw-Hill Book Co.

Bruck, Connie. 1975. "Women Against the Law," *Human Behavior,* December.

California Bureau of Criminal Statistics. 1969-72. *Crime and Delinquency in California,* Sacramento, California, Department of Justice, State of California.

Chesney-Lind, Meda. 1973. "Judicial Enforcement of the Female Sex Role: The Family Court and the Female Delinquent," *Issues in Criminology,* Vol. 8, Number 2, Fall.

Epstein, Cynthia F. 1975. "Ten Years Later: Perspectives on the Woman's Movement" *Dissent,* Spring.

Ferris, Abbot L. 1971. *Indicators of Trends in the Status of American Women,* Russell Sage Foundation, New York.

Glick, Ruth. 1974-76. "National Study of Women's Correctional Programs," funded by the Law Enforcement Assistance Administration, U.S. Department of Justice, Washington, D. C.

Heide, W.S. 1974. "Feminism and the 'Fallen Woman'," *Criminal Justice and Behavior,* Vol. 1, Number 4., December.

Hovey, Marcia. 1971. "The Forgotten Offenders," *Manpower Magazine,* U.S. Department of Labor, January.

Klein, Dorie, and June Kress. 1976. "Any Woman's Blues: A Critical Overview of Women, Crime and the Criminal Justice System," *Crime and Social Justice,* Spring-Summer.

Levitin, Teresa, Robert Quinn, and Graham Staines. 1973. "A Woman is 58% of a Man," *Psychology Today,* March.

Milton, Catherina, and Catherine Pierce. 1976. *Female Offenders: Problems and Programs,* Washington, D.C., The American Bar Association.

Philips, Norma, director of research, Division of Correctional Services, telephone interview, 1976.

Rans, Laurel. 1975. "Women's Arrest Statistics," *The Woman Offender Report,* March-April.

Rogers, Kristine O. 1972. "For Her Own Protection . . .": Conditions of Incarceration for Female Juvenile Offenders in the State of Connecticut," *Law and Society Review,* Winter.

Simon, Rita. 1975. *Women and Crime,* Lexington, Mass., Lexington Books, D.C. Heath and Co.

U.S. Bureau of the Census. 1975. *Statistical Abstract of the U.S., 1975,* 96th ed., Washington, D.C.

Velemesis, Margery. 1969. "Criminal Justice for the Female Offender," vol. 63, *AAUW Journal,* 13, 15.

Ward, D., M. Jackson, and E. Ward. 1968. "Crime and Violence by Women," *Crimes of Violence,* 13, Appendix 17, President's Commission on Law Enforcement and Administration of Justice.

Wickersham Commission. 1968. "Report on the Causes of Crime," U.S. National Commission on Law Observance and Enforcement, Montclair, N.J., Patterson Smith.

Wilson, Nanci, and Constance M. Rigsby. 1975. "Is Crime a Man's World? Issues in the Exploration of Criminality," *Journal of Criminal Justice,* Vol. 3.

Women's Bureau. 1975. *Handbook on Women Workers,* Employment Standards Administration, U.S. Department of Labor.

Wooden, Kenneth. 1976. *Weeping in the Playtime of Others,* New York, McGraw-Hill Book Co.

Part II

**Law and the Courts as They Affect
Female Criminality**

Introduction to Part II

In the past, little was known about the impact of judicial and legislative decisions on female offenders. Only as members of the women's rights movement began to examine differential civil laws affecting women in such areas as employment and financing did they begin to notice criminal laws that differentiated between the sexes. Further research revealed a plethora of laws penalizing both men and women for activities relating to their distinct roles in society. As these roles become less distinct and "woman" and "man" both become "human," such laws will be viewed as increasingly inappropriate. One by one, states are now gradually removing them from their statutes. Many still remain, however.

Chapter 3 examines those laws and judicial practices that penalize females because of the "nature of their sex." Carolyn Temin details statutes that justify longer sentences for women, and describes unsuccessful efforts to have these laws ruled unconstitutional. She makes the case for passage of the equal rights amendment as a means of permanently overruling individual judges and law makers who would use the "chivalry factor" as a means of administering an extra dose of punishment to the "fallen," deviant woman.

At the same time that laws exist to punish the fallen woman, similar laws exist to halt the descent of her younger sister. In chapter 4, Rosemary Sarri describes laws used by the juvenile justice system in its frantic effort to save the virtue of female adolescent offenders—laws that call for incarceration of girls in danger of leading a lewd or immoral life, of girls who walk with a "lascivious carriage," or those accused of promiscuity. It is clear in her discussion that what is normal, sexual acting out for boys is considered deviant behavior for girls.

Chapter 3 and 4 offer compelling evidence in favor of the equal rights amendment.

3

Discriminatory Sentencing of Women Offenders: The Argument for ERA in a Nutshell

Carolyn Engel Temin

Introduction

In 1963, the President's Commission on The Status of Women published the following statement in its report, *American Women:*

> Since the Commission is convinced that the U. S. Constitution now embodies equality of rights for men and women, we conclude that a constitutional amendment need not now be sought in order to establish this principle. But judicial clarification is imperative in order that remaining ambiguities with respect to constitutional protection of women's rights be eliminated.[1]

This statement is now familiar to all those who are active in the fight against legally sanctioned sex-based discrimination. It provided a theme with which to unite all the painstaking case-by-case legal battles of the sixties. It encouraged lawyers, regardless of their area of expertise, to seek out discriminatory legislation and bring it into the courts so that the hoped-for constitutional standards could be applied to forever nullify statutory inequalities.

It was against this background that the attack on statutes prescribing longer sentences for women offenders than for male offenders convicted of the same criminal conduct was launched. Although earlier decisions militated against success,[2] the issue seemed to be the perfect one for achieving the desired constitutional construction. The issue embodies the deprivation of personal liberty— a right that came to the forefront in the sixties; and the statutes being attacked discriminated solely on the basis of sex. To uphold them, a court would have to find that something in the very nature of being a woman justifies a legislature in maintaining that a woman be incarcerated for a longer period than a man. It was hoped that the shock value of raising the equal protection issue in this context would produce the desired judicial reaction—the application of the "overriding legislative purpose" doctrine to sex-based discrimination. The precedents thus established could then be applied to other areas (such as employment discrimination) where the issues were not always so finely chiselled.

Suits were brought challenging the sentencing statutes of Pennsylvania[3] and

Carolyn Engel Temin, "Discriminatory Sentencing of Women Offenders: The Argument for ERA in a Nutshell," *The American Criminal Law Review* vol. 11: 355–372, 1973. Reprinted with permission of the American Bar Association, Section of Criminal Justice.

Connecticut.[4] In both cases, *Commonwealth v. Daniel*,[5] and *United States ex rel. Robinson v. York*,[6] the courts held that there could be no rational basis for statutory classifications which impose longer sentences on women than on men convicted of the same offense. The statutes were found to invidiously discriminate against women in violation of the equal protection clause of the fourteenth amendment.[7] While the immediate objective of overturning these statutes was achieved, the battle for the ultimate goal, judicial recognition that classification by sex alone violates the fourteenth amendment, was lost. Both courts agreed that sex-based discrimination in sentencing statutes was unreasonable, but neither would hold that *all* sex-based discrimination was unreasonable.[8]

Daniel and *Robinson* were a great disappointment to those involved in the "fourteenth amendment approach" to equality under the law since they had very little applicability to situations not involving criminal sanctions. Nevertheless these opinions did achieve an important and much desired end which raised hopes of future successes. They discredited the earlier cases[9] which had blindly approved discriminatory sentencing statutes without conscientiously examining the state's purported justification for the classification. Even more encouraging was the suggestion by the *Robinson* court that discrimination on the basis of sex is no less inherently suspect than racial classification.[10] The adoption of this reasoning would have subjected other statutes which draw lines on the basis of sex to exacting judicial scrutiny and required the states to justify them by a compelling state interest.[11]

The hopes raised by the modest achievements of *Daniel* and *Robinson* were short-lived. On October 27, 1971, the Supreme Court of New Jersey handed down its appalling decision in *State v. Costello*,[12] refusing to hold that a sentencing statute similar to the Pennsylvania and Connecticut laws violated the equal protection clause on its face. Distinguishing *Robinson*, it criticized and discarded the precedent of *Daniel* and resurrected the decaying corpses of *Heitman*, *Platt*, *Brady* and *Gosselin*.[13] What had been so slowly and painstakingly accomplished was undone. The lesson is explicit and unavoidable. Freedom from sex-based discrimination will not come through judicial expansion of existing constitutional guarantees. The history of the fight against sex-based discrimination in criminal sentencing statutes presents a strong example of the absolute necessity for the Equal Rights Amendment.

Early History

It is one of the often encountered ironies of history that statutes imposing longer sentences on women than on men convicted of the same offense grew out of an effort to improve the lot of the female prisoner. The movement dedicated to this purpose had its origins somewhere around 1869 when Indiana became the first state to establish a separate reformatory for women. Prior to this, women prisoners had been incarcerated in the same county jails and penitentiaries housing male convicts.[14] By 1917, fourteen states had established similar institutions.[15] They were usually referred to as "reformatories" or "industrial homes" to distinguish them from penitentiaries.[16]

The reformatory ideal embodied much more than a physical plant. It embraced the notion—then revolutionary—that women criminals should be "rehabilitated" rather than "punished." It therefore followed, according to the correctional thinking of that period, that women should be detained in the institution for as long a time as necessary to achieve the desired level of "rehabilitation." In order to accomplish this, the statutes which established these "rehabilitative homes" also contained special sentencing provisions which applied only to the women sentenced to the particular institution.[17] Since most of these statutes required the courts to sentence to the "reformatories" all women over sixteen years of age who had been convicted of any crime,[18] the practical result was sex-based differential sentencing.

Pennsylvania's Muncy Act

If the sentencing statutes had merely been different they might not have been such a problem. The difficulty arose from the fact that either on their faces or in practical application, they resulted in women getting longer sentences than men. In fact, in the early twentieth century it was thought that the ideal sentence to a women's reformatory should be "indeterminate" with no limits at all on the minimum and maximum terms that an inmate could be forced to serve. Fortunately, most states put some limit on the maximum sentence—usually the maximum term prescribed by law for the particular offense.[19]

Pennsylvania created the State Industrial Home for Women by the Act of July 25, 1913, P.L. 1311,[20] known colloquially as the "Muncy Act" (after the geographical location of the institution). The sentencing provision of this Act is an excellent example of the type of statute being discussed here.[21] It required that all women over the age of sixteen years who had been convicted of an offense punishable by more than one year imprisonment be given a general sentence to Muncy. If the offense was punishable by a term of three years or less, they could be confined for three years. If the crime called for a term longer than three years, then the maximum punishment prescribed by law for the offense was the maximum sentence.[22] The judge possessed neither the discretion to impose a shorter maximum sentence than the maximum provided by law nor the power to fix a minimum sentence at which the woman would be eligible for parole.

By contrast, the Pennsylvania statute for sentencing male offenders to a penitentiary permits the judge in his discretion to impose a shorter maximum sentence than the maximum prescribed by law. In addition the judge is required to set a minimum sentence which can be no longer than one-half of the maximum sentence actually imposed.[23] Where the statute prescribes "simple imprisonment," the judge may impose a flat sentence (stating the maximum term only), but may not exceed the maximum term provided by law for the offense.[24]

The sentencing laws of Pennsylvania discriminated against women in five ways:

1. They permitted a court to send a woman to Muncy for three years even if the maximum for the offense was less than three years, whereas a man could not be sentenced to more than the maximum punishment prescribed by law;
2. They mandated that women receive the maximum legal penalty if convicted of a crime punishable by more than three years, whereas a man could be sentenced to less than the maximum prescribed by law;
3. A woman was not to receive any minimum sentence, whereas a man was to have a minimum sentence not to exceed one-half of the maximum sentence imposed except in those cases where the judge in his discretion could impose a flat sentence stating a maximum only.[25]
4. Under Pennsylvania law, where a sentence is imposed for less than two years, the jurisdiction to parole is in the sentencing judge; whereas, if the sentence imposed is two years or more, jurisdiction to parole lies exclusively with the parole board.[26] Since all sentences to Muncy were for more than two years, they came under the jurisdiction of the parole board. A person sentenced to less than two years may engage a lawyer to present and argue a petition for parole on his behalf. The prisoner may also present witnesses and enjoy the full panoply of due process rights. The Pennsylvania Board of Probation and Parole, on the other hand, makes its decisions in closed sessions and does not permit representation by counsel at its hearings.[27]
5. Under Pennsylvania law, where a statute prescribes "simple imprisonment" the sentence must be served in the county jail rather than in a state correctional institution.[28] Under the Muncy Act only women sentenced for offenses punishable by one year or less were eligible to serve their sentences in the county jail. There are very few such offenses in the Pennsylvania criminal code. Therefore, many women ended up in a penitentiary (i.e. Muncy) for offenses which would have merely sent a man to the county jail.[29]

Statutes similar to the Muncy Act are still in effect in Massachusetts,[30] New Jersey[31] and Connecticut.[32] Iowa law permits women to be confined up to five years for a misdemeanor,[33] whereas men can only be imprisoned for a maximum of one year unless otherwise stated in the statute defining the offense.[34] In Maine, women between the ages of 17 and 40 can be sentenced to reformatories for up to three years even if the maximum punishment for the offense is less.[35] Men, on the other hand, can only receive such treatment between the ages of 17 and 26.[36] Maryland permits judges to sentence women convicted of crimes punishable by three months imprisonment to the state women's reformatory for an indeterminate period not to exceed the maximum term of imprisonment provided by law.[37] Men are subject to such sentences only between the ages of 16 and 25.[38] Men over the age of 25 who are sentenced to the penitentiary receive a term stating both minimum and maximum limits.[39]

Some state legislatures have seen fit to change previously discriminatory sentencing provisions. Arkansas originally permitted women misdemeanants to be sentenced to confinement in the women's penitentiary,[40] whereas only male felons could be so confined. This was changed in 1971 specifically because it discriminated against women.[41] The discriminatory statutes which were upheld in *Dunkerton*, [42] *Heitman*[43] and *Brady*[44] have been repealed by the legislatures of Kansas and Ohio respectively and replaced by non-discriminatory measures.[45]

The Case of Commonwealth v. Daniel

On May 3, 1966 Jane Daniel was convicted of simple robbery[46] —an offense carrying a maximum penalty of ten years under Pennsylvania law.[47] The trial judge sentenced her to serve one to four years in the County Prison. Thirty-one days later[48] her sentence was vacated on the grounds that it was illegal and she was given the required ten-year sentence to Muncy. The opinion of the trial court makes it clear that there were no other reasons for the change in sentence.[49] An appeal was taken to the Superior Court of Pennsylvania on the sole ground that the Muncy Act constituted a denial of equal protection of the laws under the fourteenth amendment of the United States Constitution by arbitrarily discriminating against women as a class.

This case was the first attack ever launched against the Muncy Act. The facts of the case were particularly helpful since they presented a situation where the defendant would clearly have received a much shorter sentence if she had been eligible for sentencing under the statute for men. If the judge had been permitted to exercise his discretion, Ms. Daniel would have served a minimum of one and a maximum of four years, but under the Muncy Act she was required to serve a minimum of three and one-half and a maximum of ten years.[50]

The main obstacle to the appeal was the fact that all previous attacks on similar sentencing statutes in other jurisdictions had failed,[51] for the courts which had faced this question had uniformly held that differential sentencing was constitutional on the ground that women constituted a reasonable class for discriminatory treatment in sentencing statutes. The following language illustrates the "legal" reasoning which produced this doctrine:

It requires no anatomist or physiologist or psychologist or psychiatrist to tell the Legislature that women are different from men. In structure and function human beings are still as they were in the beginning "Male and female created He them." It is a patent and deep-lying fact that these fundamental anatomical and physiological differences affect the whole psychic organization. They create the differences in personality between men and women and personality is the predominating factor in delinquent careers. . . .

. . . [T]he female offender not merely requires, but deserves, on account of matters touching the perpetuation and virility of the species, correctional treatment different from the male offender, both in kind and degree; . . . . Let it be conceded that the industrial farm for women may fail to accomplish the results hoped for; the statute represents a serious effort on the part of the Legislature to deal justly with a subject of great public concern, . . . and this Court is not authorized to declare that the classification . . . is either arbitrary or unreasonable."[52]

The Superior Court of Pennsylvania denied the relief requested and adopted the reasoning of the earlier cases. It held that the legislative distinction which imposed longer sentences on women than men was reasonable in view of the state's purpose of providing more effective rehabilitation for women. The opinion relied on the same factors which the prior decisons had found persuasive: the inherent physical and psychological differences between men and women.[53] The decision was particularly disappointing because of its complete disregard of any of the legal reasoning presented by the appellant's brief and oral argument. The case presented one of the earliest opportunities for a practical application of the arguments outlined in the seminal article, *Jane Crow and the Law* by Pauli Murray and Mary Eastwood.[54] It was a dismal failure.

The only ray of hope was the opinion of Judge J. Sydney Hoffman, the lone dissenter.[55] He argued that the majority was wrong in merely applying the traditional rational basis equal protection test to legislation which impinged on the fundamental right to personal liberty.[56] He contended that where basic civil rights are involved, it should be incumbent upon the state to show a compelling state interest which justifies the legislative classification. Judge Hoffman recognized that there could be no overriding justification for a statute which, "under the guise of special rehabilitative treatment for women, . . . accomplishes little more than the imposition of a harsher punishment for women offenders."[57]

Daisy Douglas. Although this opinion could not become the law of the commonwealth, it was extremely helpful in convincing the Supreme Court of Pennsylvania to allow an appeal from the decision of the superior court. While the appeal was pending, a second attack on the Muncy Act was begun in the case of Daisy Douglas.

Daisy Douglas and here paramour, Richard Johnson, were tried together and convicted of robbery. Ms. Douglas, whose past record consisted of a number of arrests for prostitution, was duly sentenced to Muncy for the maximum term allowed by law for the offense of aggravated robbery—twenty years. Her codefendant, whose past record consisted of six prior convictions for burglary, received a sentence of not less than three nor more than ten years in the men's penitentiary. A petition under Pennsylvania's Post-Conviction Hearing Act was filed on behalf of Ms. Douglas on the ground that her sentence constituted a denial of her fourteenth amendment rights. Her petition was dismissed on the sole ground that the judge was "constrained" to follow the decision of the superior court in the *Daniel* case.[58]   An appeal was taken and the case was consolidated with the *Daniel* case for argument before the Supreme Court of Pennsylvania.[59]

For some reason, the *Douglas* case is never mentioned in articles which discuss *Daniel*, but it played an extremely important role in obtaining the successful result in the supreme court. The superior court in *Daniel* had said that a major flaw in the appellant's attack on the Muncy Act was her failure to substantiate the claim that if she were a man she would have received a maximum sentence of four years. Actually the court misunderstood the appellant's claim. Her argument was that if Jane Daniel could have been sentenced under the statute which applied to male offenders, she would have received a lesser sentence. Nevertheless the appellant's failure to produce data which supported this assertion prevented the court from overturning the Muncy Act on the basis that it discriminated against women.[60]

The facts of *Douglas* presented the unequivocal proof of the discriminatory effect of the Muncy Act which had been found lacking in the superior court. Male and female co-defendants were jointly tried and convicted of the same offense. The male, with a serious past criminal record, was sentenced to ten years. The female was required by statute to be sentenced to twenty years even though her past criminal involvement was extremely minimal. The male was eligible for parole after three years; the female was technically eligible for parole at any time but in practice was not considered eligible for three and one-half years.[61]   Further proof of sex-based disparity in sentencing was provided by statistics kept by the Pennsylvania Board of Probation and Parole.[62]   These showed that men on parole, convicted of a second similar offense, were rarely, even under these circumstances, sentenced to the maximum punishment permitted by law for the offense.

The consolidated appeals were argued on January 5, 1968 and on July 1, 1968 the supreme court reversed the judgments below and remanded the cases for resentencing. The court held that, while legislative classification on the basis of sex alone did not violate the equal protection clause, it could find no reasonable justification for a statute which imposed longer sentences on women than men convicted of the same crime. Acknowledging that

... there are undoubtedly significant biological, natural and practical differences between men and women which would justify, under certain circumstances, the establishment of different employment qualification standards.[63]

the court specifically found that

... the considerations and factors which would justify a difference between men and women in matters of employment, as well as in a number of other matters, *do not govern* or justify the imposition of a longer or greater sentence on women than is imposed upon men for the commission of the same crime.[64]

With these words, the Supreme Court of Pennsylvania emphatically stated that the Constitution of the United States does not embody equal rights for women, although it does prevent the imposition of longer sentences on women than on men convicted of the same offense. A similar result was reached by the United States District Court for Connecticut in the case of *United States* ex rel. *Robinson v. York*[55] decided on February 28, 1968. That case struck down a Connecticut statute relating to the sentencing of women misdemeanants which was exactly the same as the Muncy Act Provision.[66] Since both courts reached the same conclusion independent of each other, it appeared, at the time, that the issue of the constitutionality of disparate sentencing statutes had been layed to rest forever. In the words of Leo Kanowitz, the *Robinson* and *Daniel* decisions appeared to be the "early heralds of a new day."[67]

Muncy Act Amendment

But then came the backlash. On July 16, 1968, just a little more than two weeks after the Supreme Court of Pennsylvania handed down the decision in *Daniel*, the legislature passed a new version of the Muncy Act. The amendment provided that in sentencing a woman for a crime punishable by more than one year, the court "shall not fix a minimum sentence, but shall fix such maximum sentence as the court shall deem appropriate, so long as such maximum sentence does not exceed the maximum term specified by law for the crime for which the prisoner is being sentenced."[68] Thus the small victory achieved by *Daniel* was narrowed still further. Although women would not have to receive a longer maximum sentence than men, they were still to be denied the right to have their minimum sentence set by a judge. By retaining this type of so-called "indeterminate" sentence at Muncy, women were still being denied equal treatment.[69]

The 1968 amendment to the Muncy Act has been challenged in Pennsylvania courts on two occasions. Immediately after its passage, in the case of *Commonwealth v. Blum*,[70] the superior court was asked to find that the new statute discriminated merely because it was different than the statute which applied to men and because it had been shown in the *Daniel* case that women serving indeterminate sentences were held in prison for longer periods of time before being released on parole than men who had been given minimum sentences.[71] The superior court affirmed the judgment of the trial court per curiam.[72] Subsequently the Supreme Court of Pennsylvania denied allocatur[73] and the Supreme Court of the United States denied certiorari.[74] Actually this issue would appear to have been disposed of in the *Daniel* case where as part of its discussion the court indicated that the only part of a sentence which has any legal validity is the maximum sentence and that the minimum sentence is only an administrative notice that the person is eligible for parole consideration.[75]

In the more recent case of *Commonwealth v. Piper*[76] the superior court once again avoided facing the issue by rendering a per curiam opinion. Judge Hoffman, however, wrote a dissenting opinion in which he stated that the 1968 Muncy Act is unconstitutional because the minimum sentence significantly affects parole eligibility and therefore the act results in discrimination between men and women in terms of consideration for parole.[77] The case is now pending on appeal to the Supreme Court of Pennsylvania.

It should also be noted that due process constitutes another basis for arguing that the 1968 Muncy Act is discriminatory. In Pennsylvania a man is entitled by law to have his minimum sentence set by a judge, at a hearing where representation by counsel is constitutionally mandated,[78] in open court and with the full panoply of due process rights; whereas a woman's minimum sentence is decided by the parole board, at a closed session, where she has no representation, or any other procedural rights.[79] Arguably, this constitutes as much a denial of equal protection as the imposition of mandatory maximum sentences.

New Jersey and State v. Costello

An even more devastating blow to the *Daniel* doctrine was dealt by the Supreme Court of New Jersey in the recent case of *State v. Costello.*[80] This case, the first since *Daniel* and *Robinson* to treat the issue of differential sentencing, involved a constitutional attack on a New Jersey statute similar to the Muncy Act.[81] The law requires that women convicted of crimes punishable by five years or less be sentenced to the Women's Correctional Institution for the maximum prescribed by law. If the offense is punishable by more than five years, then the judge may either sentence them to five years imprisonment, or to anything over five years but not to exceed the maximum prescribed by law. Men, on the other hand, receive a sentence stating a minimum and maximum within the limits prescribed by law.[82]

The court dismissed the *Robinson* case as inapplicable to this situation because it involved a statute which sentenced women to a longer maximum term than a man *could* have been sentenced for. Technically, this distinction is correct, since the New Jersey statute, unlike the Connecticut law, does not actually increase the maximum provided by law for the offense. It does, however, force judges to impose the maximum in all cases where they are sentencing a woman for an offense punishable by five years or less, and the result, as it was in *Daniel* is that women receive longer sentences than men convicted of the same offense.

Robinson, like *Daniel*, dealt with the issue of the constitutionality of the result of such statutes (i.e., longer sentences for women) and not with the method by which this result was obtained. The New Jersey court's reading of *Robinson* appears far too narrow.

The court refused to follow the ruling in *Daniel* that there could be no rational basis for a legislative classification which imposed longer sentences on women than on men for the same criminal conduct. Instead it remanded the case to the Appellate Division to give the state the opportunity to show a substantial justification for the sentencing scheme.[83] The opinion relied to a large extent on the reasoning of a recent case comment in the *Harvard Law Review*.[84] This article critized the *Daniel* court's holding that statutory provisions like the Muncy Act would be arbitrary under all circumstances and suggested that such statutes could be sustained upon a showing of a "substantial empirical basis" for the classification. The author argued that social and psychological differences between men and women which rendered the latter more susceptible to rehabilitation might be a substantial justification for differential sentencing.[85]

If this reasoning sounds familiar, then it should come as no surprise that the court dredged up *Heitman*, *Platt*, *Brady* and *Gosselin*[86] as precedent for the proposition that sex-based discriminatory sentencing is not constitutionally prohibited.[87] The fact that most of the statutes vindicated in those cases are no longer on the books either never came to the court's attention or was not deemed significant.

A fifth case cited by the court in favor of this proposition was *Wark v. State*.[88] This 1970 decision from the Supreme Judicial Court of Maine upheld a statutory scheme whereby men could receive an unlimited sentence for jail break, whereas women could receive no more than eleven months for the same offense.[89] The Maine Court indicated that even if its previous decision in *Gosselin*[90] would have to be reexamined in the light of *Daniel* and *Robinson*, these cases were not controlling.[91] The court held that the legislature could reasonably have concluded that since men are stronger, more aggressive and more disposed toward violent action than women, they constituted a greater risk of harm upon their escape and required a longer sentence to deter them from such conduct. The Supreme Court of the United States denied certiorari.[92]

The *Costello* case was remanded and the defendant was given a chance to have her sentence reconsidered.[93] Ultimately, the defendant received a sentence which did not involve the issues raised here and the case was not appealed further.[94]

Slightly less than a month after the *Costello* decision, the United States Supreme Court decided in *Reed v. Reed*[95] that the states may classify on the basis of sex if the criteria for the classification bear a reasonable relation to the objective of the statute whose constitutionality is in question. Nothing in that decision is helpful in predicting the outcome of an appeal on the *Daniel-Costello* issue. It merely reaffirms the standard used by both the Pennsylvania and New Jersey courts to reach their disparate conclusions.

Conclusion

The inconsistent positions taken by the courts on the issue of differential sentencing demonstrate the need for the equal rights amendment. As one commentator put it:

> . . . one cannot say that the possibility of achieving substantial equality of rights for women under the Fourteenth and Fifth Amendments is permanently foreclosed. But the present trend of judicial decisions . . . indicates that any present hope for large-scale change can hardly be deemed realistic.[96]

Any case by case attack is subject to the same pitfalls as the one described here. A favorable decision in one jurisdiction is not binding on any other. Courts may interpret precedents too narrowly, thus diminishing the effect of an important decision. And a victory in the courts can be undone by the legislature. The fight must then begin again for territory already won.[97]

Only by ratification of the Equal Rights Amendment can we assure that statutory schemes such as discriminatory sentencing acts will cease to exist. The question remains as to the effect that the ERA will have on such statutes. It has been suggested that under ERA, special sentencing statutes relating to women would fall, leaving them subject to the "standard laws."[98] Another analyst states that where there are no conflicting laws, one for men and one for women, the one containing the most beneficial provisions will survive.[99] The question will then be which type of sentencing scheme is preferable.[100]

Regardless of the result, the Equal Rights Amendment will bury for all time, the useless, chauvinistic discussions in the cases concerning the "unique" physiological, psychological and sociological aspects of women. These learned, intellectual acrobatics which have been used for so long to justify the demeaning, condescending and crass treatment of humans who are female by humans who are male have no place in a society seeking equality of treatment of all its members.[101]

Notes

1. Established by Exec. Order No. 10,980, 3 C.F.R. 138 (Supp. 1961).

2. *See, e.g.*, State v. Heitman, 105 Kan. 139, 181 P. 630 (1919); *Ex parte* Dunkerton, 104 Kan. 481, 179 P. 347 (1919); Platt v. Commonwealth, 256 Mass. 539, 152 N.E. 914 (1926); *Ex parte* Gosselin, 141 Me. 412, 44 A.2d 882

(1945), *cert. denied sub nom.* Gosselin v. Kelley, 328 U.S. 817 (1946); *Ex parte* Brady, 116 Ohio St. 512, 157 N.E. 69 (1927). These cases upheld discriminatory sentencing acts against constitutional challenges.

3. Pa. Stat. Ann. tit. 61, § 566 (1964).

4. Conn. Gen. Stat. Ann. § 17-360 (1958). (Now Conn. Gen. Stat. Ann. § 18-65 (Supp. 1972).)

5. 430 Pa. 642, 243, A.2d 400 (1968).

6. 281 F. Supp. 8 (D. Conn. 1968).

7. 430 Pa. at 648, 243 A.2d at 403; 281 F. Supp. at 17.

8. 430 Pa. at 649-50, 243 A.2d at 403-04; 281 F. Supp. at 13.

9. *See* cases cited note 2 *supra.*

10. 281 F. Supp. at 14. The court said:

This statute, which singles out adult women convicted of misdemeanors for imposition of punishment by imprisonment for longer terms than may be imposed on men, must be supported by a full measure of justification to overcome the equal protection which is guaranteed to them by the fourteenth amendment. In Loving v. Virginia, 388 U.S. 1, 87 S.Ct. 1817, 18 L.Ed. 2d 1010 (1967), where penalties were imposed on the basis of racial classification, the Supreme Court enunciated a strict standard for testing equalprotection:

. . . .

While the Supreme Court has not explicitly determined whether equal protection rights of women should be tested by this rigid standard, it is difficult to find any reason why adult women, as one of the specific groups that compose humanity, should have a lesser measure of protection than a racial group.

11. Leo Kanowitz summarized the importance of *Daniel* and *Robinson* in this manner:

The various opinions in the *Daniels* [sic] and *Robinson* cases are of extreme importance for a number of reasons. For one thing, they undermine earlier cases in other jurisdictions upholding sex-based discrimination in sentencing rules and practices. They also represent a significant breakthrough . . . in the undifferentiated "sex is a reasonable basis for classification" approach that has held sway for so long in this area. What is more important is that their analytical approach— emphasizing the greater burden of justification to sustain an unequal deprivation of a "basic" civil right or analogizing a female group to a racial group—creates the possibility of successfully attacking, on constitutional grounds, a variety of other sex-based discriminatory rules and practices. In their own way, this handful of decisions may be the early heralds of a new day in the general treatment of men and women in American law and life.

L. Kanowitz, Women and the Law 172 (1969).

12. 59 N.J. 334, 282 A.2d 748 (1971).

13. 59 N.J. at 343-44, 282 A.2d at 753-54. *See* cases cited note 2 *supra.*

14. Rogers, *A Digest of Laws Establishing Reformatories for Women in the United States*, 8 J. Crim. L.C. & P.S. 518 (1917).

15. *Id.* at 520. In addition to Indiana these included Massachusetts (1874), New York (1881), Iowa (1900), New Jersey (1910), Ohio (1911), Pennsylvania (1913), Wisconsin (1913), Maine (1915), Minnesota (1915), Connecticut (1917), Kansas (1917), Michigan (1917), and Rhode Island (1917).

16. *Id.* It is interesting to note that in most cases the names of these institutions have been changed and today most of them bear the designation "state correctional institution for women." In these cases the name change reflects the true state of affairs. These are no more nor less than penitentiaries for women. *See* Commonwealth v. Stauffer, 214 Pa. Super. 113, 117, 251 A.2d 718, 722 (1969).

17. *Compare* Conn. Gen. Stat. Ann. § 18-65 (Supp. 1972) *with* § 53a-35 (Supp. 1972). *Compare* Mass. Gen. Laws Ann. ch. 279, § 18 (Supp. 1972) *with* ch. 279, § 24 (Supp. 1972).

18. *See, e.g.,* Conn. Gen. Stat. Ann. § 18-65 (Supp. 1972).

19. Rogers, *supra* note 14, at 526, 535. But Minnesota law originally provided that women could be sentenced to the reformatory for a term which would be "without limit as to time." Min. Laws 1915, ch. 324, § 1, *as amended* Minn. Stat. Ann. § 243.90 (1972).

20. Pa. Stat. Ann. tit. 61, ch. 7 (1964). A 1959 amendment changed the name of the institution to the State Correctional Institution at Muncy. Act of October 22, 1959, P.L. 1356.

21. Pa. Stat. Ann. tit. 61, § 566 (1964). *See also* Conn. Gen. Stat. Ann. § 18-65 (Supp. 1972); Mass. Gen. Laws Ann. ch. 279, § 18 (1972); N.J. Stat. Ann. § 30:4-155 (1964).

22. These were the sentencing provisions in force at the time the *Daniel* case was brought in 1966. They were later changed by case law and statutory amendment as will be discussed *infra.*

23. The statutory language refers to this as an "indefinite" sentence. In this article I have refrained from describing sentences as indefinite, indeterminate, definite or otherwise since these terms are not used uniformly throughout the states.

24. Pa. Stat. Ann. tit. 19, § 1057 (1964). Note that although the statutory language states "any person," prior to the *Daniel* case it only applied to men.

25. Under Pennslyvania law a minimum sentence is the time a person must serve before becoming eligible for parole. Flat sentences are only available for a small number of minor crimes. Since the repeal of the "good time" statute in Pennsylvania on July 22, 1965, flat sentences have fallen into disuse. (Before its repeal, Pennsylvania's good-time statute only applied to flat sentences and enhanced their appeal in the eyes of criminal defendants who often requested them at the time of sentencing.) Since women have no minimum sentence under the Muncy Act they are theoretically eligible for parole at any time after

sentencing. On its face this appears to discriminate in favor of women. The actual effect of this provision will be discussed *infra.*

26. *See* Pa. Stat. Ann. tit. 61, § 331.1 *et seq.* (1964).

27. The hearings referred to here are those where the decision to parole from a sentence is made. Pennsylvania does permit representation of counsel at hearings which consider technical violations of parole. *See* Commonwealth v. Tinson, 433 Pa. 328, 249 A.2d 549 (1969).

28. Pa. Stat. Ann. tit. 19, § 891 (1964).

29. This effect of the Muncy Act was declared unconstitutional in Commonwealth v. Stauffer, 214 Pa. Super. 113, 251 A.2d 718 (1969). In Pennsylvania the county jail is preferable to Muncy because of its location and other less tangible reasons which make "county time" less onerous to serve. A person incarcerated at Muncy is almost always cut off from her relatives and friends.

30. Mass. Gen. Laws Ann. ch. 125, § 16 (1958).

31. N.J. Stat. Ann. § 30:4-155 (1964).

32. Conn. Gen. Stat. Ann. § 18-65 (Supp. 1972). Although the *Robinson* case declared the provision relating to misdemeanants to be unconstitutional, the felony sentencing provision has never been attacked. It is exactly the same as that provided under Pennsylvania's Muncy Act.

33. Iowa Code Ann. § 245.7 (1969).

34. *Id.* at § 687.7 (1950).

35. Me. Rev. Stat. Ann. tit. 34, § 853-54 (Supp. 1972).

36. *Id.* § 802. This provision is similar to the provision complained of as being discriminatory in *Ex parte* Gosselin, 141 Me. 412, 44 A.2d 882 (1945), but discrimination still exists based on the different age eligibility limits for the sexes.

37. Md. Ann. Code art. 27, § 689(e) (1957).

38. *Id.* § 689(d).

39. *Id.* § 690.

40. Ark. Acts 1939, No. 117, § 1, at 270.

41. Ark. Stat. Ann. § 46-804 (Supp. 1971).

42. *See* note 2 *supra.*

43. *Id.*

44. *Id.*

45. Kan. Stat. Ann. § 21-4601 *et seq.* (Supp. 1970); Ohio Rev. Code Ann. § § 5145.01, 5143.23 (Anderson 1970).

46. Brief for Appellant, Commonwealth v. Daniel, 430 Pa. 642, 243 A.2d 400 (1968) [hereinafter cited as Brief for Appellant].

47. Pa. Stat. Ann. tit. 18, § 4704 (1963).

48. If the sentence had not been illegal, it would have become final after 30 days. Pa. Stat. Ann. tit. 12, § 1032 (Supp. 1972); Commonwealth *ex rel.* Perotta v. Myers, 203 Pa. Super. 287, 201 A.2d 292 (1966).

49. Brief for Appellant, *supra* note 46, at apps. 1, 2.

50. Although theoretically a woman sentenced under the Muncy Act was eligible for parole at any time, in actuality the authorities at Muncy required that a certain amount of time be served before parole was considered depending on the offense for which the woman was convicted. *See* Commonwealth v. Daniel, 210 Pa. Super. 156, 167, 232 A.2d 247, 253 (1967) (Hoffman, J., dissenting).

51. *See* cases cited *supra* note 2.

52. State v. Heitman, 105 Kan. 139, 146-48, 181 P. 630, 633-34 (1919).

53. This court is of the opinion that the legislature reasonably could have concluded that indeterminate sentences should be imposed on women as a class, allowing the time of incarceration to be matched to the necessary treatment in order to provide more effective rehabilitation. Such a conclusion could be based on the physiological and psychological make-up of women, the type of crime committed by women, the relation to the criminal world, their role in society, their unique vocational skills and pursuits and their reaction as a class to imprisonment, as well as the number and type of women who are sentenced to imprisonment rather than given suspended sentences.

Commonwealth v. Daniel, 210 Pa. Super. 156, 164, 232 A.2d 247, 251-52 (1967). It should be noted that the defendant's name was Jane Daniel. The superior court opinion incorrectly spelled her name as Daniels. It appears correctly in the opinion of the supreme court.

54. Although blacks have successfully invoked the protection of the Constitution, women have been unable to do so. The difficulty in asserting women's rights lies not in the limited reach of the fourteenth amendment, but in the failure of the courts to isolate and analyze the discriminatory aspect of differential treatment based on sex. Laws discriminate by defining crimes to the acts of one sex but not the other and by differenciating in the punishment of criminals of different sexes. The Civil Rights Act of 1964, Title VII prohibits employment discrimination based on sex, however the Act does not totally preempt state laws which discriminate by sex (*e.g.*, laws prohibiting women from working at night in certain industries, weight lifting limitations for women, and maximum hour laws). The recent increase in activity concerning the status of women indicates a gradual trend in the law not to protect women by restriction and confinement, but to protect both sexes from discrimination. Murray & Eastwood, *Jane Crow and the Law: Sex Discrimination and Title VII*, 34 Geo. Wash. L. Rev. 232 (1965).

55. 210 Pa. Super. at 167, 232 A.2d at 253.

56. In my view, the "any rational basis" formula is inadequate to test the validity of the Muncy Act against the present challenge. That doctrine derives from a number of cases upholding economic regulatory measures or statutes not directly impinging on personal liberties or fundamental rights . . . . Surely, the proper inquiry here . . . is whether there clearly appears in the relevant materials some "overriding statutory purpose" requiring the imposition of more severe penalties on women than on men and requiring the delegation of the sentencing power to a nonjudicial agency in whose hands it is manifestly susceptible to abuse.

210 Pa. Super. at 169-70, 232 A.2d at 254 (Hoffman, J., dissenting).

57. . . . [U]nder the guise of special rehabilitative treatment for women, the legislature, in the Muncy statute, has adopted a system which accomplishes little more than the imposition of a harsher punishment for women offenders. As such it denies them the equal protection of the laws guaranteed by the Constitution of the United States.

210 Pa. Super. at 172, 232 A.2d at 255 (Hoffman, J., dissenting).

58. Brief for Appellants at app. 8, Commonwealth v. Daniel and Douglas, 430 Pa. 642, 243 A.2d 400 (1968).

59. Since Daniel was already pending before the supreme court it was possible for Douglas to skip the usual necessary stop at the superior court and proceed directly to the supreme court.

60. . . . [A]ppellant argues that because she is a woman she has received a maximum sentence of ten years; . . . that if she were a man she would have received a maximum term of four years . . . . This argument rests on an invalid assumption, viz., that a man committing this crime would have received a maximum term of four years. Judge Stern's prior sentence of one to four years was imposed upon Jane Daniels, a female, and we cannot speculate as to what the sentence would have been had the person robbing the bar in question been a male.

210 Pa. Super. at 165, 232 A.2d at 252.

61. See Brief for Appellants, supra note 58.

62. Id. at app. C.

63. 430 Pa. at 649, 243 A.2d at 403.

64. 430 Pa. at 650, 243 A.2d at 404.

65. 281 F. Supp. 8 (D. Conn. 1968). Apparently this decision had no influence on the ruling of the Pennsylvania Supreme Court as it was not cited in its opinion.

66. Conn. Gen. Stat. Ann. § 17-360 (1958).

67. L. Kanowitz, supra note 11, at 172.

68. Pa. Stat. Ann. tit. 71, § 566 (Supp. 1972).

69. For a general discussion of the effect of the indeterminate sentence at Muncy see Temin, The Indeterminate Sentence: The Muncy Experience, Prison Journal (1972). In Commonwealth v. Stauffer, 214 Pa. Super. 113, 251 A.2d

718 (1969), the court, relying on Daniel, held that women could not be sentenced to Muncy for crime that was punishable by simple imprisonment since a man in that case could only be sent to the county jail. *See* Commonwealth *ex rel.* Monaghan v. Burke, 169 Pa. Super. 256, 82 A.2d 337 (1951). The effect of Stauffer is that women can get a minimum-maximum sentence for crimes punishable by "simple imprisonment" since the indeterminate sentence is only for sentences served at Muncy.

70. 220 Pa. Super. 703, ____ A.2d ____(1972).

71. See Commonwealth v. Blum, Brief for Appellant, Superior Court of Pennsylvania, October Term, 1969 Nos. 208, 209.

72. 220 Pa. Super. 703, ____ A.2d ____(1972).

73. 221 Pa. 691, ____ A.2d ____(1972).

74. 408 U.S. 516 (1972).

75. 430 Pa. at 647-48, 243 A.2d at 403.

76. 221 Pa. Super. 187, 289 A.2d 193 (1972).

77. 221 Pa. Super. at 290, 289 A.2d at 196-97.

78. Mempa v. Rhay, 389 U.S. 128 (1967); Gideon v. Wainwright, 372 U.S. 335 (1963).

79. *See* Temin, *supra* note 69.

80. 59 N.J. 334, 282 A.2d 748 (1971).

81. N.J. Stat. Ann. § 30:4-155 (1964).

82. *Id.*

83. 59 N.J. at 345, 282 A.2d at 755. The equal protection challenge was first raised on appeal in the Supreme Court and thus there was no record on this issue.

84. 82 Harv. L. Rev. 921 (1969).

85. Under the regimen of a "substantial empirical basis" test, the state would be required to show affirmatively that there are significant social and psychological differences between male and female offenders such that the latter are particularly susceptible to rehabilitative treatment under the "flexible" indeterminate sentence. The Daniels [sic] court stated that there are no differences which would justify the penal effect of the legislature's classification. However, there is considerable evidence that women who perform criminal acts possess as a group a number of distinct qualities and characteristics and a plausible argument can be made that the rehabilitative possibilities are greater for a class which, for example, demonstrates a noticeably lower frequency of recidivism and parole violations than the class of male offenders.
82 Harv. L. Rev. at 923-24.

86. *See* cases cited *supra* note 2.

87. 59 N.J. at 344, 282 A.2d at 754.

88. 266 A.2d 62 (Me. 1970).

89. *Id.* at 64. Maine is not alone in prescribing longer sentences for men convicted of prison breach than for women. *See, e.g.*, Conn. Gen. Stat. Ann. § 18-66 (Supp. 1972) and § 53a-169-70 (1958).

90. *See* note 2 *supra.*

91. 266 A.2d at 64.

92. 400 U.S. 952 (1970).

93. 59 N.J. at 347, 282 A.2d at 755.

94. Citizen's Advisory Council on the Status of Women, Item No. 24-N, February 1972.

95. 401 U.S. 71 (1971).

96. Brown, Emerson, Falk & Freedman, *The Equal Rights Amendment: A Constitutional Basis for Equal Rights for Women*, 80 Yale L.J. 871, 882 (1971) [hereinafter cited as Brown].

97. As in the case of the "new" Muncy Act. *See* notes 71 & 72 *supra* and accompanying text.

98. Brown, *supra* note 96, at 966. The authors of that article were evidently not aware that the legislature passed a new Muncy Act and that in Pennsylvania, at present, women are still given special sentences. (A new sentencing code presently pending in the legislature would apply equally to men and women and would give the sentencing judge the option of imposing a minimum-maximum sentence on a Muncy-type sentence. S.B. 440.)

99. Eastwood, *The Double Standard of Justice: Women's Rights Under the Constitution*, 5 Valparaiso L. Rev. 281, 298 (1971).

100. The author of this article has discussed her preference in Temin, *The Indeterminate Sentence: The Muncy Experience*, Prison Journal (Spring 1972).

[101. Since the date of original publication of this article, both the New Jersey and Pennsylvania supreme courts have held differential sentencing of men and women to be unconstitutional. State v. Chambers 63 N.J. 287, 307 A.2d 78 (1973); Commonwealth v. Butler 458 Pa. 289, 328 A.2d 851 (1974). It is interesting to note that the Pennsylvania Supreme Court held that the change from its holding in *Daniel supra* was mandated by the enactment of an equal rights amendment to the Pennsylvania constitution on May 18, 1971. (See Article 1, Section 27). Sentencing of criminal offenders in Pennsylvania is now controlled by a new sentencing code. The act of December 30, 1974 (P.L. 1052, No. 345 Section 1; 18 Pa. C.S.A. Sec. 1301) provides for equality of treatment of men and women offenders. These recent determinations further underscore the theory outlined here that equality for women depends heavily on constitutional amendments.]

4

Juvenile Law: How It Penalizes Females

Rosemary C. Sarri

In myriad ways statutes governing juvenile justice systems have discriminated against females. Any historical examination of law in the Western world documents sexism in both law and legal practice. Which comes first—the perspectives about female criminality, or statutes defining female crime—matters very little, because once the ideology and law are established, each reinforces the other. The processing of females into and through the justice system manifests some marked contrasts between adults and juveniles. It is frequently observed that adult females have been treated more leniently by the system, when comparisons can be made with males for the same offenses (Simon 1975; Singer 1973; Arditi et al. 1973). For example, the population of state correctional facilities was 97 percent male in 1974 when the male proportion of all adult arrests was 85 percent (U.S. NCJISS 1975, 1976). At the same time, women are arrested, tried, convicted, and incarcerated for behavior (e.g., promiscuity and prostitution) for which men are not prosecuted in the vast majority of jurisdictions.

In contrast to adults, juvenile females are dealt with more stringently by the juvenile justice system than juvenile males, for the arrest ratio of males to females is approximately 4 to 1, but the ratio of detention and incarceration is 3 to 1 (Sarri 1974). Obviously such contradictions are not the result of rational decision making about criminal justice processing. Moreover, these practices are the opposite of those that would probably be recommended if a system were designed for more effective intervention based on scientific knowledge available regarding criminal careers, deterrence, and recidivism. But as we shall note subsequently, this society is ambivalent in its perspectives toward adolescents. On the one hand they are to be socialized in a nurturant manner; on the other hand they are viewed as disruptive persons to be controlled by adults.

This chapter highlights what appear to be the more problematic aspects of sexism in the juvenile justice system. Statutory and case law is examined with respect to jurisdictions, legal authority, and sex-linked differentiation. The impact of equal rights legislation is also considered. Last, representation of females in the juvenile justice system is examined, along with operational differences in the processing of females by law enforcement, judicial, and correctional agencies, using data from the National Assessment of Juvenile Corrections.

The author wishes to acknowledge the comments and criticism of Elaine Selo, Josefina Figueira McDonough, William Barton, Vann Jones, and Paul Isenstadt of the National Assessment of Juvenile Corrections staff.

67

Females and the Administration of Justice

The diversity of judgments in alleged sex discrimination cases arises from the
application of variable standards by the court. Two tests typically are employed:

1. *Reasonableness.* Did the state have a reasonable purpose in passing the dis-
   puted law? Is there some difference between the two classes of people that
   renders the different treatment reasonable?
2. *Strict scrutiny.* Where the court maintains that the classification set up by
   the law is suspect, or that fundamental rights are affected by the law, does
   the state have a purpose of overriding public importance in passing the
   particular law? Is the classification set up by the law necessary to the
   accomplishment of that purpose?

Courts have usually used the reasonableness test in matters of alleged sex discrimination, and, as it is relatively easy to justify a law on the grounds of reasonableness, most sex-discriminatory laws have been upheld. The Fourteenth Amendment has been invoked to constrain race discrimination in voting, employment,
social welfare, education, and other areas, but only very recently have attempts
been made to employ it to prohibit or discourage discrimination against women.
Nowhere is this discrimination more apparent and of greater consequence than
in the administration of justice. Sexism is a pervasive phenomenon. It is only
recently, for example, that in some states delinquency laws discriminating against
females have been struck down as unconstitutional.

   In recent years some sex-based discrimination, particularly in military benefits and in some areas of criminal law, has been ruled unconstitutional by the
courts. For example, it has been held that laws permitting a longer sentence for
a woman than a man for the same crime contravene the Fourteenth Amendment
(*Robinson* v. *York* 1968, in Connecticut; *Commonwealth* v. *Daniels* 1968, in
Pennsylvania; and *State* v. *Chambers* 1973, in New Jersey). Similarly, it has
been held that longer sentences for female juvenile delinquents violate the equal
protection clause. Until recently a New York juvenile delinquency statute (the
PINS law) provided that girls who were "persons in need of supervision" could
be institutionalized until the age of 18, but the age for boys was 16. This law
was held to violate the equal protection clause (*In re Patricia A.* 1972). Similar
laws have been held unconstitutional also in Connecticut (*Sumrell* v. *York* 1968)
and Oklahoma (*Lamb* v. *Brown* 1972; an extended discussion of this decision
and related cases is provided by Davis and Chaires 1973).

   Juvenile delinquency laws have long discriminated against females (Davis
and Chaires 1973). A further problem remains, however, in that a law may not
be discriminatory on its face, but the attitudes and ideologies of persons administering it (i.e., judges, probation officers, or other court staff) may result in
violations of the Fourteenth Amendment equal protection clause by inducing

them to award females longer sentences than males under the guise of "protection of the female juvenile." Or the so-called double standard of morality may lead to longer terms of institutionalization for females than males committing the same acts, such as sexual delinquencies or running away. Even when laws appear to be nondiscriminatory, they are, from an operational point of view, discriminatory. One example of prima facie discrimination was the Connecticut law that until 1972 made it a crime for an unmarried woman to be in manifest danger of falling into habits of vice; it was not applicable to males in the same position.

Statutory Law

Any examination of sexism in the administration of justice must inevitably include the legal definitions outlined in the juvenile codes and the provisions established in statute and case law to govern juvenile court behavior vis-à-vis these phenomena. Of particular consequence in the processing of females are provisions assigning jurisdiction to the juvenile court for behaviors that are not violations for adults (e.g., incorrigibility, truancy, curfew violations, promiscuity, running away). Females are disproportionately processed in and through the juvenile justice system for these behaviors, usually referred to as "status offenses."

Statutory differences in jurisdiction of the juvenile court are startling with respect to age, definitions of delinquent and status offenses, offense limitations on the court's powers, jurisdictional conflicts, and permissible interaction with the adult system (Levin and Sarri 1974). At present all 50 states and the District of Columbia include status offenders within the purview of the juvenile court. In 1972, 24 states and the District of Columbia had a separate category for status offenders (PINS, CINS, MINS, etc.), with 8 other states having mixed categories. Of the 33 states with recent code revisions, only 10 have a separate category for "unruly" children. As of 1972, only 18 of the states with separate categorization of status offenders placed restrictions on disposition alternatives, and just 4 required separate detention facilities for status offenders. This is particularly serious, because the vast majority of states do not explicitly prohibit placement of children in adult jails. It is not surprising, therefore, that so many female status offenders are found in adult jails (Sarri 1974).

Four states (Alabama, Michigan, New York, and Vermont) set a higher maximum age for original juvenile court jurisdiction for those charged with status offenses. Some states also have sex-age differences for status offenses, but these are generally considered unconstitutional today because of the New York family court decision in *In re Patricia A.* (1972) and the U.S. Supreme Court decision in *Stanton* v. *Stanton* (1975).

Three states have lower maximum ages for males than females, but state courts in these states (Illinois, Oklahoma, and Texas) have declared such distinctions unconstitutional (Levin and Sarri 1974). Similarly, statutes with disparate sentences for female juvenile offenders have been struck down as being unconstitutional, such as the Connecticut law that provided for girls under 21 to be sentenced for three years but boys under 21 and convicted for the same offense to be incarcerated for only two years (*Sumrell* v. *York* 1968).

Fourteen states now have fairly stringent prohibitions against placement of status offenders with other delinquents in correctional facilities. Often, however, status offenders may violate probation requirements or be classified as not amenable to rehabilitation. In such cases youth often are declared delinquent and in no way differentiated from other delinquents. Thus statutory provisions do not control the negative labeling and stigmatizing processes.

One illustration of these processes is provided by recent Florida legislation (S.B. 165) initially heralded as a major reform. The new code essentially removed the status offender category known as CINS. Certain categories of status offenders (i.e., runaway, truancy, and ungovernability) were placed in a dependent child category. Services to them were to be provided by the public child welfare agencies on a voluntary basis. However, a major loophole was permitted in that the law states:

> . . . the first time a child is adjudicated as ungovernable, he may be treated as a dependent child and provisions relating to dependency shall be applicable. For the second and subsequent adjudication for ungovernability, the child may be treated and defined as delinquent.

The child thereby becomes subject to the full panoply of juvenile correctional action, including institutionalization.

Due to the potentially damaging effects of labeling (Velimesis 1975; Upshur 1973; Schur 1973; Konopka 1976; Grichting 1975), explicit reference to juveniles as delinquents may well start the process of overcriminalization by failure to distinguish properly between categories of juvenile deviant behavior. Moreover, only seven states have periodic review of probation and seven others limit the period for it; therefore it is conceivable that an "unruly" female could be placed on probation at age 12 and remain in that status until she reached the upper age limit of court jurisdiction, which in some states is as high as 21. Although male-female distinctions in juvenile codes are becoming obsolete, they have not been repealed in a number of states. Because of that lack of positive action, one might well expect to continue to find discriminatory behavior in law enforcement, courts, and correctional agencies.

Litigation

Where laws are enforced in a discriminatory manner in spite of their apparently neutral nature, the reason is often that the laws are vague or overbroad, so that the double'standard of morality' may be applied with impunity. Terms used in such statutes as being applicable to juveniles are *immoral, in danger of becoming immoral, moral depravity.* Use of such terms gives no standards for determining the type of behavior prescribed; neither the person accused, nor the judge, has any standard on which to base or judge behavior (Davis and Chaires 1973). In fact, in some states statutes framed in these or similar terms have been struck down as vague (*Gonzales* v. *Maillard* 1971, in California). However, other courts in other states have upheld such laws, stating that no question could be raised about what the terms of the statute meant. For example, in *E. S. G.* v. *State* (1969, Texas), the section provided that a child who "habitually so comports himself as to injure or endanger the morals of himself or others" may be classed as a juvenile delinquent by the court and committed to an institution up to the age of 21. *Morals,* the court held, conveys a concrete impression to the ordinary person; there could be no question as to what the term meant. Here the girl in question had been found with a young male adult in what was classified as a "transient apartment"; she had been keeping the company of a reputed prostitute and was away from home for more than a week. Although one might say that for a 14-year-old girl to be in such a position would not be in her best interests, placing the girl in an institution for up to seven years would seem to require a more definitive standard for such a drastic action.

Challenges that affect the processing of female status offenders are of particular concern, because this category includes 50-70 percent of the female offenders in the various states. These challenges have been based most frequently on vagueness, status charges that violate the Eighth Amendment, and overbreadth.

Void for Vagueness

The Supreme Court has struck down as vague statutes that "either forbid or require the doing of an act in terms so vague that men of common intelligence must necessarily guess at its meaning and differ as to its application" (*Connally* v. *General Construction Co.* 1926).

More recently the Court in vacating a California federal district court decision held that the California juvenile statute was void because it granted juvenile court jurisdiction over children who were "in danger of leading an idle, dissolute, lewd or immoral life." Such a statute was void, the Court said, because it failed to give fair warning of proscribed conduct or information to the fact finder to enable him to accurately recognize such conduct (*Gonzalez* v. *Maillard* 1974).

Punishment of a Condition

In 1962 the United States Supreme Court, in *Robinson* v. *California,* reversed a

conviction for violation of a California penal code making it a criminal offense
to "be addicted to the use of narcotics." The Court held that Robinson mani-
fested a condition—addiction—he was not able to control; thus the defendant
maintained a particular "status." Mr. Justice Douglas, in his concurring opinion,
stated:

We would forget the teachings of the Eighth Amendment if we allowed sickness
to be made a crime and permitted sick people to be punished for being sick.
This age of enlightenment cannot tolerate such barbarous action. (p. 678)

The effect of *Robinson* v. *California* was to support the argument that a
status must be differentiated from a criminal act and that punishment for a
status is in violation of the Eighth Amendment. This argument has continued to
surface in cases involving convictions of chronic alcoholics for public intoxication—*Easter* v. *D.C.* (1966), *Driver* v. *Hinnant* (1966), and the ultimate Supreme
Court decision that upheld the constitutionality of convictions of chronic alcoholics for public intoxication, *Powell* v. *Texas* (1968).

The previous constitutional arguments attacked adult system practices
punishing status rather than behavior. The last few years have seen similar
attempts to confront statutes applicable to juveniles. In a case involving an
adolescent female—*Gesicki* v. *Oswold* (1971)—the Wayward Minor statute of
New York was declared unconstitutional. The act granted adult criminal jurisdiction over youth 16-21 who were punished for being "morally depraved" and
"in danger of becoming morally depraved." The court stated that the Wayward
Minor statute permitted "the unconstitutional punishment of a minor's condition rather than of any specific action."

However, two recent decisions have supported statutes that were applicable
solely to status offenders and that were challenged by the "void for vagueness"
doctrine. In *Mercado* v. *Rockefeller* (1974) the New York State PINS statute
was upheld as constitutional.

In *Blandheim* v. *State* (1975) the Washington Supreme Court upheld the
constitutionality of the state's incorrigibility statute and ruled that punishment
for this offense was not cruel and unusual. (In this particular case a 17-year-old
female had run away from home and various placements, eight times in three
months.) The statute read:

An incorrigible child is one less than 18 who is beyond control of his parents,
guardian, or custodian by reason of the conduct or nature of said child.

The girl contended that the statute punished the "status" of being incorrigible,
in violation of the Eighth Amendment. The court, although not denying that
incorrigibility is a condition or state of being, justified the statute's legitimacy
by stating that one acquires such a status only by reason of one's conduct or a

pattern of behavior proscribed by the statute. Engaging in conduct that placed her beyond the lawfully exercized control of her mother was felt to be sufficient basis for support of an adjudication of incorrigibility. The court, however, did not show awareness of parental involvement nor did it acknowledge that the parents also could have been charged.

Overbreadth

Overbreadth may be another basis for an attack on status offense statutes. In the case of *State* v. *Mattiello* (1966) the court upheld a conviction of a female juvenile for violation of the Connecticut statute "forbidding walking with a lascivious carriage." The appellate division upheld the statute as valid under the concept of *parens patriae*, that the proceeding was civil rather than criminal, and that its end was not to punish but to rehabilitate the child through guardianship and protection.

The recency of legal changes is apparent in the U.S. Supreme Court decision in *Stanton* v. *Stanton* (1975). The Court reversed the decision of the Utah Supreme Court, which, in the case of child support payments, differentiated minority ages for males and females. The Utah statute had provided that the period of minority for males extended to 21 and for females to 18. But the U.S. Supreme Court qualified its reversal by saying, "We find it unnecessary in this case to decide whether a classification based on sex is inherently suspect." Thus, further decisions on statutes are required to clarify this matter.

Sex-Related Behavior

Prostitution and promiscuity are two behaviors for which women almost exclusively are prosecuted in spite of the obvious injustice of such processing. In the majority of American states prostitution is defined as the "engaging, offering or agreeing to engage in sexual intercourse for a fee."[a] Discrimination may arise in two ways: some laws confine "prostitution" to the activities of females—male prostitutes are not covered; second, in most jurisdictions the customer is not penalized at all. In regard to the latter, some states are now enacting, or have enacted, "John laws" or "customer laws" specifically to veto the activities of the person keeping the prostitute in business—the customer. For example, New York has recently enacted a law that states that "patronizing a prostitute" is a

---

[a]It is interesting to note that in the United Kingdom, Australia, and Canada the actual act of prostitution—exchange of the body for money—is not a crime; it is the solicitation that is prohibited, for example (sec. 32, Sexual Offences Act, 1966, U.K.), "Persistently soliciting or importuning in a public place for an immoral purpose."

violation, with a maximum sentence of imprisonment for 15 days. Even here, however, the effect of the double standard is obvious, in that in New York the penalty for the prostitute is far more severe—maximum prison sentence, 3 months.

Data reported by Dorsen (1970) for New York City in 1968 indicate that there were 3,500 convictions of prostitutes, but only 2 convictions of patrons out of the 112 arrested. Thus, far more prostitutes are arrested and convicted than customers. *Pimping,* or living off the proceeds of prostitution, is also a crime; however, it seems that here, too, the vigilance of the police is not as rigorous as in relation to the prostitute herself. New York City, 1968: 3,500 *convictions* of prostitutes; 182 *arrests* of pimps, and fewer than 50 convictions. It is reasonable to suppose that because the prostitute is more obvious in her activities she is more likely to be proceeded against than the pimp, who may be able to conceal his activities with greater ease.

One of the most problematic aspects of sex-related behavior and the law for adolescent females has been the prohibition against their obtaining treatment in their own right. Under the common law interpretation the consent of parents or a guardian has been required before a physician or agency would provide any kind of treatment, even on an emergency basis. Moreover, the court has supported the right of parents to make decisions contrary to the wishes of their children. In the *Cindy Lou Smith* case (In re Smith 1972) the juvenile court judge placed her in the custody of her parents and ordered that she submit to a termination of pregnancy in spite of her desire to have the child. On appeal the appellate court reversed the lower court judge and ruled that he did not have the power to order an abortion merely because the youth's mother wished her to have the pregnancy terminated.

In recent years there have been a number of decisions affecting the right of adolescent females to obtain sex-related medical care on their own consent (Paul 1974-75; Paul, Pilpel, and Wechsler 1976). Changes in age-of-majority laws have had a marked positive effect for those youth 18 and older, but younger youth in the majority of states still find it difficult to obtain medical contraceptive services or termination of a pregnancy without parental consent. By the end of 1975, only 26 states and the District of Columbia permitted youth under 18 to obtain contraceptive care and 25 states permitted termination of pregnancy decisions without parental consent (Paul, Pilpel, and Wechsler 1976: 16).

In the landmark decisions *Roe* v. *Wade* (1973) and *Doe* v. *Bolton* (1973) the U.S. Supreme Court held that states may not restrict the right to abortion unless the restriction can be justified by a "compelling state interest." Many courts have now interpreted that to mean that parental consent requirements are no longer necessary. In *Poe* v. *Gerstein* (1975) the Court pointed out that there were explicit limits on the conditions under which parental consent could be required. Most recently the Supreme Court ruled in a state of Utah case that family planning services could be made available to minors by the Planned Parenthood Association without parental consent (*Jones* v. *T. H.,* 1976).

The general principle involved in these cases and in other related ones is the extension of constitutional rights to minors. In *Tinker* v. *Des Moines School District* (1969) the Supreme Court ruled that minors are "persons" under the Constitution with "fundamental rights which the state must respect." Nonetheless, agencies as well as courts have been reluctant to proceed with the extension of rights to adolescents, even when the request is for medical or psychological treatment. Instead, parental rights are supported and reinforced under the presumption that youth are unable to make the proper decision (Lee and Paxman 1974-75). The problem is particularly significant in the case of adolescent female offenders because substantial proportions are referred to the court for behavior objectionable to their parents, that is, promiscuity, incorrigibility, ungovernability, and so forth. Obviously such females might encounter difficulty in obtaining parental consent for treatment—psychological, medical, or social work.

Other Supreme Court decisions that have import regarding this question involve more general extensions of rights to youth such as *In re Gault* (1967) and *Goss* v. *Lopez* (1975). These decisions have not been applied explicitly to programs for adjudicated youth, and if they were, there is little doubt that arbitrary actions by many agencies would be constrained substantially. A lower court in Wisconsin ruled in *Kidd* v. *Schmidt* (1975) that a juvenile may not be committed without a hearing on the basis of a parental or guardian signature. Unfortunately, until very recently less diligence has been shown in protecting adolescent females from abuse by parents as some tragic cases reveal (*In re Rebecca Oakes, Minor* 1974; see also *Commonwealth* v. *Bracher* 1971). Nevertheless it can be expected that courts will gradually acknowledge greater rights to youth in decision making affecting their own person, not necessarily their general status.

Equal Rights Amendment

As the words imply, the purpose of the ERA is to oust laws based on sex as being discriminatory. If the amendment is indeed ratified and becomes law, all laws determining rights and responsibilities on the grounds of sex as a sole determinant will be unconstitutional. This would mean that contrary to the present position, females would no longer be punishable for crimes not applicable to males. For example, prostitution provisions framed to make the offense applicable only to females, for example, "the engaging, by a *woman*, in the act of sexual intercourse for a fee is punishable. . . ." (Conn. Gen. Stat. Ann., sec. 17-379, 1958; repealed in 1972, P.A. 28, sec. 2), will offend the ERA. Similarly, sexual delinquency laws that make it a crime to be an unmarried girl between 16 and 20 in "manifest danger of falling into habits of vice" (supra sec. 17-380; unmarried boys are not mentioned!) would be unconstitutional.

Modifications in many civil and criminal statutes will be necessary to achieve conformity with constitutional requirements (Benjamin 1975). Historically females have been doubly disadvantaged under the criminal law. In the case of most rape, they were supposed to be protected as victim but typically were not. In the case of prostitution, only females were prosecuted, when both sexes were involved in the behavior at issue. Our earlier discussion regarding juvenile runaways and detention practices clearly documents the fact that females are more readily processed by both police and courts for behavior identical to that of males.

Another area in which the passage of ERA could be expected to have an effect would be in equalizing length of stay in correctional programs. Here too females typically remain longer than males regardless of the offense committed. The evidence presented by Wheeler (1976) documents the need for immediate action to reduce the gross inequities for female juvenile offenders. Sentencing practices based on the premise that females are more amenable to rehabilitation than males will be unconstitutional under ERA. Obviously such situations could be potentially as beneficial for males as females, since the former would be eligible to claim denial of equal rights if they were not provided treatment services. This amendment could also be expected to have significant effects on the operation of correctional programs in that sexual segregation would be drastically reduced and programs would have to be equally available to females as to males (Arditi et al. 1973). The Benjamin (1975) *Commentary* provides ample detail about the many expected effects on juvenile and criminal justice from the passage of ERA.

Representation of Females in the Juvenile Justice System

Data compiled by the National Assessment of Juvenile Corrections as well as by federal agencies and many other students of juvenile justice clearly indicate that females are overrepresented in critical areas of the justice system. One of the most critical areas pertains to placement in adult jails, lockups, and detention facilities. Females have a greater probability of being detained and held for longer periods than males, even though the overwhelming majority of females are charged with status offenses. Moreover, in the juvenile jurisdictions reporting a ratio of 1 female to 4 male arrests, the ratio for placement in detention is typically 1 to 3 (Sarri 1974).

It was recently reported by HEW that 68 percent of all runaways were females. Their data were based on police apprehension of youth. However, Gold and Reimer's (1975) national survey of youth in 1972 indicated no significant differences between males and females in self-reports of running away, nor did they observe any pattern of increase between 1967 and 1972. Clearly, the differential processing of females is a factor producing the variations in these two sets of data.

The survey of cases of "ungovernability" in the New York Family Court indicates that 62 percent of these youth were females in midadolescence, disproportionately nonwhite, and from large, poor, and single-parent or broken families (*Yale Law Journal* 1974). They further observed that 37 percent of these females were "neglected" but were classified as "ungovernable" in order to expedite processing. Sixty-eight percent were held in secure detention in spite of its obvious impropriety. Finally, they observed that higher proportions of these youth were adjudicated and committed to residential facilities than youth who committed serious property or person crimes.

Placement of *juvenile* females in jail is increasing more rapidly than that of males, in several states. In Wisconsin there were 2,875 males and 768 females in adult jails in 1961. In 1972 there were 7,032 males and 2,892 females—a 277 percent increase for females versus 145 percent for males. Some will undoubtedly assert that these increases are due to more rapid increase in serious criminal behavior by females. However, such assertions cannot be supported if systematic and comprehensive data are used. The National Survey of Youth by Gold shows increased use of marijuana, alcohol, and other drugs but no increase in other delinquent behavior by females (Gold and Reimer 1975). Comparison of adult commitments in New York State between 1969 and 1973 for females shows the largest increase in felonies in use of drugs, with much smaller increases for robbery and assault and no change in homicide. Overall there were 33,774 males handled in 1973, and 677 females (a factor of 66 to 1) (New York State Department of Corrections 1973). Obviously, percentage increases with such population differentials are totally meaningless; yet reports frequently refer to larger percentage increases of female versus male offenders.

In the evaluation of juvenile correctional programs throughout the United States recently completed by the National Assessment of Juvenile Corrections, a number of findings stand out that are relevant to anyone concerned with sexism. Some of the data about the characteristics of youth in different types of programs are presented in table 4-1.

1. Females are overrepresented in institutional populations as compared to day treatment centers or group homes. Females are more likely to be assigned to programs that involve removal from their homes, for out of a total of 444 females, 349 were in institutional programs.

2. The range of disposition alternatives appears to be more limited for females than for males—at least partially a consequence of the smaller number of females to be served in a given locality. But this phenomenon is observable also at the state level, where numerical constraints are fewer.

3. Females in these correctional programs were disproportionately committed for status offenses. Status offenders constituted 40 percent of the overall sample—28 percent of the males and 55 percent of the females. Examination of institutional populations shows that 50 percent of the females there are status offenders. These percentages are similar to those in several other censuses of juvenile institutions for females.

Table 4-1
Commitment Offense, by Program Type and Sex
(*In Percentages*)

	Status[a] Offense	Probation or Parole Violation	Mis-demeanor	Drugs or Alcohol	Prop-erty	Person	(n)
Institution							
Male	23	4	2	6	46	18	(832)
Female	50	1	3	18	14	14	(349)
Community Residential							
Male	50	3	1	10	26	10	(70)
Female	67	3	0	14	12	3	(58)
Day Treatment							
Male	45	3	4	6	30	12	(164)
Female	87	0	0	5	3	5	(37)

Source: National Assessment of Juvenile Corrections, University of Michigan, Ann Arbor, Michigan, 1976.

Note: Determination of commitment offense was based on youth response to the question, "Why were you sent here."

[a]Status offenses include incorrigibility, dependent and neglected, truancy, running away, curfew violations, disorderly, and so on.

4. Offenses for which females were committed were predominantly the following: 55 percent—status, 17 percent—drug, 13 percent—property, and 12 percent—person offenses. In all cases females were committed disproportionately for offenses that had little if any relationship to protection of the community. Yet they were placed in institutions more frequently and held for longer periods.

5. Younger rather than older youth were placed in institutions as compared to open residential or day treatment programs. Thus, the concept of "lesser penetration" is not being applied, since these younger females were most often status offenders.

6. Analysis of prior correctional experience indicates that in spite of the fact that juvenile females commit far fewer felonies and misdemeanors, they have extensive contact with the justice system. Females had a mean arrest rate of 4.6 times; an average of 3.8 times in detention, 2.0 times in jail, and 1.3 times in an institution. Foster care and probation are underused in comparison to these more stringent sanctions, with means of 1.5 and 1.4, respectively.

These data are more than sufficient to indicate that females experience institutional sexism in the administration of justice. Given the fact that the mean age of these youth is 16, one must inevitably ask if current practices and policies are not antithetical to the goals society seeks in the socialization of youth for responsible adulthood.

One additional factor that is particularly problematic for females is the over-whelming dominance of male staff in critical decision-making posts in juvenile justice agencies. Executives of all the programs evaluated were most likely to be white males. Of the 49 executives of programs, only 10 were female. In the case of coeducational programs 4 out of 10 executives were females, and in the case of 7 female institutions there were 3 male executives and 4 female executives (Vinter 1976). Although the presence of female staff in leadership positions cannot guarantee a reduction in sexism in juvenile justice, it does appear to be one of the essential preconditions.

Summary

Our review of statutory and case law as well as the findings from social science research demonstrate conclusively that the juvenile justice system penalizes female youth in significant ways. Perhaps of even greater importance is the fact that the vast majority of youth, both male and female, suffers as a consequence of the present ineffectiveness of this grossly overloaded juvenile justice system. In spite of laudatory efforts toward diversion and decriminalization, far too many youth continue to be processed through this system, at a great cost for society but of very little benefit. Unfortunately, those youth whose behavior warrants careful and thorough processing are often dismissed prematurely, and other youth charged with status offenses are held longer. Female offenders in particular suffer the consequences of this practice because the vast majority are charged with status violations. The juvenile justice system also allocates nearly unlimited discretion to the family and the public school in instigating action against youth without having to accept corresponding responsibility. Again, female youth are the particular victims of this situation, since the offenses they are charged with involve interpersonal relationships and victimless crimes more than property or person felonies (Morris 1964).

Discrimination and sexism toward female juveniles is a serious and pervasive problem in statutes, courts, and correctional agencies. Obviously, in the case of female juveniles society thinks that some of its actions all have positive consequences "in the long run." Such reasoning is clearly fallacious. All society is being harmed by a serious overkill in the processing of females, and in the long run the society will be irreversibly harmed.

References

Literature

American Criminal Law Review
   1973   Note, "Sex Discrimination in the Criminal Law: The effect of the Equal
           Rights Amendment." *American Criminal Law Review* 11:489-91.

Arditi, Ralph R.; Goldberg, Frederick, Jr.; Hartle, M. Martha; Peters, John H.;
and Phelps, William R.
    1973   "The Sexual Segregation of American Prisons." *Yale Law Journal*
           82:1229-73.

Bazelon, David L.
    1970   "Beyond Control of the Juvenile Court." *Juvenile Court Journal*
           20 (Summer):44.

Beaver, Herbert W.
    1975   *The Legal Status of Runaway Children: Final Report.* Washington:
           Educational Systems Corp.

Benjaman, Anne
    1975   *A Commentary on the Effects of the Equal Rights Amendment on
           State Laws and Institutions.* Sacramento: California Commission
           on the Status of Women.

Bertrand, Maria
    1967   "The Myth of Sexual Equality Before the Law." In *Proceedings:
           5th Research Conference on Delinquency and Criminality*, p. 129.
           Quebec: Society of Criminology.

Brennan, Tim; Blanchard, F.; Huizenga, D.; and Elliott, D.
    1975   *The Incidence and Nature of Runaway Behavior.* Final report for
           DHEW. Boulder: Behavioral Research and Evaluation Corp.

Burkhart, Kathryn W.
    1975   The Child and the Law: Helping the Status Offender. Pamphlet
           no. 530. New York: Public Affairs Committee.

Chesney-Lind, Meda
    1973   "Judicial Enforcement of the Female Sex Role: The Family Court
           and the Female Delinquent." *Issues in Criminology* 8 (Fall):51-59.

Davis, Samuel, and Chaires, Susan
    1973   "Equal Protection for Juveniles: The Present Status of Sex-Based
           Discrimination in Juvenile Court Laws." *Georgia Law Review* 7
           (Fall):494-532.

Dineen, John
    1974   Juvenile Court Organization and Status Offenses: A Statutory Pro-
           file. Pittsburgh: National Center for Juvenile Justice.

Dorsen, Norman
  1970   "Women, the criminal code, and the correction system." In *The Report of the New York City Commission on Human Rights.*

Forer, Lois
  1970   *No One Will Lissen—How Our Legal System Brutalizes the Youthful Poor.* New York: John Day.

Frankel, Lois J.
  1973   "Sex Discrimination in the Criminal Law: The Effect of the Equal Rights Amendment." *American Criminal Law Review* 11 (Winter): 469-510.

Gold, Martin, and Reimer, David J.
  1975   "Changing Patterns of Delinquent Behavior among Americans 13 through 16 Years Old: 1967-72." *Crime and Delinquency Literature* 7 (December):483-517.

Gold, Sally
  1972   "Women, the criminal code, and the correction system." In *Women and Social Services.* Edited by S. Gold. New York: Discus Books, pp. 512-15.

Gold, Sarah
  1971   "Equal Protection for Juvenile Girls in Need of Supervision in New York State." *New York Law Forum* 57:2.

Grichting, Wolfgang L.
  1975   "The State and Fate of Status Offenders." Ann Arbor: University of Michigan, National Assessment of Juvenile Corrections (mimeo).

Haft, Marilyn G.
  1973.   "Women in Prison." In *Prisoners' Rights Sourcebook.* Edited by Michele G. Hermann and Haft. New York: Clark Boardman Co., pp. 341-55.

Harvard Educational Review
  1973-74   "The Rights of Children." 2 parts. Special issues of *Harvard Educational Review* 43 (November) and 44 (February).

Hechinger, Fred, and Hechinger, Grace
  1975   *Growing Up in America.* New York: McGraw-Hill.

Hendrix, Omar
    1972   *A Study in Neglect: A Report on Women Prisoners.* New York:
            Women's Prison Association.

Hindelang, Michael J.
    1971   "Age, Sex, and the Versatility of Delinquent Involvements." *Social
            Problems* 18 (Spring):522-35.

Hoffman-Bustamante, Dale
    1973   "The Nature of Female Criminality." *Issues in Criminology* 8 (Fall):
            117-36.

Institute of Judicial Administration
    1975   *The* Ellery C. *Decision: A Case Study of Judicial Regulation of
            Status Offenders.* New York.

Juvenile Justice Digest
    1976   "Discrimination shown against female juveniles in Louisville." *Juve-
            nile Justice Digest*, (January 30):9-10.

Kanowitz, Leo
    1969   *Women and the Law: The Unfinished Revolution.* Albuquerque:
            University of New Mexico Press.

Katz, Sanford
    1971   *When Parents Fail: The Law's Response to Family Breakdown.*
            Boston: Beacon Press.

Konopka, Gisela
    1976   *Young Girls: A Portrait of Adolescence.* Englewood Cliffs, N.J.:
            Prentice-Hall.

Lee, Luke T., and Paxman, John M.
    1974/75 "Pregnancy and Abortion in Adolescence: A Comparative Legal
            Survey and Proposals for Reform." *Columbia Human Rights
            Law Review* 6 (Fall-Winter):307-55.

Levin, Mark M., and Sarri, Rosemary C.
    1974   *Juvenile Delinquency: A Comparative Analysis of Legal Codes in
            the United States.* Ann Arbor: University of Michigan, National
            Assessment of Juvenile Corrections.

MacLeod, Celeste
  1974   "Street Girls: If Nobody Wants You, Where Do You Go?" *The
          Nation* (April 20):486-88.

Morris, Ruth
  1964   "Female Delinquency and Relational Problems." *Social Forces* 43
          (October):82-89.

New York State. Department of Corrections
  1973   *Annual Report.* Albany.

North Dakota Law Review
  1975   Note, "Female Offenders: A Challenge to Court and the Legislature."
          North Dakota Law Review 51 (Summer):827-53.

Paul, Eve W.
  1974-75   "The Legal Rights of Minors to Sex-Related Medical Care."
             Columbia Human Rights Law Review 6 (Fall-Winter):357-77.

Paul, Eve W.; Pilpel, Harriet F.; and Wechsler, Nancy F.
  1976   "Pregnancy, Teenagers and the Law, 1976." *Family Planning Per-
          spectives* 8 (January-February):16-21.

Riback, Linda
  1971   "Juvenile Delinquency Laws: Juvenile Women and the Double
          Standard of Morality." *UCLA Law Review* 19 (December):313-42.

Sarri, Rosemary C.
  1974   *Under Lock and Key: Juveniles in Jails and Detention.* Ann Arbor:
          University of Michigan, National Assessment of Juvenile Corrections.

Sarri, Rosemary C.; Propper, Alice; Selo, Elaine; and Scutt, Jocelyn
  1975   "The Female Offender: An Annotated Bibliography." Ann Arbor:
          University of Michigan, School of Social Work (mimeo).

Schack, Elizabeth T.
  1973   *The PINS Child—A Plethora of Problems.* New York: Judicial Con-
          ference of the State of New York, Office of Children's Services.

Schur, Edwin M.
  1973   *Radical Non-Intervention: Rethinking the Delinquency Problem.*
          Englewood Cliffs, N.J.: Prentice-Hall.

Silbert, James D., and Sussman, Alan
    1973   "The rights of juveniles confined in training schools." In *Prisoners'*
            Rights Sourcebook. Edited by Michele Hermann and Marilyn G.
            Haft. New York: Clark Boardman Co., pp. 357-81.

Simon, Rita James
    1975   *The Contemporary Woman and Crime.* NIMH Crime and Delinquen-
            cy Issues series, DHEW Publication No. (ADM) Washington: Govern-
            ment Printing Office, pp. 75-161.

Singer, Linda R.
    1973   "Women and the Correctional Process." *American Criminal Law Re-*
            view 2 (Winter):295-308.

Skoler, Daniel L., and McKeown, Jane C.
    1974   Women in Detention and Statewide Jail Standards. *Clearinghouse*
            Bulletin #7, March. Washington: American Bar Association, Com-
            mission on Correctional Facilities and Services, Statewide Jail Stan-
            dards and Inspection Systems Project.

Stiller, Stuart, and Elder, Carol
    1974   "PINS—A Concept in Need of Supervision." *American Criminal Law*
            Review 12 (Summer):33-60.

Strouse, Jean
    1972   "To be Minor and Female: The Legal Rights of Women Under 21."
            Ms. (August):70.

U.S. National Criminal Justice Information and Statistics Service (USNCJISS)
    1975   *Sourcebook of Criminal Justice Statistics—1974,* by Michael J.
            Hindelang, Christopher S. Dunn, Alison L. Aumick, and L. Paul
            Sutton. Washington: Government Printing Office.

    1976   Survey of Inmates of State Correctional Facilities—1974. Washing-
            ton: Government Printing Office.

Upshur, Carole
    1973   "Delinquency in girls: Implications for service delivery." In *Closing*
            Correctional Institutions. Edited by Yitzhak Bakal. Lexington,
            Mass.: Lexington Books, D. C. Heath & Company, pp. 19-30.

Vedder, Clyde, and Somerville, Dora
    1970   *The Delinquent Girl.* Springfield: Charles Thomas Co.

Velimesis, Margery L.
1975   "The female offender." *Crime and Delinquency Literature* 7
         (March):94-112.

Vera Institute of Justice
1972   *Programs in Criminal Justice Reform.* New York.

Vinter, Robert D., ed.
1976   *Time Out: A National Study of Juvenile Correctional Programs.*
         Ann Arbor: University of Michigan, National Assessment of Juve-
         nile Corrections.

Wheeler, Gerald R.
1976   "The Computerization of Juvenile Corrections: Demystification of
         the Therapeutic State." *Crime and Delinquency* 22 (April):201-10.

Yale Law Journal
1974   Comment, "Ungovernability: The Unjustifiable Jurisdiction."
         Yale Law Journal 83 (June):1383-1409.

Legal Cases

In re Patricia A.
1972   31 N.Y. 2d 83, 286 N.E. 2d 432.

Blondheim v. State
1975   529 P. 2d 1096 (84 Wash. 2d 874)

Commonwealth v. Brasher
1971   270 N.E. 2d 389.

Commonwealth v. Daniels
1968   430 Pa. 642, 243 A. 2d 400.

Connally v. General Construction Co.
1926   269 U.S. 385.

Doe v. Bolton
1973   410 U.S. 179.

Driver v. Hinnant
1966   356 F. 2d 761 (4th Cir.).

Easter v. D.C.
    1966   361 F. 2d 50 (D.C. Cir.).

E. S. G. v. State
    1969   447 S.W. 2d 225 (Civ. App. Tex.).

In re Gault
    1967   387 U.S. 1.

Gesicki v. Oswold
    1971   336 F. Supp. 371 (S.D.N.Y.).

Gonzalez v. Mailliard
    1971   Civil No. 50424 (N.D. Cal., Feb. 9).
    1974   Vacated, 416 U.S. 918.

Goss v. Lopez
    1975   95 S. Ct. 729 419 U.S. 565.

Jones v. T. H.
    1976   44 U.S.L.W. 3663 (May 25).

Kidd v. Schmidt
    1975   No. 74-C-605 (E.D. Wis., Aug. 15).

Lamb v. Brown
    1972   456 F. 2d 18 (10th Cir.).

Mercado v. Rockefeller
    1974   302 F. 2d 666 (2d Cir.).

In re Rebecca Oakes, Minor
    1974   220 N.W. 2d 188 (53 Mich. app 629).

Poe v. Gerstein
    1975   420 U.S. 918.

Powell v. Texas
    1968   392 U.S. 514.

Robinson v. California
    1962   370 U.S. 660.

Robinson v. York
    1968   281 F. Supp. 8 (D. Conn.).

Roe v. Wade
    1973   410 U.S. 113.

In re Smith
    1972   16 Md. App. 209, 295 A. 2d 238.

Stanton v. Stanton
    1975   421 U.S. 7.

State v. Chambers
    1973   13 Cr. L. 2330 (E.D. N.J.).

State v. Mattiello
    1966   4 Conn. Cir. 55, 225 A. 2d 507.

Sumrell v. York
    1968   288 F. Supp. 955 (D. Conn.).

Tinker v. Des Moines School District
    1969   393 U.S. 503.

Part III

The Incarcerated Female Offender

Introduction to Part III

The "forgotten" status of the female offender is most evident as the institutional door locks behind her. Inside the institution she begins a life of boredom and in many cases vegetation. As with her male peers, whatever her role may have been on the outside—mother, lover, or dating and laughing juvenile—once inside, she loses that role and dangles in limbo. Unlike her male peers, however, she may derive little or no advantage from her term of incarceration because few if any meaningful efforts are made to prepare her with alternative, legal options when released. This is true because rehabilitation efforts are seen as too expensive for female offenders. The women are too few in number.

Helen Gibson traces the development of this response to female inmates in chapter 5, looking back to a time when the smallness of female prison populations was seen as an advantage in developing innovative programs. She describes the state of neglect that characterizes treatment of women in prison and proposes alternatives.

Perhaps the most difficult aspect of a woman's incarceration is the separation from her children. It troubles not only the mother, but can often have a severely damaging effect on the children. In chapter 6 Brenda McGowan and Karen Blumenthal describe the harm done to both mother and children during and after incarceration. Throughout the description there continually arises evidence of the lack of concern or awareness on the part of criminal justice personnel for the needs of the mother and the child. The most valuable recommendations for improving the system's handling of this mother-child relationship came from the women offenders themselves, and the chapter offers them as guidelines.

Problems of women in prison are compounded for those incarcerated in jails. The murder trial of Joan Little brought to national attention the plight of these women. But, as chapter 7, by Patsy Sims, reveals, the public soon forgets—as do corrections administrators. As an investigative journalist, Sims traveled throughout the South, visiting women in jails to determine how typical the Little case was and what reforms had resulted. She found the case was atypical only insofar as Joan Little had fought and killed her attacker. She found, also, a prevalent apathy regarding reform. Female inmates in jails continue to be sexually molested and harassed by male guards and trustees; and matrons to handle the women are no more in evidence than they were before.

Important, also, are the conditions in which the women are held in jails. Evidence from the article makes it clear that what little reform is touching the condition of women in prisons has yet to reach the women in jails.

Chapter 8 details discriminatory treatment of female juveniles both within the juvenile institutions and throughout juvenile justice processing. Paternalism on the part of criminal justice personnel has taken a pernicious turn when dealing with female juvenile offenders. Elaine Selo offers some valuable empirical evidence of differential treatment between sexes and races within the juvenile justice system.

5 Women's Prisons: Laboratories for Penal Reform

Helen E. Gibson

It is possible to be recognized as an expert in criminal law and penology and still fail to acknowledge the problems of the female offender. *The Correctional Process*,[1] a textbook for law students studying the criminal justice system, makes only one fleeting reference to women as criminal defendants. The President's Commission on Law Enforcement and the Administration of Justice published nine task force reports, none of which devote so much as a chapter or paragraph to the female offender.[2] In Wisconsin, the Citizen's Study Committee on Offender Rehabilitation recently published its report.[3] The problems of women offenders received little attention.

There are several possible reasons for this apparent invisibility of women criminals. First, women represent only a small percentage of those arrested and an even smaller percentage of those incarcerated.[4] Second, the crimes they commit are usually related to sex or property, and, instead of harming others, women criminals usually harm themselves.[5] Finally, with the public and official awareness of a general increase in violent crime and serious prison disorders,[6] the problems of women prisoners pale into insignificance.

Whatever the reasons behind this lack of concern, women's correctional institutions today are facing serious problems. Some of these problems are common to men's institutions as well; others are unique to institutions for women. All of them call into serious question whether women's institutions are accomplishing the objectives of a modern penological system—in fact, whether they are accomplishing anything constructive at all.

This comment, therefore, will focus on problems in the current operation of institutions for women. It will present historical data to show how women's institutions have helped lead the way to penal reform, and suggest changes which could once again make them models for the improvement of all correctional institutions.

I. Crime and Imprisonment Patterns of Women

The pattern of crime is very different for women than it is for men. F.B.I. statistics for 1968 show that only one out of every seven persons arrested in the

Helen Gibson. "Women's Prisons: Laboratories for Penal Reform," *Wisconsin Law Review* (1973):210-233. © University of Wisconsin. Reprinted with permission.

United States was a woman.[7] Only nine percent of all arrests for violent crimes involved women.[8] Women comprise 15 percent of those arrested for property crimes, but they concentrate on such nonthreatening crimes as forgery (22 percent of total forgery arrests), fraud (24 percent of total), and embezzlement (20 percent of total).[9] Of the 149,060 women arrested in the United States in 1968, for the seven index crimes of the F.B.I.'s *Uniform Crime Reports,* 113,110 of them, or just over 75 percent, were arrested for theft.[10] In Wisconsin, nearly 11 percent of the 138 admissions to the Home for Women in 1970 were involved in crimes of violence, 41 percent were involved in property crime, 9 percent in sex offenses, and 15 percent were juvenile delinquents.[11]

According to the most recent national data, there are roughly 15,000 women incarcerated on any one day.[12] This number represents about four percent of the total inmate population of the United States.[13] About 800 women are inmates of the two federal reformatories for Women in Alderson, West Virginia and Terminal Island, California.[14] In state institutions there are roughly 6,000; while about 8,000 adult women are locked up in county and municipal jails and detention facilities.[15]

In June, 1972, about 94 inmates were confined to the Wisconsin Home for Women at Taycheedah[16] and 99 girls were at the Wisconsin School for Girls at Oregon.[17] As of January 5, 1972, 36 women and 14 girls were confined in county jails.[18]

It is clear from the preceding statistics that women criminals rarely represent an overt danger to society. Although a woman who is convicted of a crime is somewhat less likely to be sentenced to an institution,[19] it is necessary to ask whether there is really any good reason to confine her at all. In view of the social costs of imprisoning women,[20] the psychological harm to the individual,[21] and the fact that society receives little or no benefit,[22] this question should receive more attention than it has so far.

II. History of Women's Correctional Institutions

A. The National Movement

The idea of imprisonment as punishment for crime is itself a product of reform. Instead of being thrown to the lions in the arena to provide a public spectacle, offenders were sometimes allowed to compensate the victim or his family.[23] But for poor people, who could not pay, for slaves, and for women, the cruel punishments were reserved.[24] Men were stoned to death and women were drowned or burned at the stake.[25]

In the American colonies, improved jail conditions were advocated by the Society of Friends, aided by Benjamin Franklin. Permitting prisoners to do productive work was a step forward.[26] But this reform, once it became widespread, led to overemphasis on prison labor as a profitmaking enterprise for the state.[27] Women prisoners, few in number, could not "pay their way."[28]

Because women criminals are viewed differently by our society, prison reform for women has had a different emphasis. Whereas male criminals are usually feared as dangerous men in the eyes of society, the disgraced and dishonored woman has more often been considered pathetic. This view has its roots in the fact that women's most frequent offenses were violations of the normative code with respect to sex and drunkenness.[29] Thus, reformation meant something quite different for women than for men. "Treatment" for women meant instilling in them certain standards of sexual morality and sobriety and preparing them for their duties as mothers and homemakers.[30]

This attitude was basic to the reformatory movement which supported new institutions for delinquent women and children late in the 19th century. Thus, the first reformatory for men, opened at Elmira, New York, in 1876, was intended for felons who were still young enough to offer hope of their being reclaimed.[31] But the first reformatories for women, opened at about the same time, were established from very different motives. It was young women who were "sex delinquents" and "inebriates" —not felons—for whom prison reform was considered to be most needed.

Socially minded women, (whose numbers and enthusiasm gradually increased, culminating in the suffrage movement) were horrified at the conditions in the jails and workhouses.[32] Women of all ages, including young children, were mingled indiscriminately. New reformatories for women met with some opposition,[33] but women eventually won their point,[34] and a number of states began establishing similar institutions.[35] At first, only misdemeanants were confined there, with felons remaining confined to prisons for men. Staffs were almost entirely composed of women.[36]

As a reaction to bad conditions existing in men's prisons where women had been confined, almost all of the reformatories were newly built. The forbidding castle with endless rows of cell blocks was replaced with separate buildings designed by women for women—complete living units of from 30 to 50 inmates each. This architectural innovation was entitled, with a bit of feminine exaggeration, the "cottage plan." Both the name and the plan are still very much in use today at all "reformatory" institutions, whether for men, for women, or for children.

Nearly all maintained sizeable farms, both to produce food for the institution and to provide a therapeutic work situation for the inmates.[37] Most women's institutions no longer operate farms, but farms and camps for men are more in vogue than ever, for substantially the same reasons as before.

Although conceived more to uplift the woman of fallen virtue than to change the antisocial tendencies of a dangerous felon, the rehabilitative model pioneered by the women's reformatories was adopted in institutions for men and for juveniles. Classification, parole, individualization of treatment, and

even work release were also innovations of the reformatory system.[38] Women's
reformatories were among the first to undertake criminological research.[39]
Dr. Lekkerkerker thought in 1930 that "the highest and most scientific standards of prison management are often found in the reformatories for women."[40]
The women's reformatories served to prepare the mind of a vengeful society for
the sight of offenders being treated with sympathy. Eventually, if never to the
same degree, the public has become accustomed to the idea of humane treatment for all prisoners.

B. Wisconsin Perspective in Reform

In Wisconsin, all prisoners were kept in county jails until the state prison was
established at Waupun in 1851.[41] In 1904 Waupun housed 566 men and 11
women.[42] The State Board of Control urged the establishment of a reformatory
for women. The argument echoed the protective attitude of the reformatory
movement:

The only thing that may be done with a woman who has gone wrong is to send
her to the State Prison at Waupun or to release her on probation; . . . To release
a female criminal on probation means, in the majority of cases, to permit her to
return to her vicious and immoral practices.[43]

   The first inmates were admitted to the Wisconsin Industrial Home for
Women at Taycheedah in December, 1921. They were women aged 18 to 30
years who were first-time felony offenders. Second offense felons and all
women convicted of murder in any degree were still sentenced to the women's
prison in the state prison at Waupun.[44]
   The women's prison was maintained as part of the state prison at Waupun
until 1933.[45] In that year, those inmates were moved to a new building on the
grounds of the Industrial Home for Women at Taycheedah, but the two institutions were kept separate until about 1945.[46] Of the 58 admissions to the
Industrial Home for Women for the biennium of 1925-1926, over half were for
sexual improprieties of some type, including 12 committed for treatment of
venereal disease pursuant to section 54.01(2) of the 1923 Wisconsin Statutes.[47]
   From time to time after 1924, volunteer teachers from Fond du Lac conducted classes, and cooking, sewing, laundry, and practical nursing were taught
by institution matrons.[48] By 1930, vocational training had expanded to include sewing, needlework, rugmaking, embroidery, tatting, crocheting, and
quilting.[49] Approximately 36 percent of the residents of the Industrial Home
and 50 percent of the women in the prison were reported to be mentally
deficient.[50]
   While women's institutions in other states were setting an example of

rehabilitation according to the most enlightened theories of the day,[51] they never achieved that position of leadership in Wisconsin. Almost from the beginning,[52] when the appropriation for education at the Wisconsin Home for Women was terminated after the first biennium of its existence, the needs of men's institutions were accorded higher priority.[53] Women failed to rise in the corrections hierarchy as they had in some other states, although a few women were consistently appointed to the Board of Control, particularly in the 1920's.[54]

C. The Present Inertia

The women's institutions elsewhere did not maintain their position of leadership. A Citizens Task Force assigned to study the State Correctional Institution for Women at Muncy, Pennsylvania in 1970 found the institution "completely inadequate in concept, policy, personnel, and resources. . . ."[55] California is regarded by many as the most progressive state in corrections, but the chief psychiatrist at the California Institution for Women complained recently that judges commit women assuming that a full staff of psychiatrists and adequate treatment facilities are available. In fact, during one year, no contact whatsoever was made with 75 percent of the population of 1,000 women.[56] City and county jails are worse, so much so that when Sara Harris wrote a book about the New York City House of Detention, she entitled it *Hellhole.*[57] Former Attorney General Ramsey Clark commented critically in his book, *Crime in America:* "The federal system has too few women prisons to offer needed services to them. . . . The whole system of corrections for women needs analysis."[58]

Work release is a prime example of a reform pioneered by women and now scarcely available to them. The Massachusetts Reformatory Prison for Women at Framingham pioneered a work release program as early as 1880.[59] Yet in 1913, when Wisconsin enacted its famous Huber Law, women were not even included.[60] When, finally, in the 1950's and '60's, legislatures began providing for work release of felons confined to prison, women were all but ignored. If they were included, their programs met difficulties. A Pennsylvania work release program was discontinued because "too many girls escaped."[61] A successful California program was dropped because of administrative problems.[62]

The Minnesota Correctional Institution for Women, with about half the population of the Wisconsin Home for Women, has had more women on work release than has Wisonsin.[63] An official in the Wisconsin Division of Corrections told this writer, "Women don't seem to be suited to work release." That would come as a surprise to Dr. Mary Harris, who wrote with pride of the young women she sent to work outside the New Jersey State Home for Girls in 1920.[64]

Women's correctional institutions are at a low ebb, and the trend is downward. Not surprisingly, some judges are losing faith in the curative powers of

prison, and are less willing to sentence women to institutions unless convinced
that their actions are a menace to the public.[65] This changing attitude, coupled,
in Wisconsin, with a court decision forbidding transfer of juveniles to adult institutions,[66] is resulting in lower populations, increased concern with costs, and the
multiplication of resulting difficulties.[67]

III. Scope of the Problems Inherent in Women's
Correctional Institutions

A. The Limitation of Size

Women inmates and superintendents of women's institutions agree on one thing:
The small institutional population is their worst problem. This condition is
frequently cited as a reason for lack of financial support,[68] as an administrative
stumbling block,[69] and as an excuse for neglecting the inmates' needs.[70]

   In 20 states, separate facilities are not available for women prisoners. Five
states house female felons in city or county jails or board them in the prisons
of neighboring states.[71] In 15 states, they are relegated to a corner of the state
prison for men.[72] There they do not have equal access to educational and
vocational programs.[73] When not busy scrubbing floors, women prisoners pass
the time mending or ironing the male officers' uniforms or doing nothing.[74]

   Another serious side effect of decreased population is the increase in cost
per inmate. Some states which have operated separate institutions for women
are now closing them because of rising costs, leaving the women prisoners in
county jails.[75] At the Wisconsin Home for Women, while budgeted staff positions remain at 116,[76] average daily population for June, 1972, dropped to 93.[77]

   In fiscal 1970-71, when average population was still 139.4, the cost of
maintaining an inmate for one year at Taycheedah was over $10,000.[78] Today,
with population reduced, it is certainly higher. These figures compare with a
cost of $4,500[79] for the same period for the Correctional Institution for Men
at Fox Lake. Yet few would deny that Fox Lake provides more treatment,
educational, and vocational facilities than does Taycheedah. The high cost of
women's institutions is not the result of waste or malfeasance, but rather the
result of efforts to provide a small population with individualized services amid
tight security within prison walls. And when economies are necessary, the educational program is reduced,[80] but not security.[81]

B. The Oppressive Institution

One of the most serious and least understood problems of women's institutions
today is the psychological harm done to the inmates. Arguably all prisons are

psychologically harmful,[82] but the typical women's institution inflicts graver
damage,[83] in spite of its more attractive appearance. In fact, the outward
attractiveness of the prison for women not only confuses the inmates,[84] but
works to deaden any impetus for change.[85]

"The first impression I got of the facility was a good one . . . no gun
towers, stone walls, uniforms, armed guards, nor barred windows,"[86] wrote
novelist William Murray of the California Institution for Women. "C.I.W.
could be taken for a bucolic college campus."[87] The Wisconsin Home for
Women is frequently mistaken for nearby St. Mary's Springs Academy. The
resemblance is superficial. Walls are replaced by personnel, guns are replaced by
stringent rules,[88] bars are replaced by constant vigilance.[89] William Murray's
account describes it this way: "The jailhouse atmosphere didn't really hit me
until I got inside and . . . gradually became conscious of the dozens of rules
. . . ."[90]

While convention requires women's prisons to *look* like minimum security
institutions,[91] economic reality decrees that they cannot *be* minimum security.
A minimum security institution can choose the best risks, and send its failures
somewhere else; a women's institution must accept every woman offender in
the state.[92] Because all women sentenced to prison must be housed in one
institution, all must live by rules which are established for the control of a very
few.[93] At the Wisconsin correctional institution at Fox Lake, a medium
security institution for men, there is one correctional officer for every six inmates. At the maximum security prison for men at Waupun, there is one
correctional officer for every four inmates. But at the medium security
Wisconsin Home for Women, there is one correctional officer for every two
inmates.[94] While officials at the men's institution at Fox Lake, accept a certain
number of "walkaways" as inevitable, officials at the Wisconsin Home for
Women, also a medium security institution, do not. Security is tight, and
escapes are rare.[95]

The result is an atmosphere that in spite of attractive facilities and peace-
ful surroundings is really very tense and oppressive.[96] The rules and regimenta-
tion restrict the inmate's ability to make choices. She is reduced to the status
of childlike dependency,[97] when her greatest need is to acquire independence.
The multiplicity of rules makes it possible for authorities to "get" any inmate
they wish.[98] In short, the reduction of women to a weak, dependent, and
helpless status is brought about by more subtle means than by the gun or the
high wall.[99]

Another of the subtle means of repression employed is the enforcement
of exaggerated standards of neatness and cleanliness.[100] Ruffled curtains are
washed and ironed monthly.[101] Floors and walls are maintained spotless and
shining.[102] Inmates perceive these duties as a feminine version of the "rock
pile," now disapproved in prisons for men.[103] While housework is claimed to
be part of vocational training, it is also used as punishment. A reporter visiting

the maximum security punishment section at the State Correctional Institution
for Women at Muncy, Pennsylvania was told by a matron,

They're confined except in the summertime, when we let them go out and
sweep the walk. They have kitchen work to do here . . . cleaning, trays to wash
and silver to wash, linens to distribute . . . the same as in your own house
practically.[104]

    This situation is aggravated by the decline in the number of women im-
prisoned. Even though inmate population is down, the institution has not
become any smaller. This means, as a practical matter, that the floors that
once were scrubbed by 150 or more women are today being scrubbed by 95[105]
or less.[106] It is true that one or two residential floors may be closed, but these
would have been maintained by the residents. There are the same kitchens,
classrooms, administrative areas and hallways to be kept clean, the same walks
to shovel, and the same yard to tend. But there are fewer people to do it. The
result is an increasing proportion of each inmate's time being taken for institutional maintenance. Even if more educational opportunities were suddenly
available, the inmate might have neither the time nor the strength to avail
herself of them.
    In assessing the harm done by the tense, oppressive atmosphere and the
multiplicity of rules and punishments, it should be noted that delinquent
women are already characteristically weak, dependent, and helpless.[107] Dr.
Seymour Halleck, in his book, *Psychiatry and the Dilemma of Crime,* describes
a typical delinquent woman: "Above all, she is dependent. Her dependency
has a demanding 'sticky' quality . . . ."[108] These characteristics may explain
why women prisoners constitute such a "manageable population." However,
women prisoners and parolees are also less likely to have someone upon whom
they can depend.[109] Margery Velimesis, in her landmark study of women
offenders in Pennsylvania,[110] found that 80 percent of all the women in jail
or prison had children to support.[111] Officials at the Wisconsin Home for
Women estimate that all or nearly all inmates leaving the institution will be
self-supporting or on welfare.[112] Thus women who have shown a tendency to
be more dependent than the average women are confined to institutions where
dependence is demanded and independence discouraged. Yet their circumstances will soon require them to be far less dependent than the average
woman.[113]

C. Inaccessibility

When the institution is located in an area of the state inaccessible to popu-
lated urban areas, its woes are multiplied. The difficulties in attracting

professional staff, of obtaining work-release positions, and of providing for family visits are all well known.[114]   But for women, the hardship is greater. Almost three-fourths of the women incarcerated in federal institutions have children.[115] While male prisoners are also parents, society does not place upon the father the responsibility for the minute details of daily care as it does upon the mother. Zalba, in a 1964 study of women prisoners and their families in California, expressed the view that

[T]he role of mother is more crucial for the mother herself than is the father's role to him, and . . . her separation from her children, and the concomitant major change in her role, more directly strike at her essential personal identity and her self-image as a woman.[116]

When distance is great and visiting hours are limited, children are seldom brought to visit. When the children are in foster homes, their social worker may discourage such visits, and even communication by letter may be forbidden, discouraged, or limited.[117]   Larger families are often broken up, siblings separated, and children moved around as relatives change their plans. Decisions are made without consulting the mother. Her feeling of isolation and powerlessness does not help her achieve the independence she will need when she leaves prison and resumes her task of daily child care and discipline.

D. Vocational Rehabilitation

Since the majority of female ex-offenders must support themselves and often others as well, vocational training is also a matter of great concern to prison officials. Unfortunately, little is being accomplished. An evaluation of vocational training at the California Institution for Women produced this discouraging conclusion:

The study failed to demonstrate that vocational training has any effect upon parole outcome. The differences in returns to prison between the vocational trainees and comparable subjects who had not received training were slight.[118]

Vocational rehabilitation programs for women share all the problems of those for men: "Training" oriented toward institutional maintenance, lack of up-to-date equipment, lack of incentive pay, and lack of placement services. However, there are peculiar problems which vocational programs for women must confront, and they are not being confronted by women's institutions today.

The first problem is that although women now constitute 38 percent of the labor force,[119] most women still do not really view themselves as wage earners.

In contrast to the male, who is expected to prepare for an occupational role, and whose prestige rank is established by the nature of his life work, the female's life goal is achieved mainly through marriage and child rearing. Society still considers a woman's role as a wage earner to be secondary to her traditional role of mother and homemaker.[120] As a result, legislators and correction officials tend to provide men's institutions with the best vocational facilities their budgets will allow, while teaching women merely to cook, sew, and clean. Unfortunately, the women themselves, often share this unrealistic view of their own future. Instead of seeking the independence of a job skill, they seek "someone" they can depend on.[121]

The second problem is that, even when efforts are made, as they are in Wisconsin, to provide reasonably up-to-date vocational skills, the available training is oriented toward "women's work," the traditional low-pay, low-status jobs that women hold in such numbers in our society. Part of the reason for this orientation is the close correlation between such training and the necessary work of institutional maintenance. Scrubbing floors becomes "vocational housekeeping."[122] Scrubbing clothing becomes "vocational laundry."[123] Another reason for the menial training orientation is probably the difficulty of procuring nonmenial job placement. Post-prison job placement assistance is practically nonexistent for women.[124] The jobseeker learns of a vacancy as cook, waitress, cleaning woman, or laundry worker by word-of-mouth, or a sign in the shop window. An applicant may be hired on the spot, and fired the same way, if she proves unsatisfactory. Whatever training is required is given by the employer himself, or by a fellow worker. The parolee with limited skills, a prison record, and a condition of parole stipulating that she must be employed is in no position to choose among employers, and she is offered little guidance in finding the kinds of job situations which offer stability and security.[125]

Efforts to provide more sophisticated, individualized skill training are stymied by the numbers problem as long as it is assumed that this training can be provided only in the institutional setting. Thus the price paid by women for being such a disproportionate minority in the prison population is high—the heaviest penalty is insignificance. Correctional officials and legislators are not unsympathetic, but they have other problems on their minds: Attica, San Quentin,[126] racial warfare, overcrowding, and public clamor for reform.

IV. Impetus for Change

Riots or demonstrations in women's institutions are extremely rare, although they do occur.[127] Yet, this type of event is what captures the attention of the public and triggers demands for reform. Thus, it naturally preoccupies the attention of responsible officials. They are never called upon to explain the conditions which led to bloody rioting and death at a women's institution, because

such things do not happen there.[128] Dr. Mary Harris, the first superintendent
of the federal reformatory for women at Alderson, West Virginia, wrote after
20 years' experience in managing correctional institutions for women: "I
learned . . . that it is riots and demoralization that elicit sympathy and attention. Appeals for help gain potency if there is a flagrant emergency."[129]

Today, attempts are being made to improve conditions in prisons and jails
through legal action. As the courts articulate and expand the concepts of
constitutional protections for the accused, legal actions originating inside
prison walls are proliferating. Class actions, civil rights actions under section
1983, title 42 of the United States Code and even civil actions for damages are
being brought by inmates trying to obtain relief from inhuman prison conditions.[130] But very few of these suitors are women. Wisconsin is probably
among the leaders in providing legal assistance for inmates and books for the
prison law library, but the Wisconsin Home for Women was assigned a law student from the law school's clinical internship program for the first time in
1971. A copy of the *Wisconsin Statutes* and a few *Wisconsin Reports* are kept
on a restricted shelf of the library.

Thus, few women are participating in the two great impulses for change in
prison life today: riots and lawsuits. They are operating effectively neither
"within the system" nor outside it. In fact, they are not operating effectively
at all, and what change there has been in their situation is largely for the
worse.[131]

V. A Solution Designed to Accomplish Modern
Correctional Objectives

The Women's Correctional Association has recommended that, when small
numbers of women inmates make it "economically unsound" to establish regional institutions, states should join together to establish regional institutions.[132]
However, this would mean additional hardship for the women inmate, since regional facilities mean still greater distances separating her from her home and her family.

Obviously, the solution is not more commitments or longer sentences. Still,
in spite of their problems, and in part because of them, women's institutions
present the greatest opportunity available today for progressive experimental
programs aimed at real change in the treatment of offenders. No one is satisfied,
least of all correctional officials themselves, with the results penal institutions
are producing today. Yet when innovation is suggested for men's institutions,
the objection is raised: It's too big; when innovation is suggested for women's
institutions, the same objectors say: It's too small!

But a small offender population can be turned into an advantage instead of
a problem. As Congressman Walter Fauntroy argued in his testimony before
the District of Columbia Commission on the Status of Women, small numbers

are more manageable, and thus the proposed change is easier to sell, easier to implement, and easier to evaluate.[133]   An innovative experimental program, which in massive jails or penitentiaries, might seem to have a negligible effect, can have substantial impact on the smaller population of the women's institution.[134]   Finally, when the change involves alternatives to incarceration, the community will be less anxious and fearful and more willing to help than would be the case if male criminals were involved.

Likewise, the peculiar traits of the female offender make her a better risk for new methods of rehabilitation. As Gloria Cunningham points out, the very habits of women (dependency, verbosity, desire for approval) which perplex male parole officers can be positive factors it they are understood.[135]   The woman offender is more ready to accept a relationship with the counselor as a "helping person," just because she is excessively dependent.[136]   If (but only if) that counselor has some real help to offer, he will find the woman offender anxious to cooperate. Too often, however, the counselors cannot deal effectively with their own feelings when confronted by a woman offender.[137]   The woman is disappointed and hurt, and she is *not* helped.

A Canadian study has noted an apparent tendency of women offenders to need and use specialized medical, psychiatric, and social treatment resources in higher proportion than is true of the same number from an undifferentiated group of men offenders.[138]   The report speculated that, because of differential sentencing practices, the sentenced women may represent a more socially aberrant and emotionally disturbed group than do the sentenced men.[139]   However, the report continued, the finding could also "reflect a general difference in attitude towards the use of such treatment resources as between women and men in the general community."[140]   It may well be that both hypotheses are true. The implication is that, if the "treatment model" can be effective at all, it can be effective with women.

While statistics on recidivism are somewhat confusing, it is safe to say that the rate for women is usually much lower than that for men.[141]   Legislators seem to believe that women and juveniles are more accessible to rehabilitation than are adult males, and more frequently apply indeterminate sentences, which are supposed to facilitate rehabilitation.[142]

It is paradoxical that while all the evidence points to the fact that women criminals are more likely to be rehabilitated,[143] and in fact are more frequently rehabilitated, the facilities which are supposed to produce rehabilitation are less available to them.[144]   The reason seems to be that they are few in number and are failing to cry out for relief. If their rehabilitation programs were to be considered laboratories, pilot projects, or "guinea pigs" for the experimentation needed to produce new concepts in rehabilitation for *all* offenders, perhaps then their problems would receive serious and sustained attention.

While prison reform is the subject of much debate today, there are several areas of general agreement among reformers. Sentences should be shorter for a definite period.[145] Correctional services should be available within the offender's own community.[146] There should be more emphasis on training in marketable vocational skills, and increased use of work release.[147] Use of probation and parole should be increased,[148] and, wherever possible, the offender should be diverted from the institutional system.[149]

All of these reforms could be implemented with less difficulty when female rather than male offenders are involved. And they would probably stand a better chance of demonstrating success. When they do succeed, the public will be more receptive to the larger and more expensive undertaking of applying them to male offenders. And in cases where they fail, the risk has been much less. The community does not perceive itself as being in such great danger from a woman or women who have escaped supervision or failed to conform to community expectations.[150]

Wisconsin is in an ideal position to embark on such a program of experimental reform in its treatment of women offenders, because present arrangements need to be changed. The Wisconsin Home for Women at Taycheedah is located too far from the metropolitan area from which over half[151] its inmates are sentenced. Morale and family problems are created by incarcerating mothers at such a distance from their children, and a host of administrative problems are caused by the distance from a large urban center.[152] With population low and getting lower, it would never be feasible to provide the individualized education and skill training that these women need within the walls of the institution. In a period of increasing cost consciousness and pressures for "austerity," continually increasing expenses will certainly be the subject of legislative scrutiny. But, were the Division of Corrections to institute a comprehensive work and study release and community treatment program, the city of Fond du Lac would not be able to provide the necessary resources. Much more could be done than is being done, but the present location of the institution places severe limits on what can be accomplished.

Some alternative must be found. Recognizing that the Wisconsin Home for Women can never accomplish its goal of rehabilitation without an expenditure of money that would be indefensible, we can proceed to consider what the alternative should be.

The best solution would be fragmentation into a number of small "community treatment centers." An excellent model is provided in the *Pennsylvania Citizens Task Force Report on Regional Community Treatment Centers for Women.*[153] The Bureau of Prisons Community Treatment Centers, which began as Pre-Release Guidance Centers for young offenders, were expanded in 1965 to include adults and those not yet paroled. They are now receiving some direct commitments of selected short-sentence prisoners and female offenders.[154] The U.S. Bureau of Prisons has also prepared a detailed handbook based on experience with this type of facility for federal offenders.[155]

The Governor's Task Force on Offender Rehabilitation recommended that all of Wisconsin's major correctional institutions be closed by June 30, 1975, and replaced by a system of community based treatment centers.[156] To house the present population of the Home for Women in community treatment centers would require four or five centers housing 20-25 women each.[157]

An obvious advantage over the present facility is that security classification would then be available, and inmates could be assigned to centers more or less secure, depending on their needs. Up to now, the custody needs of a tiny minority have determined the custodial pattern of the entire institution. The cost has been high, both in tax funds for custodial personnel, and in subversion of the rehabilitative goal.

The community treatment centers themselves must be in urban areas, either in Milwaukee or adjacent counties. They must be close to public transporation and facilities for education, job training and counseling, as well as hospitals, mental health centers, recreation, and other community services. The Pennsylvania Task Force recommends that some services be provided within the center for those who are not yet ready to take advantage of services offered in the community.[158] However, it might be more feasible to set aside a smaller center for such cases, and plan for the provision of some types of treatment on the premises. But the goal should always be maximum utilization of facilities which are already available to the general community. The rest of the centers could be operated with fewer staff as they approach this goal.[159]

Not only does the employment of fewer staff result in a saving to the taxpayer,[160] but the offender gets more benefit from counselors who do not work in the prison setting, who do not deal exclusively with lawbreakers, and who have not become institutionalized themselves. The inmate subculture,[161] which is the subject of so much study and concern by corrections officials, is subverted when the offender has daily contact at school and work with people who generally accept the standards of the outside community.

The location in urban areas makes possible greater use of volunteer workers, participation of university students and staff, and even employment of exoffenders who live in the area. Employment of ex-offenders is much talked about in correctional circles today but women are rarely included, although Minnesota is making plans to employ female ex-offenders in the correctional system.[162]

VI. Conclusion

This comment has attempted to show that change is needed in prisons for women as well as in those for men. Imprisonment is, if anything, less rational and more harmful for women than for men. For various reasons, women's institutions receive far less attention from the public and from responsible officials. While costs increase, services are not improved. Yet, with fewer facilities available, the rehabilitative ideal still seems to work better for women.

Thus, institutions for women could be an ideal testing ground for the experimentation and innovation that is necessary for the improvement of *all* penal institutions. Congressman Walter Fauntroy suggested this in his testimony before the District of Columbia Commission on the Status of Women.[163] So did the Pennsylvania Task Force on Women and Girl Offenders.[164] In fact it is an idea which has its roots in the 19th century, when activist women worked to reform women's prisons and some of their reforms were adopted in prisons for men.

Notes

1. F. Miller, R. Dawson, G. Dix & R. Parnas, The Correctional Process (1971).

2. Doleschal, *The Female Offender, A Guide to Published Materials,* 2 Crime & Delinquency 639 (1970). A brief, unpublished consultants' paper was submitted, but none of it was used. *Id.*

3. Citizens Study Committee on Offender Rehabilitation, Final Report (1972).

4. Doleschal, *supra* note 2, at 639-40.

5. Statement of Elizabeth Duncan Koontz, Director, Women's Bureau, U.S. Dep't of Labor, before the District of Columbia Commission on the Status of Women, Public Hearings on Women and Girl Offenders, Nov. 4, 1971, at 4 [hereinafter cited as Koontz].

6. Bunker, *War Behind Walls,* Harpers, Feb. 1972, at 39.

7. Doleschal, *supra* note 2, at 639.

8. A study of violent crimes in which women were involved shows that the few women who did commit robbery or burglary did so as helpers or accessories for a male principal. When the crime was homicide or assault, the victim was most often a husband, lover, or child. D. Ward, M. Jackson, & R. Ward, Crimes of Violence 867 (1969) (a staff report submitted to the National Commission on the Causes and Prevention of Violence).

9. Doleschal, *supra* note 2, at 639-40.

10. *Id.* at 640-41.

11. Division of Corrections, Statistical Bulletin C-53, Offenders Admitted to Adult Correctional Institutions, Calendar 1970 Table 5 (1971). The 15 percent who are listed as juvenile delinquents were probably admitted to the Wisconsin School for Girls at Oregon and administratively transferred to Taycheedah. Thus, their exact offenses are unknown. The Wisconsin Supreme Court ruled in State *ex rel.* Edwards v. McCauley, 50 Wis. 2d 597, 184 N.W.2d 908 (1971) that the Wisconsin statutes give the Department of Health and Social Services no authority to transfer delinquent juveniles to adult penal institutions.

12. Koontz at 2.

13. *Id.*

14. *Id.*

15. *Id.*

16. Wisconsin Dep't of Health & Social Services, Statistical Bullentin C-59, Monthly Report of Wisconsin Corrections Population (1972).

17. *Id.*

18. Division of Corrections, 1971 Population Report (1972).

19. Doleschal, *supra* note 2, at 640.

20. *See generally* S. Zalba, Women Prisoners and Their Families (1964).

21. R. Giallombardo, Society of Women: A Study of a Women's Prison 95 (1966).

22. R. Clark, Crime in America 236-37 (1971).

23. B. Odecard & G. Keith, A History of the State Board of Control of Wisconsin and the State Institutions, 1849-1939, at 195 (1939).

24. *Id.*

25. The Gauls and the Britons had prisons or jails built of wicker-ware. When the jail was filled with prisoners, logs were piled around the cage, a fire started, and the prisoners and the jail burned. *Id.*

26. *Id.* at 53.

27. *Id.* at 57.

28. Dorothea Lynd Dix, after an exhaustive tour of eastern prisons in 1845, complained that the product of women's labor in the prisons failed to meet the expenses of their department. D. Dix, Remarks on Prison and Prison Discipline in the United States 108 (1845).

29. R. Giallombardo, *supra* note 21, at 7.

30. *Id.*

31. E. Lekkerkerker, Reformatories for Women in the United States 85-86 (1931).

32. *Id.* at 91. Dr. Eugenia Lekkerkerker, a Dutch lawyer who made an

extensive survey of American reformatories for women in the 1920's, described the situation as follows:

> Though the separation of sexes was prescribed in all prisons, yet this was, in those primitive institutions, frequently not effected in such a way that women were completely removed out of sight or hearing of the men or even from other contacts with them, which led to much profanity, if not to worse. Only very few jails employed a matron to take care of the women's department, so that in most cases they were day and night under the supervision of men guards, who were as a rule not of a very high type and who frequently displayed the usual contempt of unrefined persons for women who have violated the laws of morality.

Id. at 90.

33. Prison officials said they they needed "their" women prisoners to do the house hold chores in the prisons. Otherwise they would have to hire outside help. Private contractors who had women prisoners working for them feared that a change would deprive them of profits. Some of the opposition was based on lack of confidence in the ability of women to manage prisons and control criminals. *Id.* at 92.

34. Before the Massachusetts Reformatory for Women was authorized, a jail at Greenfield was set aside exclusively for women. The work provided for these prisoners was the braiding of whip lashes. Although there were 22 women prisoners, they were supervised by one matron who taught them reading and writing, held a religious service daily and even preached on Sunday. But county authorities objected to the travel expenses of sending women to Greenfield, and the courts expressed their opposition by sentencing seven men and boys to that jail, which ended the experiment. *Id.* at 92, 93.

35. However, there are still only 29 separate women's prisons in the U.S. today. J. Eyman, Prisons for Women 172 (1971).

36. There seem to have been more professional women available in the 1920's and '30's than there are today. Possibly, because the impetus for prison reform came largely from activist women, women were in a better position to make staffing decisions than they are today. Today these decisions are made almost entirely by men and it may be that they simply overlook the availability of qualified women. The entire staff of the Massachusetts Reformatory Prison for Women, except for one utility man, consisted of women, including a full-time physician, a teacher, and a chaplain. E. Lekkerkerker, *supra* note 31, at 93.

37. M. Harris, I Knew Them in Prison 204 (1936).

38. *See* Grupp, *Work Furlough and Punishment Theory*, 8 Criminology 63, 65 (1970).

39. E. Lekkerkerker, *supra* note 31, at 173. The reformatory at Beford Hills, New York, engaged a psychologist (a woman) in 1910, and in 1912 it obtained its Laboratory of Social Hygiene. At about the same time, a research department was established at the Massachusetts Reformatory Prison for Women.

40. *Id.* at 113.

41. Law of March 14, 1851, ch. 287, [1851] Wis. Laws 281 (repealed 1945).

42. G. Küstermann, Catechism of Wisconsin Institutions 55 (1904). B. Odegard & G. Keith, *supra* note 23 include a detailed history of the Waupun State Prison, but make only a few references to the women confined there. Delinquent girls were sent to the Wisconsin Industrial Home for Girls, in Milwaukee, opened in 1875. Previously they had been set free, sent to the Industrial School for Boys, opened around 1859, or, if guilty of a crime which aroused the public, sent to the state prison. The first superintendent of the School for Boys complained about the admission of girls:

> Surely it was never intended that this School should be the receptable of abandoned females, nor that the denizens of every low brothel should be thrown into our family circle.

Id. at 233.

43. B. Odegard & G. Keith, *supra* note 23, at 227.

44. By 1926, the new institution had 84 inmates. Third Biennial Report of the Wisconsin Industrial Home for Women 467 (1926).

45. These women are not mentioned anywhere in the report of the warden of that institution. A statistical table covering all institutions reveals that at the end of 1932 there were 38 women at Waupun. Only three were lifers. Some of the 38 were babies, but the table does not show how many. Twenty-First Biennial Report of the State Board of Control 244 (1932).

46. The two institutions were consolidated by Law of June 22, 1945, ch. 343, § 1, [1945] Wis. Laws 522. The 1944 *Wisconsin Blue Book* lists both institutions, but the 1946 *Wisconsin Blue Book* lists only one, with the new name, Wisconsin Home for Women. 1946 Wisconsin Blue Book 330 (1946).

47. Law of June 16, 1919, ch. 349, § 2, [1919] Wis. Laws 455 (repealed 1945):

> The board of control shall equip and maintain one ward or department of the said industrial home with suitable hospital facilites for the treatment of women afflicted with venereal disease; and shall also equip and maintain a psychological laboratory for the study and treatment of mental disorders to which women and girls addicted to immoral practices are subject. Such females shall be committed for treatment and such industrial training as shall enable them to support themselves properly, and shall be subject to such examinations, treatments, operations and tests, under the regulations of the board as may be deemed necessary by the state board of health to improve their physical and mental condition.

Comparable legislation affecting male sufferers could not be found, The Superintendent of the Industrial Home for Women voiced this complaint in her 1926 report:

Many times commitants for violation of health regulations of this character relate that their consent to "plead guilty" is based upon representations of attorneys, social workers and others interested, that the condition is not serious and that three or four weeks time will "complete the cure." . . . Patients under treatment place reliance on these promises and grow restive under the prescribed course of treatment.

Third Biennial Report of the Wisconsin Industrial Home for Women 469 (1926).

48. In 1932, the superintendent's report pleaded for an educational program like those available in men's institutions. Twenty-First Biennial Report to the State Board of Control 261 (1932). In 1936, the superintendent, still without an appropriation for education, reported, "[C]urrent events are informally discussed by the various groups during their stocking-mending and sewing periods." Twenty-Third Biennial Report of the State Board of Control 494 (1936).

49. Twentieth Biennial Report of the State Board of Control, 404 (1930).

50. *Id.* Insight into the connection between mental deficiency and "crime" is found in Odegard and Keith's *History of the Board of Control*:

"[T]he occasional publicity given to the act of some sex pervert, referred to as a moron, promotes the idea that the feeble-minded are very sexual. . . . This may be true in a few cases, but the vast majority of feeble-minded are sexually immature and rarely if every sexually aggressive." However, the mentally deficient are easily persuaded. "The feeble-minded woman is perhaps the worst offender. She cannot resist the persuasions and temptations that beset her. *Society needs to be protected from her.* She often is the source of corruption of young men and boys. Irresponsible and innocent of intentional wrong, she brings to our very doors the most destructive and insidious of evils."

B. Odegard & G. Keith, *supra* note 23, at 177 (emphasis added, footnotes omitted) *quoting* Beier. *The Operation of Northern Colony and Southern Colony School,* 2 The Rebuilder 1, 6 (1924).

Furthermore, a sterilization law was passed in 1913. B. Odegard & G. Keith, *supra* note 23, at 13. By June 30, 1936, 735 persons had been sterilized, of whom 644 were women and only 91 were men. Twenty-Third Biennial Report of the State Board of Control 13 (1936). This in spite of the fact that the surgeon charged a flat $20 per operation, whether vasectomy of salpingectomy. B. Odegard & G. Keith, *supra* note 23, at 75.

51. For a discussion of innovations in other states see notes 38-50 *supra* and accompanying text.

52. Third Biennial Report of the Wisconsin Industrial Home for Women 468 (1926).

53. For an example of this point see note 48 *supra.*

54. B. Odegard & G. Keith, *supra* note 23, at 255-57.

55. Citizens Task Force Report on State Correctional Institution at Muncy, Pennsylvania iii (1971) [hereinafter Pennsylvania Report].

56. Doleschal, *supra* 2, at 639, 643. William Murray refers to California as

a "notorious . . . penitentiary state with . . . a judiciary quick to imprison."
Murray, *Women in Prison,* Cosmopolitan, Feb., 1972, at 145, 146.

57. Doleschal, *supra* note 2, at 639, 643 n. 16.

58. R. Clark, *supra* note 22, at 236.

59. *See* Grupp, *supra* note 38 at 65.

60. The law was changed in 1919 to allow women to participate. However, even today, not all counties allow Huber release for housework and child care responsibilities. Presumably this is because the system does require extra work, *e.g.* transportation, and the Huber Law prisoner's earnings are used to pay his board at the jail, as well as contribute to the support of his family. On the other hand, the housewife earns nothing, even though her family or the county will probably have to pay someone to care for her children in her absence. Division of Corrections surveys of Huber Law operation make no mention of women.

61. Of course women inmates working in the fields and on the grounds can also escape, but they rarely do. Pennsylvania Report 8.

62. C. Spencer & J. Berecochea, Vocational Training at the California Institution for Women: An Evaluation 32-33 (1971).

63. Wisconsin initiated work release in 1966, and Minnesota in 1967. The Minnesota Correctional Institution for Women at Shakopee has had an average daily population of 56 to 59 in the years since 1967, compared with about 140 decreasing to 120 or less for the Wisconsin Home for Women. Since the start of the program in 1967, Minnesota has had 59 women on work or study release, while Wisconsin has had only 49. In December, 1971, Minnesota, with a population of 56, had six on work or study release. Unpublished research materials supplied by Division of Research and Planning. Department of Corrections, St. Paul, Minnesota. In February, 1972, Wisconsin, with a population double that of Minnesota, had five on work release, with a waiting list of three. All five were doing cleaning. *Hearings before the Citizens Study Committee on Offender Rehabilitation,* held at Wisconsin Home for Women, Taycheedah, Wisconsin, February 15, 1972.

64. M. Harris, *supra* note 37, at 205, 206.

65. There are still judges who take the older view of a reformatory institution as protection from a bad environment. One inmate told the Citizens' Task Force on Offender Rehabilitation at hearings conducted at the Wisconsin Home for Women in August, 1971:

I was sentenced here because I made the mistake of telling the social worker how often we moved when I was a child. She told the judge I needed a structured environment.

66. State *ex rel.* Edwards v. McCauley, 50 Wis. 2d 597, 184 N.W.2d 908 (1971).

67. For a discussion of these problems see notes 69-72 *infra* and accompanying text.

68. "The county can't afford programs for a few women who are often here for a short time," was a jailer's comment reported in a Pennsylvania study of facilities for women. Velimesis, *Criminal Justice for the Female Offender,* 63 Am. Ass'n of U. Women J. 13, 15 (1969).

69. "[W]hen the population is low, it is very difficult to do a good job in classification and assignment," Wisconsin Dep't of Health & Social Services, Annual Report, Wisconsin Home for Women 10 (1971).

70. An inmate at Taycheedah remarked, "There's a bus that takes families to visit at Waupun, but I guess there are too few of us to make that worth while." *Hearings before the Citizens Study Committee on Offender Rehabilitation, supra* note 63.

71. D. Ward, M. Jackson & R. Ward, *supra* note 8, at 846.

72. Koontz, *supra* note 5, at 4.

73. A Williams, Criminal "Justice" System, Off Our Backs 2 (1972). A Wisconsin corrections official has said "the numbers of men make it relatively easy to justify spending money on special educational programs." Milwaukee Sentinel, Jan. 27, 1972, at 6, col. 1.

74. Burkhart, *Women in Prison,* Ramparts, June, 1971, at 21, 22.

75. An example of this is the District of Columbia, which formerly operated a reformatory for women at Occoquan, Virginia. The reformatory has been turned into an alcoholic treatment center for men. Women offenders are now sentenced to the Women's Detention Center, a jail.

76. Wisconsin Dep't of Health & Social Services, *supra* note 69, at 7.

77. *See* Wisconsin Dep't of Health & Social Services, *supra* note 16.

78. Governor's Task Force on Offender Rehabilitation, Report of Subcommittee on Programs and Personnel 90 (1972).

79. *Id.* at 91.

80. Wisconsin Dep't of Health & Social Services, *supra* note 69, at 10.

81. *Id.* at 11.

However, a recent drastic reduction in population has resulted in the closing of one residential building and a one-third cut in staff at the Wisconsin Home for Women. Thirty-five staff members will be dismissed, including 21 of 56 custodial officers, five of 13 teachers plus one sewing instructor who is listed as a therapy assistant, one of three registered nurses, two of six cooks, the storekeeper and her assistant, and two social workers, leaving only an administrator in the social service program, and the personnel director. Milwaukee Journal, Sept. 3, 1972, at 14, col. 2.

82. S. Halleck, Psychiatry and the Dilemmas of Crime 286-87 (1967).

83. *See* R. Giallombardo, *supra* note 21, at 99; D. Ward & G. Kassebaum, Women's Prison, Sex and Social Structure 14 (1967).

84. D. Ward & G. Kassebaum, *supra* note 83, at 5.

85. Dr. Mary Harris, writing of Alderson, put it this way:

[I] mprisonment itself, entailing loss of liberty, loss of citizenship, separation from family and loved ones, is punishment enough for most individuals, no matter how favorable the circumstances under which the time is passed. "Don't they all want to stay here when their time is up?" "Probably this is better than anything most of them have had in their own homes." "I think I'll do something to get sent here myself." These are remarks and questions that recur so frequently from casual visitors that we always expect them; and we try not to appear weary when we explain that, no matter how pleasant a place is, loss of liberty takes away its charm; that imprisonment even under luxurious conditions would press on the nerves; and we remind our questioner that children run away from home and from expensive boarding schools.

M. Harris, *supra* note 37, at 385-86.

86. Murray, *supra* note 56, at 145-47.

87. *Id.*

88. "Basic rules and routines of jails are designed to control the behavior of male inmates." Velimesis, *supra* note 63, at 13.

89. "Doors should be so arranged to give supervisory personnel maximum view into rooms without obviously going out of their way to observe. . . . Security should be built in and available if it becomes necessary but should not be too evident." J. Eyman, *supra* note 35, at 99.

90. Murray, *supra* note 56, at 147.

91. American Correctional Association, Manual of Correctional Standards 561 (1966).

92. One state has two institutions for women, but they are divided on the basis of geography. J. Eyman, *supra* note 35, at ix.

93. When asked how many inmates at Taycheedah really require close confinement for the protection of society, a staff member replied, "Perhaps one or two." *Hearings before the Citizens Study Committee on Offender Rehabilitation,* *supra* note 63.

94. Figures obtained from the Bureau of Planning, Development, and Research, Wisconsin Division of Corrections, August, 1971:

	Waupun	Fox Lake	Taycheedah
Inmates	972	522	118
Custodial Staff	219	84	57
Treatment Staff	59	63	30
Other staff (clerical, plant, etc.)	91	41	29
Total staff	369	188	116

Recent staff reductions at the Home for Women will not affect this ratio very much. With population down to 75, the number of custodial officers will be reduced from 56 to 35. Milwaukee Journal, *supra* note 81, at col. 1.

95. F. Baldi, My Unwelcome Guests 121 (1959).

96. A sociologist, Sr. Esther Heffernan, has described Taycheedah as "marvelous for tours" but a "very tight" institution in spite of the absence of prison walls. Milwaukee Sentinel, *supra* note 73.

97. R. Giallombardo, *supra* note 21, at 95.

98. E. Heffernan, Making It In Prison: The "Square," The "Cool," and "The Life" 182 (1972).

99. R. Giallombardo, *supra* note 21, at 8.

100. I thought I could get rehabilitated here, but all I'm doing is mopping floors in the administration building, cleaning their toilets and scrubbing the steps seven days a week. Do you think I can get rehabilitated here? I'm trying . . . . I sing in the choir and I'm taking an English class. My back hurts a lot from scrubbing the floor . . . .
Interview with a 19-year-old drug addict in Burkhart, *supra* note 74, at 21.

101. Interview with a correctional officer at the Wisconsin Home for Women, August, 1971. A later conversation with an inmate on the same day corroborated the officer.

102. "[T]he pungent order of floor wax always hangs heavily in the air. The ability to maintain a clean cottage is considered to be one of the marks of a good officer, and is a measure of how well she can 'control' the group." R. Giallombardo, *supra* note 21, at 27.
Wisconsin Home for Women, General Rules and Policies 3 (mimeo.):
It is our general policy that if you smoke you will be expected to wash your room walls once every other month. If you do not smoke, you should wash them once every three months. You may wash your room walls on a more frequent basis if you so desire. If the housekeeper or other staff member in your residential building determines that your room is in need of washing earlier than provided, you will be asked to do so.

103. American Correctional Association, *supra* note 91, at 418.

104. Burkhart, *supra* note 74, at 23.

105. Wisconsin Dep't of Health & Social Services, *supra* note 69, at 12.

106. *See* Wisconsin Dep't of Health & Social Services, *supra* note 16.

107. Payak, *Understanding the Female Offender,* 27 Fed. Probation 7, 10 (1963).

108. S. Halleck, *supra* note 82, at 140.

109. A study at the California Institution for Women showed that only 24% of inmate-mothers had left their children in the care of the father. The other 76% had left children with other relatives or in foster homes. A later

field investigation showed that only 11% of the fathers actually were caring for the children. S. Zalba, *supra* note 20, at 44, 83.

110. *See* Velimesis, *supra* note 68.

111. *Id.* at 14.

112. *Hearings before the Citizens Study Committee on Offender Rehabilitation, supra* note 63.

113. In 1965, Rose Giallombardo reported about Alderson inmates:

[E]vidence strongly suggests that the majority of female inmates must seek some form of employment when released. The marital status of the inmates indicated that 27.1 percent were single; 31.5 percent were married; 20.7 percent were separated; 16.4 percent were divorced; and slightly over 4 percent were widows.

R. Giallombardo, *supra* note 21, at 86. In the same year, figures for the female population at large were as follows: Single, 18.8 percent; married, 66 percent; widowed, 12 percent; and divorced, 3 percent. Bureau of the Census, U.S. Dep't of Commerce, 1970 Statistical Abstract of the U.S. 32 (1970).

114. For a discussion of the difficulties involved when correctional facilities are located in rural areas see note 152 *infra.*

115. Koontz, *supra* note 5, at 6.

116. S. Zalba, *supra* note 20, at 2, 3.

117. *Hearings before the Governor's Task Force on Offender Rehabilitation, supra* note 63.

118. C. Spencer & J. Berecochea, *supra* note 62, at 30.

119. Women's Bureau, U.S. Dep't of Labor, Women Workers Today 1 (1971).

120. R. Giallombardo, *supra* note 21, at 14.

121. Payak, *supra* note 107, at 11. Bertha Payak writes: "The female offender's goal, as is any woman's, is a happy and successful marriage, so her self-image is dependent upon the establishment of satisfactory relationship with the opposite sex." *Id.*

An institution counselor put it more bluntly in a conversation with the writer. "They don't seem ambitious to learn a trade," she complained, "but why should they? They'll be back on the street soon and they can always find some guy that will keep them."

122. C. Spencer & J. Berecochea, *supra* note 62, at 1.

123. Inmates at Taycheedah called it "scrubology," *Id.* at 3.

124. Cunningham, *Supervision of the Female Offender,* 27 Fed. Probation 12, 13 (1963).

125. C. Spencer & J. Berecochea, *supra* note 62, at 31.

126. Bunker, *supra* note 6, at 39.

127. M. Harris, *supra* note 37, at vii, 64.

128. J. Martin, Break Down the Walls 200 (1954).

129. M. Harris, *supra* note 37, at 237.

130. *E.g.,* Sostre v. McGinnis, 442 F.2d 178 (2d Cir. 1971); Morales v. Schmidt, 340 F. Supp. 544 (W.D. Wis. 1972), *rev'd and remanded,* No. 72-1373 (7th Cir., filed Jan. 17, 1973); Landman v. Royster, 333 F. Supp. 621 (E.D. Va. 1971).

131. Elizabeth Gurley Flynn was sentenced to Alderson in 1955 after a conviction under the Smith Act. In the prison library, she found a copy of Dr. Mary Harris' book, *I Knew Them in Prison.* She also talked to inmates and officers who had been at Alderson during Dr. Harris' regime. Mrs. Flynn believed that Alderson had changed substantially for the worse. E. Flynn, The Alderson Story 106-15 (1963).

132. J. Eyman, *supra* note 35, at x.

133. Testimony of Congressman Walter E. Fauntroy, before the District of Columbia Commission on the Status of Women, Public Hearings on Women and Girl Offenders, Nov. 3, 1971, at 1.

134. *Id.*

135. Cunningham, *supra* note 124, at 16.

136. A woman parole officer in Madison, Wisconsin told the writer that she and other women parole officers have lighter caseloads than the male officers. Because the women offenders accept the parole officer as counselor, they make more demands on her time. An American Bar Foundation study reported the same situation in Detroit and in Milwaukee. R. Dawson, Sentencing: The Decision as to Type, Length, and Conditions of Sentence 127, 129, 135 (1969).

137. Cunningham, *supra* note 124, at 13.

D. Ward & G. Kassebaum, *supra* note 84, at 241 give a vivid example of this kind of occurrence at the California Institution for Women. A male staff member, who was later dismissed, annoyed inmates who had been prostitutes by asking them to describe the details of their sexual experiences. They were able to discern that his interest was not really in helping them.

138. Canadian Committee on Corrections, Toward Unity: Criminal Justice and Corrections 398 (1969).

139. A Wisconsin corrections official expressed this view in an interview with the writer on February 29, 1972. He regarded women offenders as more, not less, challenging than men, from a treatment standpoint.

140. Canadian Committee on Corrections, *supra* note 138, at 398.

141. Recidivism rates are usually stated in percentages. However, percentages are inaccurate when numbers are small. Furthermore, there are many different kinds of institutions where women are kept. On June 30, 1971, 92 percent of the women incarcerated at Taycheedah were there for the first

time, and only 8 percent were re-admissions. On the same day, only 74 percent of all males incarcerated in state institutions in Wisconsin were in for the first time and 26 percent represented re-admissions. Division of Corrections, Statistical Bulletin C-57, Offenders Resident in Wisconsin Adult Correctional Institutions on June 30, 1974, at 4 (1971).

But at the Women's Detention Center in Washington, D.C., a study of 116 releasees in 1969 showed that 36 percent had been booked back in at the end of 18 months. C. Barros, V. McArthur & S. Adams, A Study of Post-Release Performance of Women's Detention Center Releasees 11 (1970).

142. Nagel & Weitman, *Double Standard of American Justice,* Society. March, 1972, at 18, 21. This supposition dates back to the earliest days of the reformatory movement. One of its earliest advocates supported indeterminate sentencing for prostitutes. E. Lekkerkerker, *supra* note 31, at 88.

143. For a discussion of rehabilitation of women offenders see notes 135, 138, 140, 141 *supra* and accompanying text.

144. For a discussion of the availability of work release programs see notes 60-63 *supra* and accompanying text.

145. *See generally* Testimony of Professor Marshall B. Clinard, Professor of Sociology, University of Wisconsin, *Hearings on Prisons, Prison Reform, and Prisoners' Rights: Wisconsin Before the Subcomm. on Corrections of House Comm. on the Judiciary,* 93d Cong., 1st Sess., ser. 15, pt. 4, at 72 (1971). E. Heffernan, *supra* note 98, at 181.

146. Citizens Study Committee on Offender Rehabilitation, Interim Report 2 (1972).

147. Canadian Committee on Corrections, *supra* note 138, at 316.

148. *See id.* at 196, 330; Citizens Study Committee on Offender Rehabilitation, *supra* note 146, at 7.

149. *Id.* at 17.

150. For a discussion of the types of offenses committed by women see note 29 *supra* and accompanying text.

151. Divison of Corrections, *supra* note 11, Table 6.

152. A comprehensive list of reasons for locating correctional facilities in or near major urban centers is given in Canadian Committee on Corrections, *supra* note 138, at 325.

153. Citizens Task Force Report on Regional Community Treatment Centers for Women, Pennsylvania (1970) [hereinafter Report on Treatment Centers].

154. U.S. Bureau of Prisons, Dep't of Justice, The Residential Center: Corrections in the Community 3 (1969).

155. *Id.*

156. Citizens Study Committee on Offender Rehabilitation, *supra* note 3, at 7-10.

157. If the recommendations of the *Interim Report* were followed with regard to elimination of criminal prohibition of certain sex behavior, as well as the recommendation that for certain property crimes, civil remedies be substituted for criminal prosecution, population would drop substantially and fewer centers would be needed. Citizens Study Committee on Offender Rehabilitation, *supra* note 146, at 14-17.

158. Report on Treatment Centers 11.

159. The U.S. Bureau of Prisons even suggests that meals be taken at nearby restaurants and cafeterias. This results in significant savings in costs of food and supplies, kitchen equipment, and food service staff, although some still believe that meals together provide a "family" atmosphere and establish a setting for interpersonal relationships. U.S. Bureau of Prisons, *supra* note 154, at 10, 20.

160. *See id.* at 9; Report on Treatment Centers 6.

161. Canadian Committee on Corrections, *supra* note 138, at 314.

162. *See* Division of Research and Planning, *supra* note 63.

163. Testimony of Congressman Walter E. Fauntroy, *supra* note 133, at 1.

164. Report on Treatment Centers 6-7.

6

Children of Women Prisoners: A Forgotten Minority

Brenda G. McGowan and
Karen L. Blumenthal

In spite of the recent surge of interest in women's rights, prisoner's rights, and children's rights, there is one group whose lives remain relatively unnoticed and unchanged—the children of women prisoners. There are a number of reasons why this population has failed to attract any widespread attention.

First, this is a group of unknown size that is not easily identified or mobilized. The children cannot speak for themselves; and the various rights groups that might be expected to focus public attention on their needs have just begun to acknowledge and deal with their own oppression. They cannot yet be expected to perform an advocacy function for others.

Second, leaders in the movement for social change are often just as wedded to and blinded by the pervasive American philosophy of individualism as those they are trying to challenge. As a result, they tend to voice their goals in terms of the rights of the individual, not the family unit, and to judge their results in terms of the behavior of their individual members of society at large.

Third, because of the lack of a national family policy, no effort is made to evaluate policies and practices in the criminal justice system in terms of their impact on family life. Every component of the correctional system is oriented toward the punishment—and perhaps rehabilitation—of the offender. Success is measured in terms of recidivism rates, not in terms of the degree to which offenders can be reintegrated into society or in terms of the impact of their experiences in the correctional system on their families or communities. The idea that the criminal justice system should take any responsibility for what happens to children of offenders is totally alien to the traditional concept of police, the judiciary, or corrections.

It should be noted that although most communities have a wide range of social services agencies, these tend to be highly specialized and fragmented. Each is organized to deal with a specific problem, a single aspect of clients' lives or a specific diagnostic category. There is no one agency or organization with responsibility for inmate mothers and their children. Instead, a number of different bureaucracies are expected to deal with each of the various problems presented by this population. This means that it is difficult to fix blame or demand any sort of accountability. More often, these children simply fall between the cracks. Finally, children of women prisoners are usually poor, often nonwhite, part of the group of children whose needs are consistently ignored by the larger society. Their plight stems so clearly from social and familial causes, it is difficult to treat them the way so many other groups of children are handled, by "blaming the victim." Instead, these children are simply ignored, although for children this may be the most severe form of punishment.

However, this is too large a population to ignore. Although the actual number of children of women prisoners can only be estimated because these children have been overlooked statistically as well as in every other way, there is evidence that they form a large group that is likely to continue growing. The Women's Bureau of the U.S. Department of Labor estimates there are approximately 15,000 women imprisoned on any one day.[a] The best available data suggest that 70 percent of female inmates are mothers and that the average inmate mother has two dependent children. Therefore, on a conservative basis, we estimate there are approximately 21,000 children in this country whose mothers are incarcerated on any one day.

On an annual basis, this figure rises steeply. Because statistics vary so widely regarding the number of persons detained or imprisoned annually, we can only approximate the number of children whose mothers are incarcerated during the course of a year. For example, almost 14,000 women were confined in state and federal prisons during 1970 (Hindelaing 1973). It has been suggested that local jails and lock-ups may hold 15 times as many persons during a year as all state and federal prisons (Flynn 1973). On that basis we can estimate that perhaps an additional 210,000 women were confined in local jails and lock-ups during 1970. Because of the lack of data regarding recidivism, we have no way of determining an unduplicated count. However, even if we deliberately overestimate recidivism and assume a 100 percent failure rate within a single year, we can assume that approximately 78,400 mothers with 156,800 children were incarcerated during 1970.[b]

To find out about this neglected segment of the population, the Children's Defense Fund of the Washington Research Project initiated a study of children of women prisoners in 1974. This was an exploratory study, which had four major components: (1) national mail survey of administrators and women prisoners in correctional facilities reported to hold 25 women or more; (2) prestructured interviews with 65 women at the New York City Correctional Institution for Women; (3) site visits to a number of innovative programs for inmate mothers and their children; and (4) open-ended interviews with a number of professionals in the child welfare and criminal justice fields, primarily in the New York City area.

Perhaps the most striking finding of this study was the range of problems

---

[a]Of these, it is estimated that 800 are in federal reformatories, 6,000 in state institutions, and 8,000 in more than 3,500 county and municipal jails.

[b]To arrive at this estimate, we have again assumed that 70 percent of female inmates are mothers and that inmate mothers have an average of two children each.

children and families experience at every point in the criminal justice process because of the lack of appropriate services and social concern. For example, police officers generally display an appalling lack of sensitivity to the needs and fears of children when they arrest a woman. Since their first concern must be apprehension of the alleged offender and community safety, they are unlikely to think about the possibility of children when there are no children present at the time of the arrest. If they do think to ask about a woman's responsibility for dependent children, given all the other tasks they must perform while effecting and processing an arrest, they are unlikely to view their responsibility for the children as a high priority unless the children are present *and* obviously in need of care.

The needs of these children continue to be ignored during the pretrial period, particularly when their mothers are detained. Depending on the judge who is present at the arraignment or at the preliminary hearing, a woman who has responsibility for minor children may be somewhat less likely than other defendants to be detained during this time. However this is the only recognition given to the needs of the woman's children prior to trial. No effort is made to ascertain that the children are receiving adequate care or to make plans for their future should their mother be sentenced. Detention procedures and policies clearly exacerbate the problems already created. Children under 16 are frequently prohibited from visiting and inmates are often not permitted to make any phone calls to their children or their children's caretakers. If children are permitted to visit, the visits are usually brief and conducted through a screen or glass under circumstances that may be quite upsetting and frightening for children. Little effort is made during this period to help mothers reassess the adequacy of their children's temporary living arrangements.

During the trial and at the sentencing, judges do appear to be somewhat more lenient with women. Nevertheless, the existence of dependent children influences a judge's decision regarding sentencing only in borderline cases. The time of sentencing is often a particularly stressful time for families because offenders are frequently taken directly from the courtroom to prison and not given any time to talk with their children or to make any plans for them.

Incarcerated mothers and their children face a number of special problems. As one woman commented, "Besides hurting us, they are hurting our children." The most critical problem is the enforced separation. Visits, phone calls, and letters help, but they cannot substitute for ongoing, daily contact. Many of the women's children are too young for letters, and opportunities for telephone contact are usually very limited. Although more facilities are now experimenting with open or "contact" family visits, many institutions still permit only visiting across a table, glass partition, or screen, which is generally very upsetting to children. Also, visiting hours are generally quite restricted, and transportation of children tends to be a major problem because distance and costs are often so great. All of these difficulties may be compounded if the children's current caretakers are angry or disapproving of the mother or if they simply feel that children should not be exposed to prison conditions. Because of restrictive prison policies regarding communications as well as the punitive attitude of many of the children's caretakers, mothers in prison frequently find they are unable to obtain sufficient information about their children's development, school problems, health needs, and so forth. Consequently, they are unable to have full input into the decisions and plans that must be made for their children. They are likely to feel guilty about what their children may be suffering because of their own failures; yet they are restricted from fulfilling their parental responsibilities and even from comforting their children and offering them the support they may need.

Although all women who are released from prison face many difficulties, mothers must cope with a number of additional problems. There are very real barriers to the women's plans to reunite with their children. A number of women do not even know where their children are. Relatives or friends caring for the children may have moved away and not informed the mother. Other times, the caretakers may refuse to return the children or create obstacles to their return. Even if there are few problems concerning a mother's "physical" reunion with her children, there may well be a myriad of emotional problems. Children may be angry or hurt because their mothers have been away; they have been left alone and feel rejected. Some children have had painful experiences while their mothers were incarcerated. As a result, many mothers must handle highly stressful situations with their children while they are trying to cope with all the other problems of the postrelease period. They receive little help from parole officers, social service agencies, and even self-help organizations of ex-offenders with these family-related problems.

One of the purposes of our study was to address the problem of the almost total lack of data about inmate mothers and their children. The U.S. Bureau of the Census provides the most complete demographic data about female inmates, but it does not provide any information about the children of women prisoners. To obtain basic statistical data about this population, we conducted a national mail survey of administrators and residents in correctional facilities reported to hold 25 or more female inmates. Responses were obtained from every state, 4 federal facilities, the District of Columbia, and Puerto Rico. We received data on 74 facilities in which approximately 9,379 women were confined at the time of the survey. Based on other national estimates, we believe our sample represents slightly over one-half of all women who are incarcerated on any one day. The many women confined in small local facilities with less than 25 residents were not included in our survey. Moreover, not all of the inmates' questionnaires were complete and a number of the administrators provided estimates rather than actual counts, so the data are of uncertain reliability.

To summarize our national findings briefly, approximately two-thirds

(67.1%) of the women in our survey were mothers;[c] the average inmate-mothers had an average of 2.4 dependent children.[d] Almost two-thirds of the children for whom age was reported (N = 4,461) were under ten (62.4%) and nearly one-fourth were under four. Although this is not surprising in view of the relative youth of the inmate population, it suggests that a significant number of children of prisoners are separated from their mothers during their early formative years when a positive, nurturing relationship is considered essential to child development. Most children of women prisoners lived with their mothers prior to arrest, but approximately one-fourth did not. Those children not living with their mothers prior to arrest generally lived with relatives (68.4%); a large percentage of those cared for by their mothers also lived in extended family situations. Consequently, many children did not experience any change in residence after the arrest of their mothers, but this does not mean they were not traumatized by the arrest of their mothers or hurt by the loss of an ongoing relationship with their mothers. Children who had to be moved after their mothers were arrested most frequently went to live with relatives; about 12 percent or one out of eight were placed in foster care. Approximately 85 percent of the inmate mothers maintained some contact with their children during the time they were incarcerated, and almost as many (82.6%) were in regular contact with their children's caretaker. However, many women indicated that because of geographic distance and restrictive visiting and telephone policies, their contacts were not as frequent or as satisfactory as they would have liked. Almost four out of five of the mothers (78.9%) said they planned to reestablish a home for their children after their release; only two (<1%) said they planned to place their children for adoption. Certainly these findings suggest that inmate mothers feel responsible for their children and regard their current separation as only temporary.

Because we held lengthy interviews with inmate mothers at the New York City Correctional Institution for Women, we were able to obtain more extensive information about this population than about the women in our national survey. Since our sample was relatively small (65 mothers of 112 children) and New York City is somewhat atypical of the rest of the country, the reader is cautioned about drawing generalizations. However, a brief overview of our findings in instructive:

1. These women were responsible for very young children; almost half of their children were under 5 and about 90 percent under 12. Hence these children were very vulnerable to separation problems.

---

[c]Excluding the four youth facilities in which there are only a small number of mothers, 3,121 or 67.1 percent of the women in the 46 facilities that provided this information were mothers. Most of the estimated percentages provided by the administrators clustered around 70-80 percent.

[d]The mean number of children per inmate mother was 2.4 in the 41 facilities that reported number of children. This figure is relatively similar to other estimates.

2. Although many of the women had prior records, these were not "dangerous" offenders; 40 percent were charged with property offenses and an additional 39 percent were charged with "victimless" crimes such as prostitution. Therefore one must ask if incarceration is the most appropriate penalty for this population. The primary reason that most were in prison was probably drug related since it is estimated that 85 percent of the population in this facility are addicts.

3. Because of the frequent use of extended family living situations, two-thirds of the children did not have to be moved after the arrest of their mothers. Of those who were moved, only three were placed in foster care and the remainder went to live with relatives or friends. The mothers of six children did not know what had happened to their children.

4. While their mothers were in prison, over 80 percent of the children were able to have some contact with their mothers and over half were in contact at least weekly. Over half of the mothers expressed positive feelings about their child's current living situation, but one-third expressed real concerns. Over 90 percent of the mothers planned to reunite with their children sometime after release, but many saw the need for some period of readjustment before taking their children.

5. Given what is known about the potentially injurious effects of abrupt separation, it was disturbing to find that the younger the child, the less likely he was to have frequent contact with his mother after arrest. Moreover, the younger the child the more likely the mother was to be planning an immediate reunion with her child, thus risking another abrupt separation from his current caretaker. The one important mitigating factor in this regard is that young children were most likely to be living with relatives and least likely to have experienced a move after the arrest of their mother. However, the lack of regular contact between mothers of young children or their caretakers, who are usually relatives, raises serious question about the quality of many of these family relationships.

6. In general, the mothers tended to be much more satisfied with the children's current living situation when the children were living with grandparents than with anyone else, including fathers or other relatives. Mothers expressed the most negative feelings about foster care.

7. A period of incarceration seems to strongly effect the likelihood that a mother will experience future separation from her child. For example, the more prior incarcerations a mother had, the less likely she was to be living with her child at the time of arrest and the less likely she was to be planning an immediate reunion, no matter whether she had been caring for her child at the time of arrest or not. We, of course, have no way of knowing whether the mother's incarceration in itself is sufficient to cause family break-up or whether there may be other factors such as drug addiction that lead both to incarceration and to long-term separation of mother and child. However, this finding suggests

that women prisoners and their children are families very much at risk; unless there is some positive intervention, the incarceration of a mother is likely to create not only temporary distress for the child, but also long-term strains on the mother child relationship.

Our study clearly indicated the harm suffered by both mothers and children when the mothers are imprisoned. To summarize, the children are often removed abruptly from their homes, schools, and communities. They may be shuttled from one caretaker to another, teased or shunned by their peers. Often they have no knowledge of what is happening when their mothers are first arrested; they are simply left alone in terror and confusion. Later, they may be deprived of any opportunity to talk or visit with their mothers. If they are permitted to visit, this is likely to involve long trips to the prison and brief, stilted, closely guarded visits behind a glass screen or across a large table. If they are placed with relatives or friends, they may hear barbed comments about their mother and feel they are a burden; or they may even be told that if their mother really loved them, she would not have gone to prison. Often there is no one with legal authority to enroll them in school, sign their report cards, or secure the medical care they need. If they are placed in foster care, they may never be permitted to return home. There is always the uncertainty about their future. When their mothers are released, they face the difficult problem of trying to reestablish a relationship, always wondering if their mother is really bad, if she is likely to leave them again. Consider for example, Beth's story:

Beth is an 11-year-old youngster who was placed in a foster home one year ago, after her mother, Mrs. Jarmin, was convicted of possessing stolen property. A week before Mrs. Jarmin was to be sentenced, she took Beth to stay at her mother's, assuming that Beth would remain there throughout her prison term. About two weeks later, a worker from the welfare department arrived at Beth's school and simply took her to the foster home. Neither Mrs. Jarmin nor her mother were told about this plan until later, at which time the welfare department claimed that since Beth had been in foster care briefly about two years prior to this, they still had custody and did not believe that her grandmother could provide a suitable home.

In Beth's own words, "When my mother was arrested . . . they just came in and took her away. . . . I was at school, but my grandmother guessed what had happened. Then my mother called after a few days. A week later, the welfare worker just came to school and told me I was going to the home. I was pretty scared at first because I didn't know anything about this place. But after I found out they would treat me OK, I didn't mind too much."

Beth says that the home hasn't been as bad as she thought it would be. However, her foster mother feels that she has had a very difficult time adjusting to the placement. When she first arrived, she was very friendly and anxious to please, but she was frequently moody and hurt herself in temper by banging her head against the wall. Midway through the school year, as she seemed to become more comfortable in the home, she started to have difficulty in school, refusing to do her homework, acting up in class, and getting into fights with other students. The foster parents held a number of conferences with the

school staff but nobody seemed able to reach her. Finally in March after a fight
with another student, she was suspended. At that point, the agency supervising
the placement decided that Beth should be sent to the girls detention center for
a week. They felt that she was starting to behave like her mother and would
have to learn some realistic limits. Since that time, the foster parents feel that
her behavior has improved. This is attributed to the fact that she has acquired
a boy friend, which has improved her self-image.

In discussing the suspension incident, however, Beth explains that the kids
in school often teased her about her mother and that one girl, with whom she
had all the fights, kept calling her mother a jailbird. Since she got back from the
detention center, the kids have left her alone.

Beth says that she doesn't have anyone she can talk to about her worries.
Her foster parents are all right, but they are very strict and don't talk too much.
And although she now has a boy friend and a best friend in school, she isn't
allowed to see them much and couldn't talk to them anyway. Therefore, she
just keeps things to herself.

When asked what was going to happen after her mother was released from
prison, Beth put her head down and said, "I don't know. It's kind of scary. I
want us to live together, but . . ." and her voice trailed off.

Inmate mothers also suffer a great deal of uncertainty and anguish. They
often feel that enforced separation from their children is one of the most difficult aspects of their incarceration (Zalba 1964; Bonfanti 1974), and several
studies have documented that official agencies consistently fail to address this
problem (Women's Prison Association 1973; Van Nuland, N.D.). As one woman
commented, "By taking away our rights to see our children, they're killing us."
The women often feel it will be difficult for their children to get to know them
or trust them again in the future. They worry about who is going to protect
their children's interests and make certain they get the education, health care,
and social services they need. They are concerned that their children will be
confused by having two mothers or that the children's caretakers will turn them
against their mothers.

At present, almost nothing is being done for inmate mothers and their
children. At each point in the criminal justice system (arrest, pretrial, detention,
sentencing, and imprisonment), policies and procedures seem oriented toward
undermining mothers' capacities to fullfill their parental responsibilities. The
child welfare system almost completely ignores the offender population; and
other community agencies that do work in the correctional system pay little
attention to the needs of prisoners' families—although several studies have documented that the maintenance of family ties is the most important component
of rehabilitation. Holt and Miller, for example, have commented as follows:

The positive relationship between strength of social ties and success on parole
has held up for 45 years of releases across very diverse offender populations
and in different localities. It is doubtful if there is any other research finding
in the field of corrections which can approximate this record. (1972:61)

There are a few innovative programs aimed at serving inmate mothers and their children. These programs are based on varying philosophies, operate under different auspices, and serve different size populations. For example,

1. Purdy Treatment Center for Women in Washington is a state correctional center that has both a philosophy and a program that reflects the importance of the family in the treatment process (Buckles and La Fazie 1973; Wolfram 1973).
2. Oregon Women's Correctional Center is a state correctional facility that has developed an "integrated services project" in which one member of the team is a social worker from the public child welfare department (Toombs, N.D.).
3. Family and Children's Services of Minneapolis, a private family service agency runs mother discussion groups that are educational, therapeutic, and change oriented at the Minnesota Correctional Institution for Women (Daehlin 1974)
4. The Women's Prison Association in New York City, a private community service agency for female offenders, recently completed a three-year research-advocacy project for children of offenders (1973).

There are other programs such as these that could serve as models for new services. However, it must be recognized that these are very limited efforts, primarily in the voluntary sector, which do not begin to address the needs of the total population of children of women prisoners.

Both the inmate-mothers and the correctional administrators who participated in our national survey recognized the current dearth of useful services; yet they had thoughtful and imaginative suggestions regarding policy changes and service programs they would like to recommend. The recommendations made by inmate mothers are presented in table 6-1.

There was a high degree of congruence between these recommendations of the mothers and those made by correctional administrators who participated in our survey. As might be expected, the mothers vigorously stressed areas relating to visiting and programming for children's visits. The correctional authorities put greater emphasis on (1) parent education programs such as child-care and family-law classes; (2) child welfare workers who could serve as a liason among mothers, their children, and community service agencies; (3) provision of better substitute care for children; and (4) services for the children in the community such as financial and medical assistance, protective services, and counseling. They also offered other suggestions such as establishing a coordinating body for all family-oriented programs and services within the prison; initiating programs to help families deal with the problems they may be having with their inmate relatives or with prison staff; encouraging agencies that sponsor child advocacy programs to include these children as a top priority in their advocacy efforts; development of a handbook for inmate-mothers on their legal rights in regard

Table 6-1

Recommendations for Program Changes made by Inmate - Mothers

1. Visiting

    a. Longer and more frequent visiting hours
    b. Overnight visits
    c. Weekend visits
    d. Family visiting programs (child, caretaker, and resident)
    e. Visits in which physical contact is permitted
    f. Better physical settings for visits on facility's grounds
    g. Occasional visits with children off prison grounds, e.g., park
    h. Fewer correctional staff present during visits
    i. Varied visiting days and times, e.g., weekdays, after school hours, so it is easier for caretakers to bring children
    j. Provision of financial assistance and escort service to facilitate visiting by children
    k. Transportation pools
    l. Establishment of mandatory visiting policy so that visitation rights may not be denied by the prison or by the agency or person(s) with custody of the children
    m. Positive efforts by correctional officials to encourage caretakers (especially husbands and foster parents) to bring children to visit

2. Parent education:

    a. Child psychology classes
    b. Family-planning classes
    c. Family-living classes
    d. Small groups dealing with questions such as how to explain incarceration to children of various ages and how to maintain an effective parent role with children when they are being cared for by other people
    e. Opportunities to work in day-care centers for experience with children
    f. "Help" to be a better mother

3. Counseling-therapy:

    a. Mothers' discussion groups
    b. Family counseling
    c. Parents without partners chapter

4. Provision of information to mothers on matters related to the conditions of their children:

    a. "Someone" (occasionally respondent specified a social worker, a case worker, or welfare) to check to see if the children are being cared for properly and to inform the mother about their conditions at regular intervals
    b. Full-time representative of the public child welfare agency at the correctional facility
    c. Better communication between the public department of social services and the prison
    d. "Someone" to help mothers locate their children

5. Programming for children's visits:

    a. More planned activities for mothers and children during visits
    b. Playroom, playground for children during visits
    c. Children's day
    d. Picnics for mothers and children
    e. Family "get-togethers"
    f. Group overnight outings for mothers and children
    g. Holiday dinners at prison for families
    h. Tours of facilities for children
    i. Photographs of children when they visit

6. Housing children with mothers serving time:

   a. Nurseries on prison grounds for infants up to one year of age
   b. Separate cottage on prison grounds for mothers and their children
   c. Special apartments on prison grounds for families
   d. Cottages or apartments for families located near, but not on, prison grounds for pre-parole or work-release women

7. Substitute caretakers

   a. Information concerning availability of foster homes
   b. Foster homes and group homes for children of inmate mothers located closer to prison
   c. Foster homes for sibling groups
   d. Sufficient numbers of foster homes (so children need not be institutionalized)
   e. Improved relationships between foster parents and mothers
   f. Rap sessions for inmate-mothers whose children are in foster care and for foster parents caring for children of inmate-mothers
   g. Tours and rap sessions for prospective foster parents and for residents considering using foster-care services
   h. Community speaking engagements for residents concerning foster-home program
   i. Meetings between mothers and foster parents prior to child's placement for purposes of sharing information and planning
   j. Visits to mother by child's case worker
   k. "Someone" to keep child aware of whom his real mother is
   l. Concrete help to regain custody of child and reestablish the home

8. Services for children in the community:

   a. Special educational programs
   b. Day-care services
   c. Preschool programs
   d. Prison workers to serve as liaison between teachers and inmate mothers
   e. Provision of gifts to children on birthdays and holidays

---

to their children; and increased research and dissemination of findings on the effects of incarceration on parent-child relationships and methods for dealing with the problems that may result.

These responses clearly suggest that the two groups who have the most intimate knowledge of the problems of children of women prisoners recognize the need for change and have a large number of innovative ideas about how it might be accomplished.

Consideration of the policy issues related to children of women prisoners raises all the classic child welfare dilemmas in terms of the need to balance the rights of parents against the rights and responsibilities of the state and the best interest of the child.

How can the state's responsibility to protect the public interest be balanced against the child's right to care and nurturance by his natural parents? Since the state has the duty under law to provide for dependent children, in situations in which the only parent is incarcerated, what is the oblication of the state, through its courts, probation, public welfare, child welfare, or other state agencies:

1. To identify and locate dependent children of the incarcerated parent
2. To provide financial assistance and special services as needed to the children
3. To investigate whether the caretaker is providing adequate care
4. To implement the right of children to the least detrimental placement usually with relatives where available and appropriate
5. To file neglect petitions on behalf of children if the caretakers are found inadequate
6. To provide counsel for the children at any court or administrative hearings to determine alternative placements

How can these obligations be balanced against the mothers' right to privacy and self-determination?

What are the affirmative obligations of the state to work with incarcerated mothers to strengthen family ties and prepare them for return to the care of their children? Does the child's right to enjoy a continuous relationship with parents place an obligation on the state to provide whatever resources are necessary to enable offenders to fulfill their parental responsibilities? How can the mothers' rights and responsibilities to know what is happening to their children, to have contact with them, and to plan for their futures be protected?

What happens when the best interests of the children suggest the need for differential treatment of women who are mothers and those who are not? Does this constitute unequal treatment?

What happens when the best interests of children suggest the need for termination of parental rights because of the length of their mothers' sentences, the age of the children, and the availability of suitable alternative living arrangements? When should the children's needs for continuity of care supersede the mothers' right to custody? Does termination of parental rights under such circumstances constitute cruel and unusual punishment for the mothers? Should conviction of a felony constitute sufficient grounds for terminating parental rights?

What are appropriate standards for the return of children to mothers following incarceration? Should the state or the mother have the burden of proving whether the mother is fit to resume care? How much weight should be given to a finding of neglect or abuse by the mothers prior to the incarceration?

There are no easy answers to these questions, nor satisfactory resolutions for the dilemmas they pose. However, we do support the following as guidelines for the treatment of this population:

First, there must be some consideration of the child's welfare at each point in the criminal justice system. This would require, for example, that police officers be trained to consider the needs of dependent children at the point of arrest and that attorneys consider the needs of these children when preparing cases involving mothers. It is also important that the pretrial investigation report and the presentence investigation report include specific mention of the defendant's family responsibilities and that this factor be weighed when recommendations are made to the court.

Judges, as well, should consider the needs of the children when making decisions about pretrial release, bail, and sentencing. Responsibility extends to correctional facilities where staff should be trained to adopt a family-centered approach to inmates, rather than viewing them as isolated women whose primary needs are only for work training and/or individual counseling. Such training would hopefully preclude the punitive attitude of one matron who responded "they should have thought of this earlier" when asked about visiting rights of inmate-mothers.

At the final point, parole, we urge that parole boards be encouraged to consider a woman's family responsibilities and the needs of her children when making decisions about parole.

Second, within the institution, many beneficial programs should be developed. Although the correctional system may not have the capacity to improve poor mother-child relationships, it has a responsibility to maintain whatever family ties exist and to minimize any potential damage to the child resulting from the incarceration of the mother. Specifically, facilities should permit open and extended visiting between inmates and children. The inmate recommendations detailed earlier should be considered. Other modes of communication, such as telephone and letters should be encouraged. Educational programs for the women in such areas as child development, child care, family life education, and family law should be available as well as family counseling, especially in the area of making realistic future plans for the children.

In order to alleviate the mother's concern over problems her child experiences on the outside, a child welfare liaison worker should be available to talk with mothers about family problems and to mediate between mothers, children, and community service providers. Consideration should also be given to experimenting with innovative housing arrangements for mothers and children. Where such arrangements may be impractical, facilities should experiment with "mother-release" programs as well as work release (Palmer 1972), and local administrators should be given the right to grant furloughs at any time during the mother's incarceration if a family emergency arises.

A third area of responsibility lies with state social and welfare services. If the state deprives the child of parental care by incarcerating the mother, it has a responsibility to insure the welfare of the child during the time the mother is imprisoned. This, at the very least, requires that, if the child is in the care of relatives, the state should make certain that the child and his relatives receive financial benefits to which they are entitled, and that they receive whatever supplementary services are necessary. State agencies should also insure that children receive help for problems that have been created or exacerbated by the mother's incarceration. Such help could include counseling, day care, and special education.

Finally, the criminal justice and social service systems must develop closer policy coordination and service integration if women prisoners and their children are to be treated more appropriately. This requires the development of linkages between these two systems and allocation of responsibility for the provision of needed services at every point in the criminal justice process.

In conclusion, it is easy to romanticize the situation of women prisoners and their children. Some of these women neglected or abused their children before they went to prison because of drugs, alcoholism, or other problems; however, many provided excellent care for their children. Many mothers had inadequate mothering themselves and lacked appropriate parental role models; others had and still enjoy strong support from their families. The vast majority of these women are poor, have limited education and few work skills. Some have long criminal histories, are involved in self-destructive relationships and behavior, and have little hope or desire for change. Many mothers have not thought much about future plans for their children. Some cannot dare to dream; others have inappropriate plans. Still other mothers are handling their present situation in as constructive a way as possible and have realistic future plans for themselves and their children.

Clearly, the factors characterizing the life of each inmate-mother and her child are different. Generalizations such as "it is best that the inmate-mother and her children reunite immediately after the mother's release" or "a mother who commits a crime should automatically lose all parental rights" are meaningless. But we do believe that the familial responsibilities of inmate-mothers and the best interests of their children should be considered at each point in the decision-making process. It may be too much to hope that the correctional system can overcome poor mother-child relationships or create family life where none existed before; but it is the responsibility of the community to make certain that the criminal justice system does not destroy family life through ignorance or indifference and that each woman who comes into the system is helped to make the best plans possible for her children.

References

Bonfanti, Marcia et al. 1974. "Enactment and Perception of Maternal Role of Incarcerated Mothers" Masters Thesis, Louisiana State University, May.

Burkles, Dorene, and Mary Ann La Fazie. 1973. "Child Care for Mothers in Prison," *Social Work Practice and Social Justice*, ed. by Bernard Ross and Charles Chireman (New York: National Association of Social Workers).

Daehlin, Diane, and Jane Hynes. 1974. "A Mothers' Discussion Group in a Women's Prison," *Child Welfare*, LIII: 7 (July).

Flynn, Edith. 1973. "Jails and Criminal Justice," in *Prisoners in America*, ed. by Lloyd E. Ohlin (Englewood Cliffs, New Jersey: Prentice-Hall).

Hindelang, Michael J., et al. 1973. *Sourcebook of Criminal Justice Statistics, 1973* (Washington, D.C.: U.S. Department of Justice, Law Enforcement Assistance Administration, National Criminal Justice Information and Statistics Service, August), Table 6.16.

Holt, Norman and Miller, Donald. 1972. *Explorations in Inmate-Family Relationships,* Prepared by Research Division, Department of Corrections, State of California, Report #46.

Palmer, Richard. 1972. "The Prison Mother and Her Child," *Capital University Law Review.*

Toombs, Thomas G. N.D. "Integrated Services Project: A Review" (Superintendent, Oregon Women's Correctional Center, mimeographed).

Van Nuland, Jan. N.D. "The Problem of Prisoners' Children," (International Programme for Prisoners' Children, Ecole de Criminologie, Tiensestraat 41, B 3000, Louvain, Belgium).

Wolfram, Essey. 1973. "Developing Values Through Milieu Therapy," *Social Work Practice and Social Justice*, ed. by Bernard Ross and Charles Shireman (New York: National Association of Social Workers).

Women's Prison Association. 1973. *A Study in Neglect: A Report on Women Prisoners*, Prepared by Omar Hendrix on a Ford Foundation Travel Study grant.

Zalba, Serapio. 1964. Women Prisoners and Their Families (State of California, Department of Social Welfare and Department of Corrections, June).

7

Women in Southern Jails

Patsy Sims

No one knows how many there are. No one seems to care. One woman here; two there; sixty, seventy, a hundred, maybe, crammed into the larger, city jails. Nameless numbers; numbers too long to remember; forgotten women in southern jails. Forgotten—unless they become Joan Littles.

There are, an Atlanta attorney estimates, a thousand Joan Littles all over the South, in the small county jails. What happened in North Carolina is typical. Another attorney, from Mississippi, says that sexual abuse of female offenders is "common practice."

Driving through the South, stopping at 20 jails and talking to women who have spent time in another 60 or more places, the comments become more real than exaggerated. One realizes that they *are* there—the Joan Littles of tomorrow— that the South is ripe for more Beaufort County incidents; that many of its jails are in fact the hell holes, the repositories of human misery, that they were reputed to be in the past.

In my interviews with more than 50 women serving time in southern jails or work-release programs, inmate after inmate repeated virtually the same stories of what happened to them, or to the woman in the next cell: the oral sex through bars; the constant intrusion of male trustees who slither in and out of the women's cells as unrestricted as the rats and roaches; the threats of "you do, or else"; the promises of "Girl, you got thirty days, we'll knock off ten if you take care of my friend here."

Their stories are substantiated by numerous attorneys, correction officers, and law enforcement agents, who tell still more stories of jailers boasting to friends about "getting some" from female prisoners, of suits filed and dropped against sheriffs and deputies accused of rape, of men being allowed "informal" conjugal visits in return for letting the jailer have intercourse with the wife or girl friend.

Stories abound—of how Clarence Alligood propositioned other women in the Beaufort County jail, offering a sandwich or whiskey for the touching of a breast; of how an Alabama inmate testified that a sheriff forced women to have sex, with no formal charges ever following; of how a mulatto woman became pregnant in a south Louisiana jail and a black deputy, later found sterile, was blamed; of male inmates exposing themselves through bars to the women nearby.

Research for this article was funded in part by the Southern Investigative Research Project of the Southern Regional Council, Inc., Atlanta.

137

The stories go on and on, so much that responsible people are beginning to believe them, people like U.S. Attorney Ira DeMent, who feels sexual abuse of females in jail occurs "not infrequently" and even more than the complaints his office in Montgomery, Alabama receives.[1]

Improvements at the prison level—brought about largely by Attica and an influx of relatively reform-minded commissioners—have simply not taken place in jails. They have received neither attention nor money. When legal reform bills have been passed—as in North Carolina, Georgia, and Texas—conditions are little or no better than before.

There are times, too, when even the most needed prison reforms only add to the jails' problems. A case in point is the recent court order by U.S. District Judge Frank Johnson barring further admissions to Alabama's prisons until the "intolerable" conditions are corrected, an order that will force many inmates back into the state's equally deplorable jails, which are also under federal suit.

The problem with jails is due partly to a reluctance of taxpayers and politicians to spend money on them, partly to a "we're not running a Holiday Inn" attitude, and partly to the fact that they are operated independently, county by county, answerable to almost no one. Where a state regulatory agency does exist, it seldom has the staff or the enforcement power to effect change, as the Joan Little case proved.

So jails continue to be among the worst of Southern institutions, particularly for blacks and women. Although the plight of blacks has to a degree been publicized, the plight of women has not. Yet they, even more than black men, have been and are subjected to the most deplorable conditions, treatment, and attitudes, to squalid facilities, and to verbal and often sexual abuse from jailers.

"Women are the 'forgotten group' in corrections," says jail expert Robert Sarver of the University of Arkansas. "Most jails simply are not programmed, not built, and not staffed to look after female prisoners because they haven't been accustomed to dealing with them. Because there have been few women in comparison to the number of men, jails have been built traditionally to accommodate male felons while pending trial. Women have come along incidentally."[2]

In the meantime, women are no longer "incidental." Between 1960 and 1973, according to the FBI's *Uniform Crime Report*, their arrest rate for serious crimes—armed robbery, murder, theft, assault—went up by 277.9 percent, nearly three times faster than it did for men. In property crimes alone, the increase in arrests of women in 1972-73 was more than twice that of men.[3]

Although the crimes and arrests among women have escalated, jails have failed to keep up, either with adequate facilities or staff or programs. In metropolitan areas, the biggest problems in the jails are crowding and idleness. Sometimes 10 and 15 women are crammed into unair-conditioned cells originally built for 8. They sleep 2 to a bunk or on the floor, at times without mattresses. They stay locked in, day and night, because there are few recreational or educational programs for women. They are seldom allowed to become trusties and to work outside their cells.

Yet in the rural, out-of-the-way jails that handle one or two women at a time—maybe as few as a half dozen a year—females suffer the most and sexual abuse or misuse is many times part and parcel of being behind bars. The old situations of women at the mercy of the jailer, once thought to be only material for movies and books, still exist in these places.

The facilities are often filthy and makeshift, with little or no separation of women and men, be they jailers or inmates. Yet staff is an even bigger problem. Because of meager pay scales and the remoteness from city conveniences, most small-town jails can attract only what one expert describes as "people who can't do anything else." Some are even operated without staff. "The janitor at the courthouse keeps the keys," explains Robert Sarver. "At night, there is no one at all. That's when anything can happen, and that's when it usually does . . . inmate on inmate."[4]

A woman in one such jail in North Carolina complained to a state official, "They don't have a jailer from 5:00 p.m. on. No one cares whether we live or die after 5:00 p.m. I know I have done wrong, but this is no reason to be treated like a dog."[5]

It is the almost total lack of matrons that makes the small jails targets for sexual abuse. In my own travels in the South, I saw few matrons, and many inmates complained—as did Joan Little during her trial—that they were taken care of almost exclusively by men.

In North Carolina, a *Raleigh News and Observer* survey of 47 county jails in the eastern part of the state showed that fewer than half had taken any steps to lessen the likelihood of another prisoner Little-jailer Alligood incident. Only 19 of the counties had 24-hour matron service and adequate separation of women and men, in spite of a 1968 state law requiring both.[6]

At North Carolina's Hillsborough and Greensville jails I saw no signs of female employees even though they were included on a state list as providing full-time matrons. At the Wake County jail in Raleigh, Administrator William T. Threewitts was unaware of the provision requiring around-the-clock matrons.[7] According to Joan Little's attorney, Jerry Paul, at least 15 of the state's minimum standards were not being followed at the Beaufort County jail at the time of the Little-Alligood incident.[8]

Enforcement of the standards is the duty of Woodburn Williams, head of the North Carolina Jails and Detention Services, who has a mere three inspectors to cover the state's 190 jails, little enforcement power, and even less inclination to get tough with jails that fail to comply. Although Williams could bring misdemeanors charges against a sheriff who does not comply or even close the jail, he prefers gentle prodding to legal action.[9] There is some question, too, as to how thorough his staff investigations are. For example, in a routine report just two months before the Little-Alligood incident, the Beaufort County jail was given top ratings in every area—including the provision of matrons.

Williams blames the incident in the Beaufort County jail, only a one-year-old structure, on "a breakdown in administrative practices. A jail could report to us they have a matron, and she could quit the next day and we wouldn't know unless we caught them."[10]

Beaufort County itself has taken stringent measures to prevent another incident such as the one that put it on the map. Men now are not allowed in the women's section for any reason, not even to deliver meals, and closed-circuit monitors are placed in the all-female radio dispatchers' office to see that they don't go there. Six women who double as matrons and dispatchers or secretaries work around the clock. Sheriff O.E. ("Red") Davis, understandably touchy about the incident, warned that other counties "should take notice. Whenever they don't have matrons, they are taking a chance. I wouldn't be without them."[11]

Yet other counties, both in North Carolina and elsewhere, have apparently not learned the lesson so well. In state after state, jailers and sheriffs see no need to review their procedures for handling females. They have hired no matrons, nor have they taken steps to make keys to the women's sections less accessible to male trustees.

Many sheriffs told me they could not afford to hire matrons for the few women they do house. Some—even with new buildings and adequate facilities set aside for women—said they preferred to send females to neighboring counties because of the cost of hiring matrons. Yet I found in at least two such counties that women were kept as long as a week before being transferred to other jails, no more than 30 minutes away.

Lack of matrons and lack of adequate conditions cropped up again and again. Some officials argue that having male jailers go to the cells two at a time was sufficient, but even there officials had no idea how stringently that policy was followed. *Paper matrons*—female radio dispatchers or the wives of jailers and sheriffs—are apparently not the answer either. A paper matron was on duty—two halls and 65 feet away—the night Clarence Alligood made his way to Joan Little's cell.

There are no statistics, no figures, to fully document the extent to which sexual abuse occurs in jails; many cases go unreported, partly because of fear, partly because the jailer is considered more believable than a woman already accused of another crime. "It takes a great deal of courage for a woman to complain," says attorney Jerry Paul, "because she knows if she does, the chance of receiving worse treatment or some form of punishment is great. She realizes she could be shot and they could claim she was trying to escape. She is completely at their mercy. They can make her do most anything they want."[12] Besides the abuse revealed by the *Little* case, Paul said he has had complaints from at least five other jails in eastern North Carolina.

Much of the abuse—sexual and otherwise—is due to an attitude that women prisoners, especially black ones, are little better than animals. "The so-called fallen woman is subjected to almost any sort of humiliation and it seems to be perfectly o.k.," observes Robert Sarver. "The attitude is, she's a fallen woman and therefore you can say anything you want to her. If she has a tatoo on her arm, she'll probably do anything. Quote end quote. And if she'll do anything, you might as well go on and do it. It won't make any difference.

"I dare say the cute, sweet-looking little felon probably is treated a whole lot better than the rough one that has 'fuck' tatooed across her fingers or down her shin bone. And as far as a black woman is concerned, 'she probably gives it away anyway, so why not just take some.' " An attitude, he notes, that is as true in the North as in the South.[13]

Even the women admit that although some of the sex is by force, a lot is by consent. "Bartering," they call it—a means of getting better treatment or something they need or want, say, a Coke or a candy bar.

"That's a thing in jail," one Georgia inmate told me. "If you need something, nine times out of ten somebody comes up and propositions you. Shit, what can you lose? You ain't losin nuthin'. A feel. A pat. What have you. You can git more out of a deputy than a matron if you do what he says."

Bartering for better—in my travels, I heard and saw a lot that made me understand why the women go along, why the sex is more a matter of self-survival than immorality. I heard about filth, about going weeks—even 10 months—without a bath or shower, without towels or sheets, or even hot water. I heard about these conditions and then I saw them. In jail after jail, I thought about the Georgia inmate who spoke forcefully, "The only thing that's lighter on a woman than a man is the time of the sentences. The rest goes against a woman. It takes away your identity. They just bust you down. You get stripped of everything."

I thought of this statement in Raleigh when, on a tour of the women's area, I looked down on an embarrassed young girl squatting on a toilet and when, next door, I saw a mental patient on her hands and knees trying to claw her way out of the cell.

I thought of it when Linda, on parole in Texas, told of the indignities of being searched, of being stripped and fingered to see if she was carrying anything inside her body.

I thought of it when I read the letter from a Florida inmate complaining of being stripped in front of 15 to 25 girls and sprayed with a delouser; when a Houston inmate lamented, "I've forgot what I look like. I haven't seen my face for months"; when I heard of women enduring pain for days before being taken to a doctor or dentist; when I saw woman after woman in her bunk, the covers pulled over her head, because she had nothing to do; when a 36-year-old Georgia inmate, who looked 50, told of "holding it" all day, of waiting until the lights went out so she wouldn't have to use the toilet in front of male inmates.

"Women prisoners," says Donna, a 36-year-old former Louisiana inmate, "are at the end of the line because there are so few of them. They have no voice. If you're the only woman, they can do anything they want."[14]

Because of her family background and education, a master's degree in special education, Donna is not the typical female inmate. She is not poor or black or a high-school dropout. Yet during her 13 years in and out of at least 20 jails, she has experienced the same abuses and indignities as her less fortunate "sisters in crime."

"You feel," she reflects now, "like you're really not important enough for anybody to pay any attention to. And there's only one or maybe two of you, so you're pretty defenseless in those jails. You're going to have sexual advances made to you very often. A lot of this happens. The women just haven't killed their jailer, so it's swept under the rug.

"I don't know if it makes the police feel good or what, but the first thing out of their mouth is the 'nigger bitch' type thing. If you're white, they call you 'honky bitch,' so it's not like it's a racial thing."

Relaxing in the halfway house where she now works, Donna looked around at some of the women there, women she has come to like, and yet, unapologetically, insisted, "Women prisoners are sort of bummers. They're mean to one another. They may not actually implement their ideas, but they can be very treacherous. Jail," she concludes, "produces a particular type of front that you have to present. You have to be one of two things. You have to be underdog or top dog. There's no medium. You either have to get ready to start kicking someone or you have to be kicked."

Women also suffer in less obvious ways. "I think," said Donna, "maybe 90 percent of them and perhaps 99 percent of the black women don't have bond money. And they can't hire lawyers. We all know how the court dockets are, so you might be held six months on a charge that carries only three months' sentence. The women don't know legal procedures, either, so those who are into professional crime get out of jail a lot faster than the women who are minimally involved." To illustrate, she told of being arrested sometimes two and three times a week for transporting "hot" cars, cars loaded with marijuana, from Brownsville to New Orleans, and getting out immediately on bond. "I remember thinking, 'These poor slobs. Here I'm doing all this terrible stuff, and they never get out.'"

Donna, her hair in rollers and sleepy from working all night as housemother at the halfway house, flicked a cigarette and pondered how many times she, attractive and bright, had been sexually propositioned. Maybe even more by trustees, she estimated, than by police. She remembered the time she threw water on a persistent trustee in Pascagoula, Mississippi, and threatened to tell the sheriff; and another time, in another Mississippi jail, when deputies allowed her to roam the halls while they had intercourse with other women in her cell.

"It's the trustees, mostly," she explains. "They're given practically free reign. They have keys to the cells, and they can come and go as they want. After you've been around awhile, you can so 'no' and mean it. But if you're a young kid and you've never been in jail, they can bring you out to make a telephone call and make these advances. And some of these young girls don't know what's going on. The trustees scare them into having sex."

Yet, in spite of the often filthy jails, of being locked up 24 hours a day with nothing to do—no radio, no TV, nothing—and in spite of the rampant sexual abuse, Donna insists she would prefer to be in a rural jail, preferably one in the South. "The sheriff there is usually more easy going. He knows you're not going to take over his jail. After a couple of days, people get really lax. They're not worried about you running away."

Donna readily admits she's had "plenty" of breaks. She attributes this to southern chivalry, a mystique that has never left the South but is definitely gone in the North. Women's liberation is making it tougher on women like herself involved in crime, because judges and prosecutors are less disposed to "protect" them. Donna says, "The only thing I've ever liked about women's liberation is the salary, the wage. You might say, I'm for equal pay but I wouldn't want to be treated like a man in jail."[15]

Treated like a man in jail—was that an alternative? A black female inmate insisted, "There was more prejudice between men and women than whites and blacks. It was more a situation like a woman isn't supposed to be in jail. They fed the men three times a day; they fed us twice." Peggy McCoy, director of a halfway house in Houston now, after serving 20 of her 43 years in jails and prisons, lamented: "The men experience more brutality—physical brutality—in the jails than women do, but women, they just put them up there and seem to forget about them. 'They ain't no damn good noway,' so they just lock 'em up there and leave 'em."[16]

I thought about that when Texas attorneys told me of a bordertown jail, where a two-story stairwell, windowless and unairconditioned, had been converted into cells for women; of a jail where the women's section had no lighting at all, except for one hour a day when the sun shown through a window seven feet away.

In DeKalb, Mississippi, the Kemper County jail—two stories of crumbling concrete and rusting bars—sits on a mound of weeds, surrounded by a rusted cyclone-and-barbed wire fence, across the street from the town's historic courthouse, down the block from its new Town Hall, and less than a mile from the home of U.S. Senator John Stennis. The sheriff, H. T. ("Bud") Jarvis, figures the jail could be 75 years old or more. "Couldn't say for sure," he drawled.[17] It looks even older. Like something untouched from the Dark Ages. Some relic of hate.

Inside, women are kept, in full view of the men, in a six-by-six metal mesh cage furnished only with a bed and a slop jar that goes unemptied for days. There is no source of water—for bathing or drinking—except when the otherwise-absent jailer comes twice a day with meals.

Jarvis insisted, "We never hold women, only 'til we take 'em to Meridian (an hour's drive away), if we can't take 'em right away. We don't keep 'em at night if there's any way 'round it."[18] But there is now pending a federal lawsuit that grew out of the 13-day incarceration there last February of Clara Cotton, a young

Choctaw Indian. Harvis would discuss neither the law suit nor why Ms. Cotton was held that long, nor would he say anything about where she was confined, beyond the fact that it was "one little cell over there that we don't put no man in." When I asked to see it, he focused his eyes like a double-barrelled shotgun and growled, "Not lessen you git locked up."[19]

The class-action law suit, filed by the Southern Poverty Law Center in Montgomery, charged that Clara Cotton was arrested on February 16, that eight days later the uncovered slop jar had not been emptied and that insects swarmed about the bucket, settling on her and her food. The cage has no ventilation, the suit says, and "the oppressive stench of human waste and body odors was over-whelming."

Kemper County was the most, but not the only, deplorable jail I saw. In Union Springs, Alabama, Deputy Pete Cole politely warned, "This ain't purty," as he unlocked a gate leading to the century-old Bullock County jail.[20] Outside it is three stories of cracked and crumbling brick; inside, with gallows still intact on the third floor, it is dark and dingy, and stacked with urine-stained mattresses. The women's cell is on the first floor, next to one for men. A deteriorating space heater is the only source of heat in that area; one dusty window, the only source of light.

"There's nothing you can do to a building this old, 'cept replace it," Cole apologized. "The conditions are very poor, for both males and females. It's probably worse for a woman, though. A man can get by where a woman can't."[21]

Cole and the sheriff, H. O. Williams, insisted they seldom bring women to the jail. "It has to be something bad for us to bring a woman to jail, and then none of 'em stays for any period of time," Cole said.[22] But just a few miles away, in another jail, I had already talked to a woman who had recently been confined in Bullock County for seven days, less than two weeks before my visit. Sitting in Pike County jail, Maggie Hallford, 36 and pregnant, described her filthy cell at Bullock. She had not been allowed to shower the entire week she was there, and she'd eaten port 'n beans and bread and little else.

"You've come to the wrong jails," she said, imploring me to drive to Union Springs. "There, you have no privacy. The trustee or anyone else can come right in on you at anytime, even if you're on the toilet. And you're cursed at." She started to cry and apologized, "I'm just upset. I know we're not supposed to be treated like God, but they don't have to treat us like this."[23]

At Pike County—"a good jail"—she was housed in an area with two bunks, a metal picnic table, a shower, a toilet, and a window that looked out on a pecan tree—a nice, easy-going place, with equally easy security. The jailer, an aging man, led me to her cell and left me there without asking to see credentials and without checking my purse or briefcase. When I left her cell, I was free to wander through the jail.

The Kemper Counties, the Bullock Counties. No one knows how many there are like them, or even worse. Or how many pistol-packing deputies still

refer to their woman charges as "trash," "sluts," "bitches," "whores," even
"pussy." No one knows because few people have been interested enough to
find out.

But some observers see a change in the attitudes and treatment of women
coming about, although ever so slowly. Some credit the new consciousness to
the women's movement, some to the *Joan Little* case. Whatever the reason,
more women in jail are speaking out about the conditions and the treatment.
More suits are being filed on their behalf. Jerry Paul reports that since the
Joan Little verdict he has received an increased number of complaints about
sexual abuse in North Carolina jails. "People are beginning to believe that jailers
really do the things they are being charged with doing," says Paul. "We have
proved one time that a jailer *did* what he was charged with. That leaves open
the possibility for others. And the other jailers are now very careful that they
don't do anything to provoke or cause a situation."[24]

The *Little* case, Paul noted, has also raised public consciousness. Even
Judge Hamilton Hobgood, shortly after the *Little* trial, told reporters he hoped
the trial would result in improved treatment of women prisoners in North
Carolina, calling it "very poor procedure for males to guard female prisoners."

The case has also resulted in a suit filed by Paul and the Southern Poverty
Law Center against all North Carolina jails because of their handling of women.
Paul plans to take separate action against the sheriff of Beaufort County.

Around the South, these other cases are current:

1. In Georgia, the ACLU has filed suit against the Coweta County jail on behalf
   of a woman forced to go without sanitary napkins for three days, during
   which time she shared a bunk with another woman.
2. In Alabama, U.S. Attorney DeMent has filed suit against every jail in the
   state to establish adequate funding and minimum standards for jail security,
   inmates' legal rights, sanitation, jail administration, recreational programs,
   and food service. Adamant on the subject of matrons, DeMent hopes to
   have it declared unconstitutional for a jail to house females without a matron
   on duty.

Besides the law suits, there are other signs of hope. Whereas jails in the past
have been built almost exclusively by and for men, the National Clearinghouse for
Criminal Justice Planning and Architecture, at Urbana, Illinois, has begun getting
requests for facilities for female offenders. A $2.2 million facility on the drawing
board for Dade County, Florida would provide individual rooms with bathtubs,
picture windows without bars, and an outdoor playgound for the visiting children
of inmates. The current jail, although in an antiquated building, is already considered a model among women's facilities. It is one of the few in the nation
housed separately (two blocks away) from the men's jail. Unlike most jails, it
offers a variety of recreational and educational programs and classes in cosmetology,

office skills, industrial sewing, automotive engineering, and air-conditioning, as well as academic courses at both high school and college levels. The Dade jail also has a work-release program and indoor and outdoor recreation.

The improvements at this institution are due in large measure to Janet McCardel, a 36-year-old former policewoman with a Ph.D. in psychology, who took over as supervisor in 1972. Dr. McCardel hopes for final approval of the new facility within six months. Although Dade already has what is considered a model jail, she says, "We're about twenty years behind; everybody else is about fifty."[25]

In Richmond, Virgina, what until six or seven years ago was described as a hell hole has been transformed into a colorful jail facility for women. The entrance is bright yellow. The pastel tiers are furnished with single beds and colorful spreads, televisions and radios, sewing machines, enclosed showers, and even typewriters for working on the prison paper, *Busted*. There is a separate dining room—aqua with laminated-wood tables and orange plastic chairs; a sick room for inmates recovering from surgery; an infirmary staffed 24 hours a day by a nurse (a general practitioner comes three times a week, and a dermatologist, gynecologist, and psychiatrist once a week each).

For recreation, there is an upright piano, ping-pong, table hockey, and an air-conditioned "family room" comfortably furnished by the Helpmates, a volunteer group of women who often bring their children to their special programs and classes. The inmates are also allowed outdoor exercise once a week. Besides the usual GED (General Equivalency Degree) programs, women can attend classes at J. Sargeant Reynolds College and Virginia Commonwealth University.

In place of the usual jail uniforms, Richmond inmates wear jeans and striped tank tops in summer, sweatshirts in winter. They have unlimited access to the female area until bedtime and are allowed to use a washer and dryer. Trustees earn $6 a month and, unless they are felons, a day off for every six they work.

Most of these changes began five years ago when Andrew Winston, a former magistrate, took over operation of the jail and started working with Nancy White Thomas, wife of a local minister and organizer of the Helpmates. Although Winston has no statistics, he is confident that the new procedures and the added trust they place in the women have reduced both recidivism and internal jail problems.

Two good jails—they were bright spots in my research; yet I remember so much more vividly the bad ones. I remember them and the women, pleading for change, saying—and knowing—they were little more than afterthoughts in jail.

Then I remember Peggy McCoy, the halfway house director, toying with a scales-of-justice ring, brightening somewhat, and telling me, "In the last two years, I've seen things happen. Society is getting more willing to look at women a little bit differently."

It was, she speculated, largely because of the drug scene moving out of the ghettos and into better neighborhoods, because of young girls from richer, more prominent families going to jail.

"For us older characters, it's good," Peggy mused, "but it's a shame these youngsters had to get into this to bring the change."[26]

Notes

1. Ira DeMent, interview at Montgomery, Alabama, August 18, 1975.

2. Robert Sarver, interview at Montgomery, Alabama, August 18, 1975.

3. *Uniform Crime Reports*, 1973. Washington, D.C.: U.S. Federal Bureau of Investigation, United States Department of Justice.

4. Sarver interview.

5. Survey by Raleigh, N.C. *News and Observer*, August 24, 1975.

6. Ibid.

7. William T. Threewitts, interview at Raleigh, North Carolina, August 22, 1975.

8. Jerry Paul, interview at Chapel Hill, North Carolina, August 23, 1975.

9. Woodburn Williams, interview at Raleigh, North Carolina, August 24, 1975.

10. Ibid.

11. Sheriff O. E. "Red" Davis, interview at Washington, North Carolina, August 24, 1975.

12. Jerry Paul interview.

13. Sarver interview.

14. "Donna", interview at Baton Rough, Louisiana, August 13, 1975.

15. Ibid.

16. Peggy McCoy, interview at Houston, Texas, August 8, 1975.

17. H. T. "Bud" Jarvis, interview at DeKalb, Mississippi, August 15, 1975.

18. Ibid.

19. Ibid.

20. Pete Cole, interview at Union Springs, Alabama, August 19, 1975.

21. Ibid.

22. Ibid.

23. Maggie Hallford, interview at Pike County, Alabama, August 19, 1975.

24. Jerry Paul interview.

25. Janet McCardel, interviewed by phone, August 5, 1975.

26. Peggy McCoy interview.

8 The Cottage Dwellers: Boys and Girls in Training Schools

Elaine Selo

On June 30, 1973 over 26,000 youths were residing in "cottages in the country," or training schools as they are presently called.[1] In spite of the growing concern about the impact of the experience on all children, little attention has been paid to the possibly different characteristics, experiences, and treatment of young men and women. In part, this is a reflection of the general lack of research on the juvenile justice system in general. But also, it is a manifestation of the almost total disinterest in the correctional experiences of women.[2]

Because of the smaller numbers of women, both adult and juvenile, processed through various stages of the criminal justice system, most of the research detailing the conditions and reactions of inmates has been limited to men. The assumption has been that theories of male criminal involvement and institutional adaptation can be applied to females without basic alterations. Further, because most people believe that women are usually treated in a gentler and more benign way by the justice system, the real examination of institutional deprivation has focused on males. Research on females in institutions has largely ignored the conditions of incarceration. Instead it has dealt primarily with subcultural practices of tatooing, homosexuality, and make-believe familes, which fascinate most readers but may not really capture the essence of the experience.

In spite of the rhetoric of rehabilitation, it has become increasingly evident that institutions are perceived as places of punishment by most confined youth. Although the degree of restriction and repression may vary from institution to institution, youth of both sexes are deprived of many of the normal adolescent processes, pleasures, and privileges for fairly long periods. Because of the lack of

The collection and preliminary analysis of data reported in this chapter were conducted by the National Assessment of Juvenile Corrections project supported by a grant (76JN-99-0001) from the Juvenile Justice and Delinquency Prevention Operations Task Group, Law Enforcement Assistance Administration, U.S. Department of Justice, under authorizing legislation of the Omnibus Crime Control and Safe Streets Act of 1968 and the Juvenile Justice and Delinquency Prevention Act of 1974. The project was sponsored by the Institute of Continuing Legal Education and the School of Social Work of the University of Michigan; co-directors were Robert D. Vinter and Rosemary Sarri.

Major analysis of these data was conducted in conjunction with a study of status offenders supported by a grant (HEW 100-76-0081) from the Department of Health, Education, and Welfare; Paul Isenstadt served as director.

The contents of this chapter do not necessarily reflect the views or policies of either funding source or of either parent project.

I wish to express my appreciation to William Barton, Paul Isenstadt, and Rosemary Sarri for their helpful comments and suggestions.

comparative studies of institutions for young men and women, it has been impossible to say that girls have really been treated in a more compassionate and lenient way by prison officials and criminal agencies. Yet there is endless speculation that the "chivalry factor" operates, providing girls with more favorable treatment and ignoring their serious delinquency.[a] On the other hand, there is a contention that girls are subject to a double standard of justice and are provided with less treatment and more psychological abuse in training schools than are boys.[b]

In this chapter, we report on the similarities and differences in experiences and behavior of both boys and girls in training schools in this country. We compare their delinquent experiences and involvements with agencies of social control prior to being institutionalized as well as their perceptions of the treatment and its legitimacy and effectiveness. Moreover, we examine the disparities in the kinds of deprivations imposed on them and the kinds of misconduct they engage in during their institutional stay.

Sample

The sample consists of 1,425 youth in 16 randomly selected institutions in 11 states, selected as part of a larger set of programs for delinquent youth studied by the National Assessment of Juvenile Corrections between 1972 and 1974.[c] Since few studies had been directed at female or coed programs, and since there was an obvious need for such data, institutions housing females were deliberately over-represented in the sample.

The study was conducted by visiting each institution. Trained field teams administered questionnaires to youth and staff, and observed as many program activities as possible. They also mingled informally with youth and staff to gain a broad understanding of the institutional program. Data presented in this chapter come from the youth questionnaire, which was handled confidentially (youth were not required to sign their names) and administered to small groups of youth without the presence of institutional staff. The questionnaire was especially designed for youth with low reading levels and was read to youth by field staff.

---

[a]A classic example of this point of view is expressed by James V. Bennett, in "Women Behind Bars," in *I Chose Prison*, New York, Alfred A. Knopf, 1970, pp. 127-141.

[b]One of the more recent examples of this point of view is Kenneth Wooden, "The Sexuality of Punishment: The Juvenile Female Offender," in *Weeping in the Playtime of Others: America's Incarcerated Children*, New York, McGraw Hill, 1976, pp. 118-128.

[c]Detailed statements of the research design and sampling procedures of the larger study as well as data collection techniques for studying correctional programs can be found in three documents published by the National Assessment of Juvenile Corrections, entitled *Research Design Statement, Sampling Plans*, and *Time Out: A National Study of Correctional Programs for Youth*.

All of the data presented in this chapter is a product of youth's own self-reports about their behavior, experiences, and perceptions. There are several reasons for this preference. Much of the information we wanted was officially undetected, either prior to or during institutionalization and could only be provided by youth. Other information about reactions and responses to institutionalization are important measures of the meaning of the experience for inmates, and provide at least as much understanding of the reality as more "factual" data. In general, research has demonstrated self-report data, even from youthful populations, to be quite valid and reliable.[3]

Demographic Characteristics

Among our sample, girls committed to institutions for status offenses were on the average one year older (15.5 years for girls, 14.4 for boys) and were slightly farther behind in school relative to their age than were boys. The same does not hold, however, for criminal offenders. Among this group, there was little difference in age at entrance to the institution between males and females, (15.0 years vs. 15.4 years). Unlike male status offenders, however, these males were quite a bit farther behind in school relative to their age than were females.

Perhaps the greater discrepancy between age and school grade for female status offenders is due to the repeated episodes of running away that resulted in noncompletion of the school year. School problems that prompted the institutionalization of male status offenders did not result in failure to pass but were more likely due to behavior problems.

The age differences between male and female status offenders could be a result of various factors. They may become delinquent at a later age, or it could be that the status offenses they commit are ignored for a longer period. It may also be that juvenile courts assume a more "protective" role with girls than with boys and thereby exercise their prerogative of providing structured, residential care for older girls more often than for older boys.

For both sexes, over half of the criminal offenders were nonwhite and over half of the status offenders were white. Within each offense category, the differences in race between male and female offenders were small. Male status offenders were more often black, however, than female status offenders. Since male status offenders were most often committed for school problems and since blacks are disproportionately subjected to problems with schools in this country, we would expect to find this. Considering the proportion of blacks in the general population, it is quite clear that, in our sample at least, they are overrepresented in the institutional population as both status and criminal offenders. Information discussed later indicates, however, they are also overrepresented in the institution in relation to the seriousness and frequency of their crimes.

The social class of youth was ascertained by asking about the occupations of both parents and coding the occupation of the parent that was highest on a socio-economic scale. It is interesting that a fairly high proportion of institutionalized youth did not know what their parents did for a living or could not describe it in enough detail so that it could be coded. The vast majority of all institutionalized youth came from families at the lower end of the economic spectrum. Less than a quarter of all youth came from families holding white-collar or professional-managerial occupations.

Why Were They Sent to Institutions?

Many of the institution personnel in our sample had no idea what proportion of their population were committed for serious delinquent acts, although in most programs, files did contain the official reason for commitment. We obtained our commitment offense data directly from youth by an open-ended question: "Why were you sent here?"

Table 8-1 reveals the response. According to our findings, the proportion of girls committed to institutions for status offenses (i.e., acts not considered criminal for adults) is twice as high as the proportion of boys. Other studies have shown this proportion to be even higher. There are a number of possible reasons for the seeming discrepancy.[d] Although other studies have based their figures on official juvenile court records of legal commitment, our findings derive from self-reported offenses. It may well be that a larger number of the youth in our sample were committed for status offenses although they actually had engaged in other delinquent or criminal acts. Because of plea bargaining, inadequate evidence, or a desire to protect juveniles from criminal stigmatization, some youth who admitted committing criminal acts and thought they were institutionalized because of these acts may actually have been adjudicated as status offenders.

Even so, the disparity in the proportion of males and females committed for status offenses is consistent with every study examining sex differentials and reflects a continuing practice. Girls are institutionalized for status offenses at a *much higher* rate than boys. Furthermore, only 32 percent of the girls were institutionalized for serious person and property crimes but this was true of 72 percent of the boys. Girls were more often committed for drug offenses, and these were most often possession of marijuana or hashish, rather than possession of hard drugs or sale of any drugs. The same phenomenon holds for both blacks

---

[d]Examples of studies showing higher proportions of status offenders, both male and female in institutions are: *Children in Custody,* 1971, U.S. Department of Justice, LEAA, National Criminal Justice Information and Statistics Service, p. 9; Lerman, Paul, "The New Jersey Training School for Girls; A Study of Alternatives," Mimeographed Report to the New Jersey Department of Institutions and Agencies, July 1974; Baron, Roger et al., "Preventing Delinquency through Diversion: The Sacramento County 601 Diversion Project, *Federal Probation*, March 1973, pp. 13-18.

Table 8-1
Self-reported Commitment Offense of Institutionalized Youth, by Sex

Offense Type	Males		Females		Total	
	Percent	Base N	Percent	Base N	Percent	Base N
Emotional problems, dependent, neglect	1	(11)	4	(12)	2	(23)
Status	18	(138)	39	(126)	24	(264)
Misdemeanors	2	(13)	4	(14)	2	(27)
Drug	7	(53)	21	(69)	11	(122)
Property	51	(391)	16	(51)	40	(442)
Person	21	(162)	16	(51)	20	(213)
Total	100	(768)	100	(323)	99	(1091)

and whites, in that females committed to institutions are largely status and drug offenders and males are largely person and property offenders.

The term "status offense" is an umbrella concept embracing a multiplicity of problems. The status offenses for which girls are incarcerated differ substantially from those for which boys are committed. Over half (51%) of the male status offenders in our sample reported that they were institutionalized because of school problems, compared with only 16 percent of their female counterparts. Females, on the other hand, were disproportionately institutionalized for running away (57%). This pattern holds for black status offenders as well.

This finding of a disproportionate problem with female runaways is consistent with other studies and carries broader social implications. It is widely accepted that this society places greater restrictions on the behavior of females than on that of males. Girls are expected to be more passive, more restrained, and less sexually active. These societal and parental expectations may conflict with the behavior and desires of adolescent girls and result in the child's running away. Several studies have validated this conflict and have revealed a disproportionate emphasis on the sexuality of adolescent females. One such study in New York found that 62 percent of all ungovernability cases involve girls. It also found that 51 percent of these cases alleged potential sexual involvement.[4]

The seriousness with which sexual acting out by female adolescents is treated is further indicated in this study by the finding that "64% of the cases in which the parent, usually the mother, objects to the daughter's boyfriend and 80% of the cases in which the daughter is charged with being promiscuous go to court. . . . By contrast, only 50% of the cases in which the parent alleges arson or illegal entry go to court."[5]

Researchers in Hawaii found further evidence of this concern over adolescent female sexuality by juvenile courts. During a 26-year period, they found that 70 to 80 percent of the juvenile female defendants were ordered to receive physical examinations compared with 12 to 18 percent of the males. The doctor's notations on the forms such as "hymen intact," "hymen ruptured," or "hymen torn—admits intercourse" indicates the nature of the court's interest in the physical condition of the girls.[6]

Delinquent Experiences

Literature on the differences between the actual delinquency of boys and girls is plagued by contradictions. Some writers characterize girls as primarily "sexual delinquents" who commit more sex offenses than do boys and are committed to institutions in greater numbers for these offenses, even though labeled as "runaways" or "incorrigibles." Others support the studies cited above by maintaining that girls do not actually commit more sex-related offenses, or even the typically "feminine" acts of ungovernability and running away, than do boys, but the offenses they commit are "sexualized" by the juvenile court. Finally, writers and juvenile justice practitioners contend that girls are processed more leniently by the juvenile court. They argue that although the girls' offenses may be more criminal in nature, they are prosecuted as status offenders because there is less stigma to incorrigibility than there is to a criminal label.[7]

Martin Gold, in his study of the self-reported delinquent behaviors of a sample of youth aged 13 to 16 in Flint, Michigan, found that the nature of girls' delinquency was quite similar to that of boys, only less frequent. Girls were generally less delinquent than boys except for the fairly infrequent acts of running away from home and hitting their parents.[8]

In an attempt to settle these contradictions and establish the actual nature of male and female delinquency, we asked youth in our sample to indicate how often they had done a series of delinquent acts prior to coming to the program.

As the data in Table 8-2 indicates, more of the female population had frequently used alcohol, marijuana, and hashish, as well as other drugs, had engaged in sexual intercourse, and had run away from home before their incarceration. On the other hand, boys more often committed serious delinquent acts—stealing, damaging property, robbery, and breaking and entering.

Although this table indicates that both male and female youth charged with status offenses were less likely to have been involved in delinquent acts than were youth charged with criminal offenses, there are notable differences among this group. Specifically, male status offenders were twice as likely to have robbed someone or broken into a building to steal something than were females. Girls among this group were much more likely to have used drugs and run away from home than their male counterparts. This shows that girls had more often engaged in and were more likely to be incarcerated for self-destructive, victimless offenses.

Table 8-2
Prior Delinquency of Institutionized Youth, by Sex and Commitment Offense

	Percent Male Status (N = 132-36)	Percent Female Status (N = 120-26)	Percent Male Criminal (N = 587-610)	Percent Female Criminal (N = 177-85)
Drank alcoholic beverages more than 10 times	47	60	67	68
Used marijuana or hashish more than 10 times	28	46	56	64
Used other drugs more than one or twice	22	49	55	69
Had sex relations with someone of the opposite sex more than 10 times	35	55	61	65
Skipped school more than 10 times	54	59	68	66
Suspended from school more than once or twice	32	33	55	54
Ran away from home more than once or twice	23	53	32	64
Ever hurt self on purpose	15	23	14	26
Ever tried to kill self	10	17	9	26
Stole more than once or twice	52	35	79	52
Every damaged property on purpose	50	40	72	52
Hurt someone on purpose ever	42	44	65	57
Ever had sex relations for pay	9	12	13	18
Ever robbed someone	34	18	66	51
Ever broke into a place to steal something	50	25	84	44

Controlling for race only strengthens the differences between males and females committed for the same offenses and it further shows that white youth of both sexes and offense types were more often delinquent both in minor and serious ways than is true of blacks, with few exceptions.

The evidence is strong and compelling that girls committed for status offenses are not as seriously delinquent as either their male counterparts or as both girls and boys committed for criminal offenses. In fact, significantly fewer of them have engaged in any activity that would be considered criminal for adults. The most numerous offenses reported were drinking alcoholic beverages, skipping school, having sex relations more than ten times, and running away from home more than once or twice. This finding refutes the argument that female status offenders are generally more serious offenders who have been deliberately mislabeled by a lenient juvenile court.

Nor does the argument that girls are treated more leniently than boys hold for criminal offenders. Among this group, for every serious kind of delinquency (stealing, hurting someone, damaging property, robbery, and breaking and entering), fewer girls than boys report committing these offenses. As with their status offender sisters, these girls are much more likely to engage in self-destructive, victimless behavior such as running away from home, trying to hurt or kill themselves, and using drugs, than are male criminal offenders.

Martin Gold's findings that girls commit as great a *variety* of delinquent acts as boys but at a significantly lower rate seems to be confirmed in our sample for status offenders, but not in our sample of criminal offenders. Among the former group, females both had more *widespread* and *frequent* involvement in victimless delinquency (drugs, alcohol, etc.), but *less frequent* and *equally varied* involvement in serious delinquency (stealing, damaging property, robbery, breaking and entering, etc.).

Among criminal offenders, girls again had more widespread and frequent involvement in victimless crimes (drugs, alcohol, etc.), but had both *less frequent* and *less varied* involvement than boys in serious delinquency. For both sexes, the average proportion of both victimless and serious delinquent acts engaged in was higher for criminal than for status offenders.

Previous Correctional Experiences

The argument that females are treated more leniently by the juvenile justice system can also be attacked with statistics on previous correctional experiences. A study of 66 juvenile courts in an eastern state from 1966 to 1968 found that regardless of race and prior court contacts, females who committed juvenile code violations had a larger percentage of detentions than males who committed such offenses.[9] Our finding confirmed this when we asked youth how many times they had ever come into contact with police, courts, group or foster homes, jail, detention, or had been on probation or in training schools before coming to the training school this time.

The most significant finding was that female status offenders had been in juvenile detention an average of one more time than boys. This is particularly interesting when we consider the fact that male status offenders were more often involved in serious delinquency than female status offenders. The greater rate of detention of female status offenders holds for both blacks and whites.

The picture differs for criminal offenders. Males have considerably more previous experience in correctional settings than do females, which we would expect, considering their more widespread and frequent involvement in serious delinquent acts.

It is interesting that relative to the number of times they have been arrested by the police, males have fewer other correctional contacts than females. To be more specific, male criminals have on the average twice as many police arrests (12) as females (6), but beyond that they have only one more experience with every other process. This is true for both blacks and whites. We know from youth's own reports that acts serious enough to become detected by the police are more frequent for boys than for girls, but it is also true that past the point of police detection, there is relatively little difference in the processing of girls and boys.

Girls, on the average, have more court appearances than police arrests, but this is not so for boys, suggesting the possibility that girls are more frequently referred to the courts by their own parents, and boys are more frequently picked up by the police for delinquent acts. Since the number of correctional contacts beyond police arrest drops off very sharply for boys but not for girls, it appears that a much higher proportion of complaints filed against boys are dropped than is true for girls. This is consistent with the findings of the New York study discussed earlier where parents were more likely to report girls for ungovernability and these charges were more likely to go to court than were charges of criminal behavior such as arson and larceny.

In order to explore further the interaction of actual delinquency and the official processing of it for youth in our sample, we use a typology developed by William Barton, involving a cross-classification of delinquent history with correctional experiences prior to institutionalization.[e] For ease of presentation, the four cells of the typology can be labeled as follows:

1. *Angels:* Youth who have engaged in relatively little criminal activity and who have had relatively little prior correctional contact.
2. *Victims:* Youth who have engaged in relatively little criminal activity but who have had a lot of correctional contacts.
3. *Evaders:* Youth who have engaged in a lot of criminal activity but have had relatively little contact with correctional agencies.

---

[e]This typology is presented in an unpublished paper by William Barton entitled, "Deviance and Identity in Juvenile Correctional Programs," August 15, 1975. Basically, it involves the development of indices of prior correctional contact in detention, jail, juvenile court and prior delinquent involvement in drugs, stealing, hurting someone, damaging property, sex relations for pay, robbery, and breaking and entering. These indexes were

4. *Tough Kids:* Youth who have engaged in a lot of criminal activity and have
    had a lot of experience with correctional agencies.

As table 8-3 indicates, youth committed for status offenses are most often
"angels" or "victims" and youth committed for criminal offenses are most often
"evaders" or "tough kids," which points out the consistency between commitment
offense and prior delinquent history. What is really more interesting, however,
is the inconsistency between actual delinquency and official processing reflected
in the "victim" and "evader" categories. For youth committed to institutions
for status offenses, almost three times as many girls were "victims" as boys. That
is, three times as many girls experienced heavy correctional contact even though
they had been involved in few criminal activities. Although the difference between
male and female criminals as "victims" is slight, the direction is the same. Males
of both offense types were slightly more likely to have been able to "evade"
correctional contact than females.

When we looked at this phenomenon for both blacks and whites separately,
we found some interesting variations. Almost half of the black female status
offenders were "victims" (43%) as compared with only 27 percent of the white
female status offenders, who were instead more likely to be "angels." Few black
or white female status offenders were either "evaders" or "tough kids." Thus,
for status offenders at least, black females are the most "victimized" in terms of
correctional handling prior to institutionalization, and males, particularly white
males, are treated most leniently.

Among the criminal offenders, females of both races were more likely to be

Table 8-3
**Institutionalized Youth Classified as Angels, Victims, Evaders, and Tough Kids,
by Sex and Commitment Offense**

	Percent Male Status	*Percent Female Status*	*Percent Male Criminal*	*Percent Female Criminal*
Angels	50	40	20	30
Victims	12	32	10	14
Evaders	20	15	28	23
Tough kids	18	12	42	33
Total	100	99	100	100
N	(114)	(121)	(554)	(169)

then dichotomized near the mean, producing four levels: low criminal behavior and low
correctional contact, high criminal behavior and low correctional contact, and high criminal
behavior and high correctional contact.

"angels" and "victims" than their white counterparts. This interaction of race and sex is dramatically illustrated by the finding that 65 percent of the black females who were institutionalized for criminal offenses were "angels" and "victims" (i.e., had below average prior delinquent history); the corresponding figures for other criminal offenders were 45 percent for black males, 37 percent for white females, and 25 percent for white males.

White criminal offenders of both sexes have been able to "evade" the juvenile justice system more often than black criminal offenders. Although the differences are much less for criminal offenders, the general pattern previously observed for status offenders still holds. Blacks, but particularly black females, are the most "victimized" and white males are able to most often "evade" correctional handling for serious offenses.

This data suggests the following points. Girls, regardless of adjudication, enter institutions having engaged in less serious prior delinquency than boys, and this is particularly true of black females. Several possible explanations occur. Courts may use institutionalization as a disposition as much for victimless crimes as for serious ones or they may treat girls more punitively than boys. Perhaps it is because of the relative lack of alternatives to institutionalization for girls or because girls are viewed as needing the protection and structure of institutions more than are boys. Or perhaps it is because there is a double standard of acceptable behavior for girls and boys as discussed earlier.

Even before entering the institution, girls are apparently subject to more criminal processing for the same criminal behavior than are boys, especially white boys, so this kind of differential treatment is not a new experience for them. The suggestion that girls are treated more leniently than boys in the criminal justice system is not supported in any way by these results; in fact, we suggest the opposite: girls are really penalized by the juvenile justice system relative to their male counterparts. Blacks are penalized relative to their white counterparts.

Attitudes of Youth Toward Staff

Youth were asked a number of questions about the staff—how fair staff were, how accessible and caring they were, and whether youth could really trust them. Generally, youth thought that most staff really cared about them and were not just doing a job. But female status offenders were significantly less likely to feel this way than male status offenders. Perhaps the relative antagonism felt toward staff by female status offenders is a function of a fundamental feeling on the part of these girls that they should not be in these programs in the first place. Or perhaps it is because staff actually behave differently toward female status offenders for a variety of reasons.

Custodial Care

Youth were generally satisfied with the degree of individuality they were allowed in terms of hair and dress and being able to retain their personal possessions. In many of the programs they were allowed to decorate their rooms with posters.

There was tremendous dissatisfaction with the quality of food and the availability of snacks when youth were hungry. Less than a quarter of any youth thought that the food was usually as good as what they had been used to before and males in particular felt that snacks were generally unavailable. At the end of the questionnaire, youth often wrote spontaneous remarks about the food such as: "Food is rotten"; "I don't like it here because we don't get enough food here"; "Same food every week." In girls' programs, the complaints about the food were particularly directed to the starchy and generally fattening types of meals served. Several girls told us that they had gained over ten pounds in two months of program residence.

Lack of privacy is always a problem in congregate settings. Well over half of all youth felt that they could not be alone when they wanted to be and this was slightly more true of the girls. In one of the programs, for example, girls were not allowed to go to their room alone until they had been there for eight months.

Although most youth regardless of sex or offense share the feelings of deprivation of privacy and food, girls are significantly more likely to feel they are receiving inadequate medical and dental care. Less than a quarter of girls, regardless of commitment offense, felt they could see a doctor or dentist at the time they needed one. Although most boys also felt that such care was not immediately available, it was less of a problem for many of them. For example, 18 percent of female status offenders reported that when they needed to see a doctor they could see one soon, as contrasted to 44 percent of male status offenders.

Although the lack of accessibility to doctors and dentists may be a temporary phenomena in many of these programs, it is still a fairly standard practice for youth to have most of their complaints handled by cottage parents and nurses, with doctors and dentists coming a few hours a week at the most. For females, especially, complaints about health are often regarded as hypochondriacal or manipulative by staff and thus may be ignored for fairly long periods. Very few of the programs maintained clinics with bed space for youth with contagious diseases, so such youth were often returned to the cottages where they infected the rest of the youth or were confined in a discipline unit away from other youth.

This perceived lack of concern about general and preventive medical care is accompanied in most of the girls' programs with little attention to sex education and contraception. In at least two of the girls' programs, girls were not only not provided with contraceptive devices, but those who were taking birth control pills at the time of program entry were not allowed to continue taking them. In spite of the fact that these programs did not prepare girls by sex education or contraception, they were very concerned about the sexual behavior of youth and had very rigid procedures to check on it. The following procedures illustrate this concern:

It is important that the nurses keep a record of the girls' monthly periods in order to detect possible pregnancies. When a girl requests a kotex, make sure it is for herself. Do not give girls kotex to be given to someone else.
     Nine days after returning from truancy, a girl must undergo a gynecological examination.

     For the most part, institutions make no effort to acquaint their residents with the basic legal rights. Well over half of all youth report that no one on the staff has talked to them about their rights and most of the youth do not know if staff would even occasionally help them see a lawyer if they so desired. In fact, 72 percent of females incarcerated for status offenses indicated that staff had never talked to them about their legal rights. Youth committed for criminal offenses more often said that staff would help them see a lawyer and had talked to them about their rights than was true for status offenders. The parens patriae doctrine for status offenders, noted in the juvenile court, extends to the training school, and there is no due process for most youth.
     Custodial care for youth in institutions generally is characterized by an emphasis on demeanor and grooming, lack of privacy, food that is unappealing and often inadequate, medical and dental attention that is often very poor, and little concern for the rights of juveniles. Yet the overwhelming complaint of youth in these programs was the boredom of such a life. The recreational facilities and activities for girls were particularly uninteresting and girls spent most of their leisure time doing little more than watching television or playing cards.

Isolation from Family, Friends, and Community

Because of the nature of institutions, contact with the outside is very limited in any ongoing sense. Very few residents attend community schools or work outside the program but in several programs two or three youth were allowed these special privileges. Although it is true that most youth, regardless of sex or offense, were not regularly allowed to go off grounds for shopping, recreation or other reasons even once a week, this isolation was even more pronounced for female status offenders. Only 17 percent of these girls had gone off grounds for these reasons at least once a week.
     Moreover, girls often reported that the ways in which they were transported

Table 8-4
Measures of Isolation, by Sex and Commitment Offense

	Male Status (N = 110-37)	Female Status (N = 118-26)	Male Criminal (N = 559-614)	Female Criminal (N = 173-84)
Percent who in the last month have gone off grounds for shopping, recreation, or other reasons at least once a week	36	17	26	28
Percent who can take part in community activities enough	63	42	44	47
Average number of home visits youth in institutions had per month	0.67	0.55	0.39	0.45
Percent who can be in touch with friends enough	56	42	51	48
Percent who can be in touch with family enough	63	56	58	62
Median distance (in miles) between home and institution	84	73	77	80

on these outings tended to isolate them even more. In at least one of the programs, girls were taken on shopping and field trips as a total group and were not allowed to have contact with people from the outside. A number of girls mentioned how humiliating it was when their cigarettes were passed out to them in front of other people. Other programs transported youth by means of large vans or buses clearly labeled as from the training school and many youth felt stigmatized by these procedures. Over half of most youth, except male status offenders, felt that they could not take part in community activities enough.

Few of the institutions had well-established volunteer programs or other devices to bring community people into the institutions. So both girls and boys suffered from the lack of normal interactions with neighbors and outside friends. In part, this was intentional "treatment" for these youth. As a social worker in a girls' institution told us:

We don't involve ourselves with the surrounding community. What could the girls gain from this? We take them out shopping and so forth. Our girls would make friends that would cause no end of problems. Girls placed here are looking for as little publicity as possible.

In our sample, youth had on the average less than one visit home for every two months of program residence, but youth committed for status offenses did have a slightly greater amount than those committed for criminal offenses. In most of the girls' institutions, home visits were only granted after they had been there two months, regardless of commitment offense or conduct in the program, except in cases of home emergencies. Most of the institutions had fairly rigid guidelines for visitation of family and friends to the program. Two typical policies are as follows:

Only parents or guardians, family members, and grandparents are permitted to visit. Girl friends and boy friends *must have approval* from the superintendent before visiting. You may not visit more than an average of four hours per week. (Male institution)

We provide for visiting on each Sunday of the month from 1:30 p.m. to 4:30 p.m. However, each student is permitted one visit each month on a designated Sunday. In months with five Sundays all students are permitted an on-campus visit. (Female institution)

Phone calls to parents and friends as well as correspondence is often quite restricted. In most programs, youth could only use the phone for very special reasons, such as birthdays or emergencies, probably largely because of logistical problems, but the restriction of correspondence is less understandable. The following rules are not atypical:

With certain exceptions he may receive any letters from friends that come to him. Then he may select those he wishes to correspond with and thereafter he will be permitted to write them during the specified times (every two weeks). . . . He may not correspond with any student in another state institution or one who is on parole, except when given special permission by the superintendent. (From an information booklet for parents)

Girls may write to and receive letters from boys (boyfriends or just friends), on condition of agreement between agency worker, caseworker, and cottage director. (From a procedure manual in a girls' institution)

As shown in table 8-4, a very high proportion of youth feel deprived of enough contact with their families and particularly their friends. Although most of the youth report they get letters from family and friends at least once a week, this really does not compensate for the lack of more personal contact through visits and phone calls.

Although there are exceptions, a good proportion of institutionalized youth have been placed far away from their home communities. As table 8-4 shows, regardless of sex or offense over half of the youth live more than 70 miles away from their homes and this increases the feeling of isolation as well as the difficulties of trying to maintain parental contact. It is particularly difficult for parents who live considerable distances from these programs to conform to very rigid visitation policies.

Control and Surveillance

The searching of personal things, monitoring of correspondence, and punishing of rule violations are constant activities in institutions designed to rehabilitate juveniles. In the case of girls, there are really no distinctions in the level of control exercised on status as opposed to criminal offenders. As table 8-5 clearly indicates, as many or more status offenders than criminal offenders report that their incoming mail, outgoing mail, and personal things are searched. In fact, many more female status offenders report that their outgoing mail is read than was true of criminal offenders. Further, many more girls committed for status offenses reported this kind of control than their male counterparts. Although for boys the monitoring of correspondence is often only for the purpose of inspecting for contraband and thus consists only of opening the envelope, the surveillance is more intense for girls. The following procedure in one girls' institution illustrates the point:

All mail coming and going is to be read by the Cottage Director. Anything significant should be discussed with the girl and/or the social worker. Letters to and from the girls' outside agency social worker should be seen by our social worker.

Table 8-5
Youth Perceptions and Reports of Control, by Sex and Offense

	Percent Male Status (N = 118-38)	Percent Female Status (N = 111-24)	Percent Male Criminal (N = 537-612)	Percent Female Criminal (N = 163-84)
Staff opens incoming mail	40	78	69	76
Staff reads outgoing mail	35	51	52	39
Personal things are searched	79	84	88	88
Personal searches are done	68	46	77	54
There are too many rules here	62	72	74	73
The punishments here are too hard	33	50	44	55

Furthermore, in this same program, mail is not only read but censored. As a staff member told us:

If a girl writes a nasty letter to a parent, we don't send it. We ask her to think it over and rewrite it. I know that censorship is unconstitutional and we'd lose a test case and I have mixed feelings about it.

Although there is little difference in the proportion of youth reporting that their personal things are searched, by either sex or commitment offense, girls are searched in a more unpredictable fashion than boys. Boys more often reported that their rooms or personal areas were searched regularly at particular times, but girls never knew when it would happen. In one program, the cottage director told us that she frequently and with no announcement would dump a drawer or a set of drawers onto a girl's bed if things were not "neat or in tip-top order."

Girls, regardless of offense, are not as likely to be subject to personal searches as boys, and possibly this more chivalrous treatment reflects a general reluctance to impose really brutal control practices on them. Yet the psychological impact of the kinds of control to which they are subject can hardly be taken lightly.

Punishment for acts of misconduct within the institution can be quite severe in both girls' and boys' institutions. Discipline units, euphemistically labeled "Seclusion Rooms" and "Special Care" are an important aspect of the structure of authority. The criteria for placement in these units are often unspecified except in general terms resulting in real abuses of their usage by staff. In one of the girls' institutions, records of the discipline unit indicate that girls had been placed in it for:

. . . lending clothes, sleeping in, lying to their group, drinking glass cleaner, striking matches, being upset, stealing, fussing and arguing, fainting and hyperventilating, planning to run away, talking back to a cottage parent, cussing, slashing a wrist, smoking marijuana, and kissing another girl.

Girls do not stay in this unit for a short time. There is a minimum stay of five days, but girls have stayed as long as six weeks for poor behavior. These special-care units typically consist of about five or six cells with security screens over the windows and beds bolted to the floor. Girls in them have to wear pajamas but are not allowed to sleep during the day. In many of these units, youth are given the same meal three times a day and are required to eat it with plastic spoons.

The rigidity and harshness of the control exercised in institutions is imprinted on the minds of both girls and boys. As shown in table 8-5, most youth thought there were too many rules. But girls were much more likely to think that the punishments were too hard, regardless of offense. Whether girls are

actually subject to more brutal or more frequent punishment than boys is unknown. But it does seem that relative to their past experience, girls are treated
more punitively than boys are.

Misconduct in the Institution

Youth were asked how often they had engaged in a variety of different kinds of
misconduct in the program in the four weeks preceding our field visit. As table
8-6 shows most youth reported they had not engaged in any of the misconduct
in the last month, regardless of sex or commitment offense. Of the seven items,
boys were more likely to have participated in fighting than in any of the other
kinds of misconduct, and girls were more likely to have used illegal drugs as well
as engaged in fighting. Boys, committed for both status and criminal offenses,
had more frequently than girls committed aggressive acts, theft, and property
damage. There was no real difference in the proportion of the different sexes
and offense types running away from the program or pretending to be sick.
    The institutional misconduct of youth appears to be related at least in part

Table 8-6
Misconduct Behaviors of Youth in Institutions, by Sex and Commitment Offense

During the Last Month	Percent Male Status (N = 121-36)	Percent Female Status (N = 120-26)	Percent Male Criminal (N = 576-606)	Percent Female Criminal (N = 177-83)
Fought with youth	43	29	56	31
Stole something	22	16	34	24
Damaged property	25	20	42	28
Used illegal drugs	24	31	36	34
Pretended to be sick	21	24	26	25
Ran away	17	18	17	15
Hit staff	7	2	14	6
Have hurt self on purpose in program	17	23	22	34
Ever tried to kill self in program	9	18	14	24
Since being in program have learned to break the law	38	44	60	51

to their prior involvement in delinquency, since many of the same patterns we found related to prior delinquency occur again with regard to misconduct (i.e., the greater involvement of male criminal offenders and the lesser involvement of female status offenders). The same patterns with regard to prior self-destructive behavior occur again with regard to self-destructive behavior within the institution. That is, females are more self-destructive than males and criminal offenders are more self-destructive than status offenders. In fact, we find that more than a third of females committed to institutions have tried to hurt themselves in the program and almost a quarter have tried to kill themselves.

At this point, we have no way of knowing whether the amount of control exercised over these youth really prevents a greater amount of internal misconduct or aggravates the situation so as to produce more than would otherwise occur. But we do know that its effect on the amount of serious acts of self-destruction that occur is not positive. In fact, a higher proportion of all youth have tried to hurt themselves on purpose in the program than did prior to coming. In spite of the degree of control exercised over these youth, a fairly high proportion of them have learned new ways of breaking the law since coming to the program, particularly youth committed for criminal offenses. In spite of our expectation that status offenders would become more criminally sophisticated because of their exposure to criminal offenders, we find the opposite to be true. This may be due to the phenomenon observed by Heffernan in a study of a Women's Reformatory that subsystems exist within the inmate population based on *offense type*. The degree of interaction, she found, was higher between persons of the same offense type than with those of differing offense types, producing totally different patterns of behavior and attitudes within the same facility.[10] If youth in institutions also tend to interact more with youth who have been committed for the same reasons and who have similar delinquent histories, and form subcultures based on these differences, we would expect that the youth in criminal subcultures would be more often socialized into new ways of delinquency.

Stigmatization

A very high proportion of all youth in our sample of institutional programs felt that people thought of them as criminals because they were there. Interestingly enough, there was no difference in the feelings of stigma of girls committed for status offenses as compared to girls committed for criminal offenses. Half of both of these kinds of youth felt that people thought they were criminals. For boys on the other hand, criminal stigmatization was felt by significantly more criminal than status offenders.

In spite of the fact that most of the girls committed to institutions for status offenses had not committed serious delinquent acts, they felt they were thought of as criminals because of their experience. This of course was also true of male status offenders, but they had committed significantly more serious delinquent activities before their incarceration. Yet for status offenders, in general, the institutional experience can be thought of as one that labels them as criminals although they have been adjudicated only for acts that would not be considered criminal for adults.

Perceptions of Effectiveness of Institutions

We asked youth to tell us how much they thought they were helped by several components of the training school program: school, individual counseling, group counseling, vocational and job training, and work experience. Less than a third of all youth felt that any of these program components had helped them a lot. Status offenders were most helped by the school program, which is probably due in large part to the fact that problems with community schools accounted for the commitment of many of them, particularly males.

Less than a third of any sex or offense type felt that individual or group treatment had been very helpful to them. In many of the programs, treatment was little more than an adjunct to control. Often, youth disliked the social workers because they felt that information discussed during counseling sessions was shared with cottage parents and teachers to the disadvantage of the youth.

The vocational and job training programs as well as work experience were viewed as much more helpful by boys than by girls. This is in part due to the fact that many of the girls could not participate in these experiences either because there were no programs in the institutions or because the programs were limited to only a few girls. Vocational programs for girls were largely in the areas of traditional feminine roles, for example, cosmetology, home economics, and business education; boys' programs were more varied, including graphic arts, electricity and carpentry shops, and auto mechanics in some institutions. A boy in one of the programs told us, in fact: "I have learned a lot from the vocational rehabilitation program and it has a carpentry job set up for me on the outside." Most youth, however, were not so fortunate. Less than 44 percent of the boys and 36 percent of the girls had a job waiting for them upon release.

In order for institutions to provide effective treatment, it is probably necessary for youth to view their experience as legitimate and to view the goals of the program as desirable. Only 18 percent of the female status offenders and 26 percent of the female criminal offenders agreed strongly with the changes the program was trying to make in young people like themselves. However, 42 percent of male status offenders and 29 percent of male criminals agreed a lot with these changes. Thus, although male status offenders most often strongly agreed with the program goals, female status offenders were least likely to.

There are a number of possible reasons for this. First, female status offenders
may perceive of their institutionalization as less legitimate because of their
relatively minor delinquent history, and thus may resent having any changes
made in them by the program. Second, the kinds of control exercised over
female status offenders suggest that staff may be trying to change aspects of
their behavior such as sexual conduct, peer associations, and use of drugs and
alcohol, whereas for males in general and for criminal offenders, staff may concentrate on altering criminal behavior alone. Or perhaps staff dealing with female status offenders are just more punitive in general, resulting in less identi-
fication with their efforts by youth.

Summary

The data presented in this chapter suggests that the contention that females are
accorded favorable treatment in the juvenile justice system is untrue at least for
that portion that eventually reach training schools. Rather, girls are essentially
victimized by:

1. Being disproportionately placed in institutions adjudicated as status offend-
    ers, that is, for offenses that are not criminal for adults
2. Being placed in institutions with less frequent instances of serious criminal
    behavior than boys
3. More often being subject to correctional processing for less serious delin-
    quent behavior

Once institutionalized, there is little differentiation made between youth
adjudicated as status offenders or criminal offenders since most training schools
mix both types of delinquents and do not even separate them by cottage units.
It also appears that the distinctions between offense types are not made by
people outside the institution either, since for girls at least, stigmatization as
criminals is felt equally by status and criminal offenders. Thus for status offenders in general the experience of incarceration can be seen as especially devastating and unjust.

The situation, though, is especially oppressive for girls. Not only can their
experience often be viewed as illegitimate, but it also is more frequently restrictive and more ineffective in dealing with their problems and needs. The differences in the availability of services and the control and isolation for girls and
boys rarely work to the advantage of girls. Many of them are probably harmed
more than helped by these programs. For people concerned with the problems
of children and programs for them, it becomes essential to develop alternatives
to these total institutions. The girls and boys in our study were eloquent spokes-
men for deinstitutionalization so that other children would be spared their
experiences.

In the words of a girl we talked to in a large coed institution: "Don't ever send your kids here!"

Notes

1. *Children in Custody*, May, 1975, U.S. Department of Justice, LEAA, National Criminal Justice Information and Statistics Service, p. 9.

2. Examples of literature on male juvenile institutions: Empey, LaMar, T., and Lubeck, Steven G., *The Silverlake Experiment*, Chicago, Aldine Publishing Co., 1971; James Jones, "The Nautre of Compliance in Correctional Institutions for Juvenile Offenders," *Journal of Research in Crime and Delinquency*, 1(1964), 183-195; Polsky, Howard, *Cottage Six: The Social System of Delinquent Boys in Residential Treatment*, New York, Russell Sage, 1962; Street, David; Vinter, Robert; and Perrow, Charles, *Organization for Treatment: A Comparative Study of Institutions for Delinquents*, New York, Free Press, 1966; Rubenfeld, Seymour, and Stafford, John W., "An Adolescent Inmate Social System—A Psychological Account," *Psychiatry*, 26, 3 (August, 1963), 241-256; Fisher, Sethard, "Informal Organization in a Correctional Setting," *Social Problems*, 13 (Fall, 1965), 214-222; Baum, Martha, and Wheeler, Stanton, "Becoming an Inmate," in *Controlling Delinquents*, edited by Stanton Wheeler, New York, John Wiley and Sons, 1968, pp. 153-185.

Examples of literature on females in juvenile institutions: Catalino, Anthony, "Boys and Girls in a Coeducational Training School are Different—Aren't They?" *Canadian Journal of Criminology and Corrections*, 14, 2 (1972, 1-12; Farley, Frank H., and Farley, Sonja V., "Stimulus-Seeking Motivation and Delinquent Behavior among Institutionalized Delinquent Girls," *Journal of Consulting and Clinical Psychology*, 39(1972), 94-97; Giallombardo, Rose, *The Social World of Imprisoned Girls: A Comparative Study of Institutions for Juvenile Delinquents*, New York, Wiley-Interscience, 1974; Halleck, Seymour L., and Hersko, Marvin, "Homosexual Behavior in a Correctional Institution for Adolescent Girls," *American Journal of Orthopsychiatry*, 32(1962), 911-917; Konopka, Gisela, *The Adolescent Girl in Conflict*, Englewood Cliffs, New Jersey, Prentice-Hall, 1966; Rochelle, Phyllis Ann, "A Study of the Social System of an Institution for Adolescent Delinquent Girls," Ph.D. Dissertation, University of California at Berkeley, 1965; Trese, Leo J., *101 Delinquent Girls*, Notre Dame, Indiana, Fides Publishers, 1962.

3. Short, James, and Nye, Ivan, "Reported Behavior as a Criterion of Deviant Behavior," *Social Problems*, 5(1957), 207-213; Gold, Martin, *Delinquent Behavior in an American City*, Belmont, California, Brooks/Cole Publishing Company, 1970; Clark, and Tifft, "Polygraph and Interview Validation of Self-Reported Deviant Behavior," *American Sociological Review*, 31(1966), 516-523; Williams, and Gold, "From Delinquent Behavior to Official Delinquency," *Social Problems*, 20, 2 (Fall, 1972), 209-227.

4. *Yale Law Journal*, "Notes: Ungovernability" The Unjustifiable Jurisdiction," 83, 7(June, 1974), 1395.

5. Ibid., p. 1395

6. Chesney-Lind, Meda, "Judicial Enforcement of the Female Sex Role: The Family Court and the Female Delinquent," *Issues in Criminology*, 8, 2 (Fall 1973).

7. Arthur, Lindsay G., "Status Offenders Need Help, Too," *Juvenile Justice*, 26, 1(February 1975), 3-7.

8. Gold, Martin, *Delinquent Behavior in an American City*.

9. Pawlak, Edward, *The Administration of Juvenile Justice,* Ph.D. dissertation, University of Michigan, 1972, pp. 138-139.

10. Heffernan, Esther, *Making It in Prison: The Square, the Cool and the Life*, John Wiley and Sons, New York, 1972.

Part IV

Prostitution: Women's Crime or Crime
Against Women

Introduction to Part IV

Prostitution has long held a dominant position in discussions of female criminality. The disproportionate concern over prostitution as a form of female deviancy derives from a centuries-old concern over female sexuality. It has always been seen as the ultimate betrayal of female virtue and of male ownership of that virtue—an instantiation of the Madonna-whore conflict. Betrayed by the Madonna, while serviced by the whore, males have reconciled the conflict through demeaning the prostitute in myths. They have depicted the prostitute as feeble-minded, sexually depraved, economically deprived, morally corrupted, and brutalized by a libidinous pimp. They have made token attempts to confine prostitution through criminal justice sanctions.

Jennifer James examines these myths in chapter 9 through a review of the literature and through presentation of the women's point of view using material from original research with prostitutes. She finds that, contrary to popular belief, prostitution is an institutionalized occupational choice resulting from the same motivations that persuade other individuals to choose various careers. As such, she argues that prostitution should be decriminalized.

Marilyn Haft continues the discussion of present laws relating to prostitution in chapter 10, concluding that such laws should be declared unconstitutional on four basic grounds: equal protection, privacy, cruel and unusual punishment, and due process. She points out that France, Britain, Italy, Japan, Germany, and a total of 100 United Nations member countries have eliminated the crime of prostitution and abandoned attempts at regulation. Both authors agree that our prostitution laws are archaic and destructive.

Motivations for Entrance into Prostitution

Jennifer James

Prostitutes are not the cause of prostitution. Prostitution is more easily understood as an institutionalized occupational choice for women than a symptom of pathology. This chapter examines the motivations that persuade individual women to become professional prostitutes. "The factors that account for women becoming prostitutes, just at the factors which account for a person becoming a lawyer, a doctor, or a robber, are multiple and are often on several levels" (Pomeroy 1965:183). Because of the "immoral," illegal, "deviant" status of prostitution in our society, however, the occupational decision for prostitution has been surrounded by social scientists with an elabroate mythology of theory and analysis far removed from our usual perception of occupational choices such as law or medicine. It is true that "the conscious and immediate reasons that the prostitutes themselves are capable of giving . . . must be considered in conjunction with, and as overlaying other, more deeply hidden factors" (Pomeroy 1965:183). The same would hold, of course, if we were examining why some people become psychiatrists. Moreover, "Just because these (conscious and immediate) reasons are easily accessible does not, of necessity, mean they are not 'real' factors" (Pomeroy 1965:183). Esselstyn (1968:130) states that the "avowed reasons (of prostitutes for their choice of profession) deserve a more respectful hearing than they have received in these changing times." It is time to examine prostitution from the women's point of view rather than the traditional clinical perspective.

Benjamin and Masters (1964:91) posit a division of prostitutes into two general motivation categories: "voluntary" and compulsive." Those in the former group are acting rationally and by free choice in opting for prostitution, and those in the latter group are to some extent acting under compulsion by "psychoneurotic needs." In the majority of cases, as Benjamin and Masters point out, prostitutes cannot accurately be assigned to either of these categories exclusively. These attempts to differentiate between "conscious," "rational" motivations and "more deeply hidden," "psychoneurotic" influences appear again and again in the literature, as illustrated by table 9A-1. For the purpose of this chapter we consider 11 motivating factors, which are presented in table 9A-1. These factors have been divided into three general groupings. *Conscious motivations* include the factors of economics, the persuasive pimp, working conditions, and adventure. *Situational motivations* include early life experiences, parental abuse-neglect, and occupation. *General psychoanalytical motivations* include, along with that category itself, latent homosexuality, oedipal fixation, and retardation.

To supplement this review of the literature on prostitution motivations, we use data from our 1974-75 study (James 1976), which included in its sample population 136 prostitutes from the same large western city. Sixty-eight of these subjects were also defined as addict-prostitutes. Data were collected through questionnaires and interviews and therefore limited to "self-report." For ease of reference, the responses of these subjects to the question, "Why did you get started in prostitution?" are tabulated in table 9A-2.

Conscious Motivating Factors

Economics

Because its stock in trade is sexuality, prostitution has traditionally been both controversial and difficult to define. "The basic element in what we . . . call prostitution—the employment of sex for non-sexual ends within a competitive-authoritative system—characterizes not simply prostitution itself but most of our institutions in which sex is involved, notably courtship and wedlock. Prostitution therefore resembles, from one point of view, behavior found in our most respectable institutions." (Davis, 1937:746) More recent writers such as Winick and Kinsie (1971:3) add the criterion that prostitution is "the granting of non-marital sexual access . . . for remuneration which provides part or all of (a prostitute's) livelihood." (The similarity between prostitution and the "normal" female sex role is shown in the necessity for specifying "*nonmarital* sexual access.") Although these definitions reflect the literature's general bias toward examining prostitution through the study of prostitutes to the exclusion of their customers, they are unable to ignore the *causa sine qua non* of the profession: a consumer demand that generates a business; an institution (albeit a very individualistic one) to supply the desired service. Economics is the pervasive theme of prostitution, and this reality is indicated by the fact that money is mentioned as a motivating factor in virtually all of the literature, although some writers see the prostitute's emphasis on money as a symptom of, or less important than, certain sociological or psychoanalytical factors.

One traditional stereotype of prostitutes represents them as wretched creatures forced into prostitution by extreme economic deprivation. Opposing this stereotype is a body of research showing that the majority of prostitutes choose prostitution as the occupational alternative that affords them the highest attainable standard of living. Greenwald (1970:199) studied 26 call girls and reported that "not one of the girls I interviewed attempted to explain her choice of profession in terms of desperate economic need." As shown in table 9A-2, 8.40 percent of the prostitutes in our 1974-75 study claimed to

have started prostitution because of economic necessity, and 56.49 percent
were motivated by a desire for money and material goods. It is, of course,
very important in this context to recognize that money-making options are
still quite limited for women in this society, especially for unskilled or low-
skilled women. Recognition of this basic sex inequality in the economic
structure helps us see prostitution as a viable occupational choice, rather
than as a symptom of the immorality or "deviance" of individual women.
Pomeroy (1965:175) studied 175 prostitutes, 83 to 93 percent of whom were
motivated by economic factors; he noted that "the gross income from prostitution is usually larger than could be expected from any other type of unskilled labor." Benjamin and Masters (1964:93) were also aware of this sex-
based economic differential and its relationship to prostitution: "The economic
rewards of prostitution are normally far greater than those of most other
female occupations." According to Esselstyn (1968:129), "women are attracted
to prostitution in contemporary America because the income is high and because it affords an opportunity to earn more, buy more, and live better than
would be possible by any other plausible alternative." Davis (1937:750) sums
up the economic pull of prostitution: "Purely from the angle of economic
return, the hard question is not why so many women become prostitutes, but
why so few of them do."

Some researchers claim to find an abnormal, perhaps even neurotic
materialism among prostitutes. Jackman, O'Tool, and Geis (1967:138), for example, state that "The rationalization by prostitutes violating social taboos
against commercial sex behavior takes the form of exaggerating other values,
particularly those of financial success, and for some the unselfish assumption of
the financial burden of people dependent upon them." However, as Greenwald
(1970:200) more accurately points out, "Economic factors helped to mold the
entire society, the family structure, and therefore the very personalities of these
girls (call girls) . . . the girls were caught up in the worship of material success.
. . ." In what way is the economic motivation of these women different from
that of men who strive to attain a position on the executive level so they can
afford "the good life" and support the people dependent upon them? The
majority of Americans share the desire for financial success. Prostitutes are
women who, usually with good cause, see prostitution as their only means,
albeit illegal, for moving from a $3,000- to $6,000-a-year income to the gracious
living possible with $50,000 a year.

A person's choice of occupation is not limited solely by external realities.
One's self-image plays an important part in one's perception of viable alternatives. If a man believes himself to have a "poor head for math," he will probably
not be able to visualize himself attaining great success as a physicist. Women as
a class suffer from an especially narrow self-image in terms of occupational
choices. Traditionally, women's roles are those of wife and mother, both of
which are exclusively biological and service roles. The emphasis on service

carries over into the definition of "new" traditional women's roles, such as teaching children, serving food, and keeping track of appointments for the boss. The importance of physical appearance in many of these occupations reenforces women's self-image as physical-biological objects. As Rosenblum argues (1975: 169), "prostitution utilizes the same attributes characteristic of the female sex role, and uses those attributes toward the same ends; . . . the transition from non-deviance to deviance within prostitution requires only an exaggeration of the situation experienced as a non-deviant woman; . . . all women, to the degree to which they reflect the contemporary female sex role, are primary deviants" (Rosenblum used Edwin Lemert's definitions of primary and secondary deviance). Greenwald, perhaps unwittingly, demonstrates this fact in his effort to prove that the economic motivation is not the most important factor in the choice of prostitution as a profession by claiming that 18 out of 20 prostitutes he interviewed, none of whom "had skills to earn twenty to thirty thousand dollars a year in any other way," had had "chances either to marry or become the mistresses of wealthy men. . . ." In other words, if it's money you're after, why not be a "respectable" sexual object rather than a sexual "deviant?" Later in this chapter, some answers are provided, but for the moment our purpose is to underline the congruence of prostitution and the traditional female sex role. Stein (1974:21-22), in the course of a four-year study, found that "many of the call girls' professional techniques that had once disturbed me, began to remind me of techniques I used as a social worker" — and social work is, of course, another *service* profession. Data from our 1974-75 study show that less than one-fourth of the prostitutes interviewed had completed any vocational training program; the programs reported by those who had had vocational training were primarily in the service fields (appendix 9B, chart 1). Appendix 9B, chart 2 tabulates the occupations held by those prostitutes who were employed when they entered prostitution; again, we find the majority in low-paying, low-status, low-skilled service occupations.

Persuasive Pimp

Another erroneous conception about prostitutes sees them as defeated women cowering under the coercion of brutal pimps. Kemp (1936:214) stated that "In many cases friendship with a pimp may be considered the immediate cause of a woman's becoming a harlot. It is the man who leads her on." However, "friendship" and leading "on" are not necessarily coercive, and Kemp earlier (p. 190) stated that the influence of a pimp was the "immediate cause of prostitution" for only 8.3 percent of prostitutes. Gray (1973:412) found that the influence of pimps, when it was a factor, "was generally minimal." Data from our 1974-75 study, displayed in appendix 9B, chart 3 shows a somewhat larger role for pimps in recruiting women for prostitution. It should be noted, however, that the influence of "girl friends" was more than equal to the influence of pimps, that more than twice as many women reported choosing prostitution solely on their own initiative, and that our experience leads us to agree with Gray that the pressure applied by pimps in recruiting women is generally minimal.

Women in this society are socialized to feel they need a man to take care of them, to "take care of business," to "complete" them, to love them, to make a home with them. Prostitutes are no exception to this rule. Because of their involvement in a "deviant" life-style, however, prostitutes must share their lives with men who understand the dynamics and values of their "deviant"subculture. Any man who lives with a prostitute will be called a pimp, although usually the only factors that distinguish a prostitute-pimp relationship from that of a "normal" marriage relationship are the illegality of their occupations, the woman's status as the sole "breadwinner" and, often, the man's overt maintenance of two or more similar relationships simultaneously. As is true throughout society, womens' socialized need for men is reinforced by the fact that a woman's status is determined by that of her man. Prostitutes who can achieve a relationship with a "high-class" pimp have a higher standing in the subculture of prostitution. This rise in status pays important dividends in her interactions with other members of the culture. Thus, confounding the scenario of the coercive pimp, one can often find prostitutes actively seeking to attach themselves to those pimps whose patronage they feel will be most beneficial.

The ideal pimp fills many roles in his relationship with the prostitute; he is husband, boyfriend, father, lover, agent, and protector. As husband he may pay the bills, take care of the car, and father her children. His role as boyfriend includes taking her to parties and providing other entertainment. These two both overlap in his role of lover. As father he may discipline her for inappropriate behavior and make all her decisions. The agent and protector provides bail money, retains the services of an attorney, and protection from others on the street through his reputation as a strong man whose women are not to be "hassled." How well he fills any one of these roles depends on how "good a pimp" he is and his relationship with the woman. Although individual cases vary depending on particular circumstances, prostitutes give basic reasons for having a man: respect, business, and love.

Regardless of how people may wish to qualify the statement, women in our society feel they need a male companion if their position is to be respected. Women alone, if they are not elderly or widowed, are viewed as "needing a man." Unmarried daughters are harassed, women without men frequently feel their life is incomplete, and friends are forever trying to make a couple out of two singles. The same feelings of need for a male associate pervade the "fast life." In fact, sex-role behavior is conservative among prostitutes and a woman needs a man or she is regarded as an "outlaw," someone who is abnormal by the subculture's values. If her man is in prison or has recently been killed, she will have a period of grace, but few other excuses are acceptable.

A woman needs a man, not only because woman alone is incomplete, but for basic protection from harassment by other men. A prostitute without a pimp is considered fair game by other pimps who will attempt to "catch" her. She will be looked down on by her colleagues and be more open to abuse from others on the street. Her pimp's name is significant as a "keep away" sign in the same way that a wedding ring traditionally has been. On the street it becomes more important because of the threat of assault or robbery if a woman does not have a man "behind her." His reputation provides respect and therefore protection. He does not in fact appear on the street, but instead socializes with other pimps in bars or private homes. Protection from customers is left to the prostitute and her co-workers since the pimp is not around when she is working.

Respect has other dimensions besides a male associate and protection. A woman's status among her peers in "the life" is directly related to the status of her pimp. Just as the banker's wife is accorded more status than the truck driver's, a prostitute's reputation in large part depends on her pimp's. If he is well dressed, handsome, drives a prestige automobile, and handles himself well she will be highly respected; on the other hand, if he is less than stylish and unsuccessful in playing his role she will be looked down on. The woman is defined by the man for whom she works, and a really top pimp finds women asking and paying to be associated with him rather than waiting for him to recruit them.

A second major factor in the prostitute-pimp relationship is business. Many women feel they need a man to take care of business details that women traditionally have not felt capable of handling. They need a man to tell them when to work, how to work, to keep them in line, to give them confidence, and to take care of them. The pimp ideally takes care of all accounts. He handles the money, pays the bills, makes the investments, and gives her an allowance. He provides a place to live, food, clothing, transportation, entertainment, medical care, and makes provision for children. He is expected to take care of bail when she is arrested, provide a lawyer, and give her financial and moral support if she has to serve a sentence. The pimp takes care of her property and sees that her children are taken care of during the times she is working or serving a sentence. As one pimp put it, "I provide the mind and she provides the body. After all, that's the difference between a man and a woman." One of the older women interviewed put it this way:

I gave him all of the money and, like I say, all my business was taken care of. I didn't have to worry about it. If I went to jail I'd be right out, if I needed an attorney he'd pay for it, and he sent money to my kids, and he was always buying me something. We had our little misunderstandings but nothing really serious. We did a lot of things together. We were in New York, he sent me to business school and he went to a school of acting; we had a lot of fun. We traveled together, we even bought a house, but after the Feds were bothering me so much we had to give it up.

The third important consideration discussed by prostitutes is affection. As they point out, everyone needs someone to come home to, and for the prostitute, it has to be someone in "the life." The prostitute needs a man who understands the profession and accepts her. The pimp provides the prostitute with varying degrees of affection. He may be a wonderful lover or a controlling father. He supports her with talk of how special their relationship is and how they can make it together. To love and be loved is often stated as being the motivation to stay with a pimp.

The reasons offered by both pimps and prostitutes for this kind of relationship does not differ greatly from the reasons most men and women have for marrying. Respect, business, and love — perhaps not in that order — are major motivating factors. In reality, detailed description of the interaction between pimp and prostitute produces a picture of a relationship that is little more than an exaggeration of the male-female relationships in the larger society. Levels of love, respect, and economic exchange vary but the needs are the same.

Adventure and Working Conditions

Financial independence is a possibility not included in traditional womens' roles. In a sense, then, a financially independent woman is a "deviant" woman. These roles are beginning to shift and broaden now, but there are still virtually no occupations available to unskilled or low-skilled women that allow the independence, or provide the adventure, of prostitution. Rosenblum (1975: 177) states that the "specific precipitating factors" that cause women to choose prostitution as a profession "can be identified simply as independence and money." Data from our 1974-75 study supports the assertion that independence is highly valued by many of the women who choose prostitution. In appendix 9B, chart 4, "Why did you leave home?" the largest category of first responses was "desire for independence." The second largest category was "dispute with family," which may also imply a desire for independence from the strictures of family life. In the second responses to this same question, these two categories simply change places, with "dispute with family" having the largest percentage and "desire for independence" the second largest. The two sets of responses shown in appendix 9B, chart 5, "What are the advantages of being a prostitute?" also reveal the value independence has for these women. The economic motivation overwhelms all other categories in first responses, but in the second responses, independence has first place. Davis (1971), Benjamin and Masters

(1964), and Esselstyn (1968) also specifically mention independence as a motivating factor in the choice of prostitution.

For many women, the "fast life" of prostitution represents more than simply independence from the conventions of the "straight" world. The life-style of the prostitution subculture has itself proved very attractive to a large number of women over the years. "Fondness for dancing and restaurant life" and the tendency to vagabondage" comprise over a quarter of the "immediate causes of prostitution" listed by Kemp (1936:190). In tabulating the "factors in becoming prostitutes" of three groups of prostitutes, Pomeroy (1965:184) found 3 percent to 19 percent influenced by their perception of prostitution as "an easy life," 12 percent to 24 percent by the "fun and excite-ment" they found in the "fast life;" and 14 percent to 38 percent by the fact that prostitution enabled them to meet "interesting people." Gray, in a study examining "why particular women enter prostitution" (1973:401), reported that "many of the respondents . . . felt intrigued by the description (by pros-titutes) of prostitution which appeared exciting and glamorous . . . the initial attraction for the girls in this study was social as well as material" (pp. 410-11). Benjamin and Masters (1964:107) state that the life-style inherent in identifi-cation with the prostitution subculture continues to be a strong attraction after women have committed themselves to the profession: "There is an abundance of evidence that on the conscious level it is the *excitement* of the prostitute's life, more than any other single factor, which works to frustrate rehabilitation efforts." Referring again to table 9A-2, we see in the second responses that the excitement, adventure, and life-style of prostitution were significant motivating factors for starting prostitution among the population of our 1974-75 study. The second responses shown in appendix 9B, chart 5, on the advantages of prostitution, also support this conclusion, with the social life, working conditions, excitement and adventure of prostitution following independence as the most often mentioned advantages of the profession.

We believe the above data provide a substantial response to Greenwald's implied question on marriage versus prostitution, mentioned earlier. Neither marriage nor extralegal monogomy provides or allows for the economic independence, the excitement, the adventure, or the social life available through prostitution. The basic fact of sexual objectification may be the same in either case, but, for many women, prostitution obviously has benefits that outweigh the privileges — and limitations — of "respectable" womens' roles. Winick and Kinsie (1971:75) refer to a rehabilitation program for prostitutes in Japan in the 1950s, which included such traditional womens' activities as arts and crafts and home making. The program failed, they report, because the prostitutes were simply not interested. As Greenwald discovered (1970: 202), most prostitutes feel "overt hatred of routine, confining jobs." The traditional female occupation of housewife can be seen as one of the most "routine, confining jobs" of all, and thus presents limited temptation to women who value the relative freedom of the "fast life."

Situational Motivating Factors

Parental Abuse and Neglect

Parental abuse or neglect is widely considered a typical childhood experience of women who become prostitutes. Kemp (1936), Choisy (1961), Maerov (1965), Jackman, O'Tool, and Geis (1967), Esselstyn (1968), Greenwald (1970), N. Davis (1971), and Gray (1973) all mention unsatisfactory relationships with parents as a fact of life for these women. Whether the condition is simple neglect-by-absence or outright psychological or physical abuse, the result is generally considered to be alienation of the child from the parents, and a consequent inability — greater or lesser, depending on the circumstances — on the part of the child to adequately socialize the conventional mores of "respectable" society. Data from our 1974-75 study seem to reaffirm the prevalence of parental abuse-neglect experience among prostitutes. The mean age at which the women in our study left home permanently was 16.25 years (s.d. 2.09). As previously mentioned, "dispute with family" is one of the two major reasons given by these women for leaving home (appendix 9B, chart 4). Appendix 9B, chart 4 also shows that physical and emotional abuse was a significant factor in separating 28.84 percent of our prostitute subjects from their families. Of the study population, 65.41 percent had lived apart from their families for some period prior to moving out permanently (appendix 9B, chart 6), and 70.37 percent reported the absence from the family of one or more parent — most often the father — during the subject's childhood (appendix 9B, chart 7). On the other hand, as shown in appendix 9B, chart 8, a majority of these women felt that their childhood relationship with their general family had positive aspects. The second section of appendix 9B, chart 8 seems to indicate that neglect, as opposed to abuse, was the pattern for the majority of subjects who experienced a negative relationship with their parents, although physical abuse was reported by a significant number.

Early Life Experiences

According to Rosenblum (1975:181), "the only hypothesis that can be put forward is that access to prostitutes and perhaps specific incidents in the life of the individual provide the initiative to act upon the potential for prostitution inherent in the female sex role." Maerov (1965), Bryan (1967), and Gray (1973) also see "access to prostitutes" — whether through personal relationships with people in the "fast life" or through the overt presence of prostitution in the neighborhood — as a significant factor in many women's entrance into prostitution. In our 1974-75 study, the mean age at which the subjects became aware of prostitution was 13.75 years (s.d. 3.23); the mean age at which they began regular prositution was 18.20 years (s.d. 2.60). Appendix 9B, chart 9 indicates that girl friends, relatives, and the neighborhood were the most important sources of their first information about prostitution. The second section of that question, which is cross-tabulated by race, gives the subjects' responses to the question, "Where did you first come into actual contact with prostitutes?" The largest category for both races in this area is "friends." Black women had more first contacts than white women in their families and in their neighborhoods, and white women more often had first contact in jail. Approximately 20 percent of both races reported their first contact was "on the street."

Early sexual experience has also been cited as important in entrance into prostitution. "At what number of lovers is a girl supposed to lose the status of a decent person?" asks Choisy (1961:1). Carns (1973:680) explains, "a woman's decision to enter coitus . . . implies that she is creating for herself a sexual status which will have a relatively pervasive distribution. . . . she will be evaluated downwardly. Such is the nature of the male bond." Female promiscuity virtually guarantees loss of status in our majority culture. The labeling implied by such loss of status may be an important step in the process by which a woman comes to identify with, and thus begins to see as a viable alternative, a "deviant" life-style such as prostitution. N. Davis (1971:305) describes this process in the context of her discussion on the effects of institutionalization: "The adolescent girl who is labeled a sex offender for promiscuity . . . may initially experience a conflict about her identity. Intimate association with sophisticated deviants, however, may provide an incentive to learn the hustler role . . . and thus resolve the status anxiety by gaining prestige through association with deviants, and later, experimentation in the deviant role." Even without institutionalization, the labeling impact of status loss must strongly affect the subject's self-image. She may attempt to rebuild her self-image by moving into a subculture where the wider society's negative labeling of her will not impede her efforts toward a higher status — although that status itself will be perceived as negative by the wider society. Of the prostitutes in our 1974-75 study population, 44.85 percent reported that they had "gotten into trouble" because of their sexual activity while they were juveniles (appendix 9B, chart 10).

However negative the long-term effects of juvenile promiscuity on a woman's social status, the short-term effects of contranormative juvenile sexual activity may often appear quite positive to the young woman involved. Young women suffering from paternal abuse or neglect, which we have seen to be a common pattern for prostitutes, may be especially susceptable to the advantages of what Greenwald (1970:167) calls "early rewarded sex — that is, . . . engaging in some form of sexual activity with an adult for which they were rewarded. [These women] discovered at an early age that they could get some measure of affection, of interest, by giving sexual gratification." This type of positive sexual reinforcement, particularly when coupled with the cultural stereo-type of women as primarily sexual beings, may cause some women to perceive their sexuality as their primary means for gaining status: "Sex as a status tool is exploited to gain male attention" (Davis, 1971:304). All women in our culture must somehow come to terms with the fact that their personal value is considered inseparable from their sexual value. "While men are also concerned with their sexual desirability, their opinion of themselves is not founded primarily on that desirability, for occupational achievement provides an important alternative to a self-identification based on sexual desirability. The alternatives available to females are fewer and generally carry lower social esteem, resulting in an inordin-ately high value being placed on sexual desirability" (Rosenblum, 1975:180). Prostitution is a result of the discovery that carrying out the implications of the "normal" female sex role can pay off not only in a certain sort of social status, but also in cold cash.

Not all of the sexual contacts between juvenile women and adult males can be seen as having positive aspects for the women involved, for example, incest and rape. Maerov (1965) and Kemp (1936) mention the prevalence of these "traumatic events" (Maerov 1965:690) among prostitute populations, and data from our 1974-75 study seem to indicate that early sexual trauma may be a common experience of prostitutes. In that study, 49.1 percent of the subjects answered affirmatively to the question, "Prior to your first intercourse, did any older person (more than 10 years older) attempt sexual play or intercourse with you?" The perpetrators of these attempts were 10.60 percent fathers, 12.12 percent step-fathers, 3.03 percent foster fathers, and 15.15 percent other relatives, which makes a total of 25.75 percent for father figures and 40.90 percent for experiences that could be seen as incestuous. Of our 1974-75 sample, 46.5 per-cent reported that they had been raped, and 16.7 percent had been raped more than once. Although the ages of the subjects when these rapes occurred is not known, in an earlier study (James Basic Statistical Summary 1971) including 20 adolescent prostitutes, 72.2 percent of these subjects reported having had a "forced-bad sexual experience," and 84.7 percent of these experiences occurred while the subject was aged 15 or younger. The men responsible for these experi-ences of the adolescent subjects were 23.1 percent fathers and 15.4 percent other relatives. The long-term effects of sexual abuse of children are virtually unknown. DeFrancis (1969) found that guilt, shame, and loss of self-esteem on the part of the child victim are the immediate results of sexual abuse, and it seems likely that these reactions might have considerable impact on the victim's developing self-image, possibly leading to an abnormal degree of sexual self-objectification.

Occupation

Some researchers (e.g., Esselstyn 1968) believe that certain occupations lead women easily into prostitution. These occupations are those that adhere most closely to the traditional female service role, often emphasizing physical appearance as well as service. Clinard (1959:228) comments that "Quasi-prostituting experiences, such as those of a waitress who after hours accepts favors from customers in return for sexual intercourse, may lead to prostitution." It is not unusual for a woman who is required by her employer to flirt with customers and "be sexy" to find that the men with whom she must relate in business transactions consider her to be "no better than a prostitute." Once she has been so labeled, her loss of status is automatic, and she may decide she might as well make the best of a negative situation by accepting the "favors"—or the money—men are eager to give her for playing out the implication of the label. Again, these low-status service occupations are among the few occupational alternatives available to unskilled or low-skilled women.

Psychoanalytical Motivating Factors

Retardation and Inherited Disabilities

Theories of prostitute motivations based on inherent or inherited disabilities or mental retardation have been generally unaccepted in recent years. It is simply not true that "from 30 to 50 percent of all prostitutes must be classed as feeble-minded" (Kemp 1936:126). Nor, we hope, would most present-day social scientists accept as valid the conclusions of researchers such as Lombroso (1898), who stated that "even the female criminal is monotonous and uniform compared with her male companion, just as woman is in general inferior to man" (p. 122); and further on, "women are big children; their evil tendencies are more numerous and more varied than men's. . . ." (p. 151). Kemp and Lombroso are extreme examples of the type of studies of prostitution that are biased by the fact that the researchers apparently began with a highly prejudiced attitude toward their subjects, either because of their sex or their occupation. We find less extreme examples of this attitude in other studies that seem to be attempts to discover "what is *wrong* with these women?" (e.g., Maerov 1965; Hollender 1961; Winick and Kinsie 1971; Greenwald 1970).

Latent Homosexuality

Misogyny is not the only prejudice affecting some of the literature on prostitution motivation. The orientation of the majority culture is mirrored by
several researchers in their evaluation of "latent homosexuality" among prostitutes. Since homosexuality, like prostitution, is considered "deviance," the
temptation to put all the "bad eggs" in one theoretical basket is perhaps understandable. Rosenblum (1975:173-4), however, reacting to Lemert's positing
of prostitution and homosexuality as similar examples of sexual deviance,
argues:

> Homosexuality can be characterized as a specific, socially censured form of
> sexual desire. . . . Both society and the stigmatized individual agree on what
> is being labeled deviant — specific sexual desires as manifested in behavior.
> However, except in a few cases, prostitution is clearly not the result of unusual
> or excessive sexual desire. . . . by Lemert's own definition prostitution is char-
> acterized as emotionally indifferent promiscuity. The prostitute's most basic
> motivation is monetary gain. . . . By accepting as given the classification of
> prostitution as sexual deviation, Lemert has assumed congruence between the
> action performed and the norms violated. . . . More seriously, the classifica-
> tion of prostitution as sexual deviance means, at least implicitly, that deviance
> is not being discussed on its own terms, but rather from the perspective of the
> societal reaction to it. . . . the unequivocal classification of prostitution as
> sexual deviance seems primarily a reaction to and reinforcement of the dom-
> inance of sexuality in the female sex role. . . .

Greenwald's book (1970) is a good example of this type of analysis. He sees
homosexuality as a "confusion" — an inability to develop a "normal" sexual
identity — and prostitution as an attempt on the part of many prostitutes to
deny homosexual feelings (cf, pp. 176-79). Other researchers who view homosexuality as a "neurotic" component of prostitute motivation are Maerov (1965)
and Hollender (1961).

Data from our 1974-75 study reveal that 35.3 percent of the sample had
experienced a lesbian relationship, 7.4 percent reported "frequent" homosexual
activity, and 6.7 percent were exclusively lesbian. Although the percentages for
frequent and exclusive homosexuality in the study population are probably not
significantly larger than the percentages for the wider society, it is doubtful
whether any study of the general female population has resulted in a figure as
high as 35.3 percent for female homosexual experience. One explanation for
this discrepancy may be, of course, that "respectable" woman might be less
willing than women already labeled as "deviants" to admit engaging in "deviant"
sexual behavior. It is also possible that some aspects of the life-style of prostitutes may make homosexuality appear more feasible than it does to the majority of women, for example, the absence of conventional restraints on the open

discussion of sex and sexuality, a wider experience of different sexual techniques, and the fact that in their private lives, prostitutes often live more intimately with other women than with men. Some prostitutes may turn to lesbianism as the only sexual alternative while incarcerated and discover that they enjoy it. Finally, since their working hours are spent in the unilateral fulfillment of male sexual needs, some prostitutes may find that their own needs are better filled by the more diffuse sensuality and mutuality characteristic of lesbian sexuality.

Oedipal Fixation

Some researchers believe many prostitutes have an oedipal fixation. Winich and Kinsey (1971:83), for example, see prostitution as atonement for guilt produced by incestuous fantasies. This theory is impossible to disprove, since we cannot accurately measure the incidence of incestuous fantasies. On the other hand, it is also impossible to prove their theory, or to prove that it applies more to prostitution than to other occupations. "Money is heavily loaded with all kinds of psychological conflicts. In our civilization, among many other things . . . it sympolizes the will to power and the ensuing unconscious guilt of having taken the father's place," Choisy states (1961:1). Perhaps every woman, prostitute and business executive alike, who desires economic independence is acting out oedipal fantasies. Such theories, and the theory that prostitutes are subconsciously seeking sexual relations with a father figure, are based on the perception of prostitution as a special psychological "problem," or a form of deviance, rather than as an economic option for women.

General Psychoanalytical

The myth that women become prostitutes because they are "oversexed" has been countered by the discovery that prostitutes see their sexual activities with customers as purely business and usually get no sexual pleasure from them. Unfortunately, an opposite myth also exists: that of "the invariably frigid prostitute" (Maerov 1965:692). Responding to this myth, Pomeroy (1965:183) reports that the 175 prostitutes he studied "were more sexually responsive in their personal lives than were women who were not prostitutes [Pomeroy was using data from Kinsey et al., *Sexual Behavior in the Human Female* (1953), for comparison] and even in their contact with paid partners they were more responsive sexually than one might have anticipated." Data from our 1974-75 study also indicate a higher rate of orgasm among prostitutes than among the general female population. Appendix 9B, chart 11 shows these data compared with those from Bell and Balter (1973). Given this information, we need no longer look for "explanations" of prostitution based on the psychological effects of frigidity.

"Movies, television, popular literature and, particularly, advertising make it seem that the cardinal sin a woman can commit is to be unattractive" (Greenwald 1970:201). Some researchers believe, with Greenwald, that prostitutes are motivated by the need to prove their attractiveness through sexual contact with many men. Taking the theory a step further, Winick and Kinsie (1971:35) state that

Many prostitutes apprehended by the police tend to be overweight and short. They often have poor teeth, minor blemishes, untidy hair, and are otherwise careless about their personal appearance. Docility and indifference are common. This leads one to conclude that such women may feel inadequate to compete in more traditional activities and thus more readily accept a vocation that involves the sale of something they may not value highly.

Winick and Kinsie do not seem to consider the fact that "poor teeth" are common among lower class people, nor that a large percentage of the prostitutes apprehended by the police are "hypes" — drug addicts working as prostitutes to support their habit — who form a special, lower class in the hierarchy of the "fast life." One wonders if they even considered the effect being arrested might have on the amount of attention the suspect pays to her hairdo. In any case, since it is demonstrably true that the majority of "unattractive" women do not become prostitutes, and since it is a matter of personal opinion what percentage of prostitutes is "unattractive," the importance of the Winick and Kinsie statement quoted above lies in its assumption that women's "traditional activities" are those that emphasize physical appearance. This assumption is very pervasive throughout society and is a major influence for many women in the development of self-image — and self-image is always a factor in the individual's choice of occupation. Perhaps we could find women who became prostitutes because their "attractiveness" rating was not high enough for them to gain employment as receptionists or cocktail waitresses. On the other hand, prostitutes generally make more money than waitresses or receptionists, regardless of physical appearance, and we are inclined to believe that the economic motivation is statistically far more important than the psychological one presented by Greenwald and Winick and Kinsie. Appendix 9B, chart 5, for example, shows that a very small number of subjects in our 1974-75 study saw "being desired by men" as a significant advantage of being a prostitute. A slightly larger number believed that being a prostitute "enhances self-worth," but this response could as easily reflect factors such as independence or higher income rather than reassurance as to their physical appearance. In fact, almost two thirds as many subjects stated that *lowered* self-esteem was an effect, for them, of being a prostitute (appendix 9B, chart 13).

There is another analytic theory about prostitutes that pictures them as using their profession to act out their hostility towards men. Looking at this objectively, it would seem, except for the illegality of the profession, equally valid to suggest that some women become elementary school teachers in order to act out their hostility towards children. Perhaps this motivation is real for some women, both teachers and prostitutes, but documentation is very scarce. In our 1974-75 study, only one woman mentioned hostility towards men as a motivating factor; and it was her second response, indicating that, even for her, there was another, more immediate motivation. Myths such as this one arise because objectivity is very often lacking in our perception of prostitutes. As Stein (1974:21-22) says about her attitude at the beginning of her study of call girls, "I kept looking for signs that the women were really miserable or neurotic or self-destructive. I wanted them to be that way. I think I wanted call girls to be 'sick' because I believed that anybody — at least any woman — who sold sexual access ought to be sick." Once she had discarded these pre-conceptions, Stein discovered that

The women who became successful call girls, like those who became social workers, had to be sensitive and warm. They had to like people and feel comfortable with them. Nobody who dislikes people could succeed over a period of time in a profession that requires close body contact with strangers. Within this broad framework, the call girls' attitudes to their clientele varied, much like social workers. For some girls, the call-girl-client relationship was a purely business one. . . . Other call girls tended to become genuinely concerned with their clients. . . . Most of the call girls I met, like most social workers I knew, fell in between these two extremes. (pp. 22-23)

Discussion

Can the study of prostitute motivations tell us anything about how to "reform" prostitutes, that is, how to encourage women working as prostitutes to choose a different occupation? Certainly those young, unskilled women, for example, who are considering prostitution because of its economic potential might be lured into a "respectable" occupation if there were more high-paying, "respectable" job options available to unskilled women. For women who are already prostitutes, however, the degree of professionalization, as well as the original motivations, must be considered. The choice of prostitution may come to be seen by the prostitute as irreversible. Davis (1971:300) describes the entrance into prostitution as she perceives it: ". . . there is a 'drift into deviance,' with promiscuity initially used as a status tool, but later becoming defined by the individual as having consequences for the foreclosure of alternative career routes." Institutionalization — which often occurs because, in our society, girls can be incarcerated for being sexually active — can reinforce this "drift" towards professionalized promiscuity in two ways. First, it brings a young girl into "intimate association with sophisticated deviants" (Davis 1971:305) who may give the girl her first impression of prostitution as a viable, even an exciting and rewarding, life-style. Second, incarceration is a major part of the labeling process. A woman in jail is *ipso facto* "deviant," and whether or not she was convicted of, or ever engaged in, prostitution, "the societal reaction to women participating in deviant activities is to assume that they are also, or perhaps only, prostitutes" (Rosenblum 1975:180). Being labeled "deviant" and being assumed to be "no better than a prostitute" may remove some womens' inhibitions against involvement in the socially disreputable "fast life."

Another factor that motivates women to continue in prostitution applies to the professionals in any field, namely, once a person has developed the skills of any given occupation and becomes successful in it, she or he is naturally reluctant to change careers, especially if she or he has no other job skills. Our jobs are an important part of our lives, around which we usually organize much of our time and many of our social relationships. Prostitution, because of its "deviant" status in society, is a particularly compelling force in the lives of its practitioners: "For all prostitutes . . . the most mundane routines of living become rigidly restructured" (Rosenblum 1975:175). After years in the profession the prostitutes' contact with people outside the "fast life" is usually very limited, making reentrance into the "straight" world a difficult and lonely experience. Economics, however, seems to be the primary reason that prostitutes continue in prostitution, as shown in appendix 9B, chart 12. Of our 1974-75 sample, 68.70 percent stated that they remained in prostitution because of economic necessity or because of a desire for money and material goods. In second responses, enjoyment of the prostitution life-style is the largest category after economics. These responses, unsurprisingly, echo those in appendix 9B, chart 5 on the advantages of prostitution.

Winick and Kinsie (1971:78-79) present a "typology of prostitutes . . . in terms of their response to rehabilitation," which can be seen as a description of the effects of different levels of professionalization. Their first category might be called *short-timers*, women who have not been prostitutes long and who have developed "no habit patterns or personal involvements" related to the occupation, that is, women whose prostitution has not become professionalized. These women, Winick and Kinsie feel, can often be successfully rehabilitated. Disillusioned, older prostitutes form Winick and Kinsie's second category and can be compared to professionals ready for retirement. These women "need considerable rehabilitation," according to Winick and Kinsie, as would most people attempting to change from one fully formed career to another for which they had no training. For category three, those women who are involved in prostitution just to earn a living, economic alternatives are the answer. These women, unlike those in the first category, may have been prostitutes for some time, but their level of professionalization is not high because they look upon prostitution as "just a job," not as a career. Their final category consists of successful, satisfied, highly professionalized prostitutes who are "not likely to respond voluntarily to any rehabilitation plan." In our experience, women between the ages of 18 and 24 can rarely be reached through rehabilitation programs. They visualize success and wealth if they "hustle," and they scorn the low-paying, boring straight life. Counselors have little to offer these professionals that can successfully compete with the income, adventure, and independence they perceive in the "fast life."

Appendix 9B: charts 13, 14, and 15 show some of the negatives of prostitution revealed by our 1974-75 study. The primary "disadvantage of being a prostitute" (appendix 9B, chart 13) for the women in our sample was the intrusion of the legal system into their lives. Danger from customers and physical-emotional stress also rated high. Tabulated by race, black women felt significantly more disadvantaged by the legal system, and white women gave significantly higher importance to familial and societal reactions, physical-emotional stress, and lowering of self-esteem. "Adequate employment" was the largest category of response to the question, "What do you feel would enable you to stop prostitution?" (appendix 9B, chart 14). A change in environment, life-style, or "self" were also chosen by many subjects as responses to this question. The legal system, lack of education, lack of alternatives, and low self-esteem were among the largest categories of responses to the question, "What do you see as the primary obstacle to your future success?" (appendix 9B, chart 15). (We are deemphasizing the impact of addiction revealed in these data because it applies only to a subgroup of prostitutes—the addict-prostitute, or "hype.").

Summary and Conclusion

Prostitution is perceived by some women as their best occupational alternative. The desire for a higher income and an independent, exciting life-style are the major motivating factors for most prostitutes. Five aspects of our economic-social structure make prostitution attractive to many women motivated by these factors:

1. There are virtually no other occupations available to unskilled or low-skilled women with an income (real or potential) comparable to prostitution.
2. There are virtually no other occupations available to unskilled or low-skilled women that provide the adventure or allow the independence of the prostitution life-style.
3. The traditional "woman's role" is almost synonymous with the culturally defined female sex role, which emphasizes service, physical appearance, and sexuality.
4. The discrepancy between accepted male and female sex roles creates the "Madonna-whore" syndrome of female sexuality, such that women who are sexually active outside the limits of their "normal" sex-role expectations are labeled "deviant" and lose social status.
5. The cultural importance of wealth and material goods leads some women to desire "advantages to which [they are] not entitled by [their] position" in the socioeconomic stratification (Davis 1937:745).

The issue to which we must now speak is: how should prostitution be handled by society? There is general agreement that it cannot be eliminated without changing our entire structure of sexual socialization. "We can imagine a social system in which the motive for prostitution would be completely absent, but we cannot imagine that the system could ever come to pass" (Davis 1937: 753). As long as the definition of the "normal" male sex role is broader than that of the "normal" female sex role, there must be "deviant" women to take up the slack. At present, society deals with prostitution by declaring it a crime and prosecuting, in the vast majority of cases, only the prostitute, although her customer is usually equally culpable under the law. Prostitution is a victimless crime – a crime without a complainant, in which, typically, all those involved are willing participants – and there is a growing body of opinion that victimless crimes like prostitution do not belong under the jurisdiction of the criminal justice system. Instead of using the criminal-law system in an acknowledgedly hopeless, and therefore often cynical and hypocritical, effort to eliminate prostitution, we believe that society should limit its aim to ensuring that prostitution does not disrupt society or offend nonparticipants, an effort that could be better achieved through civil-law regulations.

Present antiprostitution laws come in two main types: (1) offering or agreeing to an act of prostitution, and (2) loitering for the purpose of soliciting for prostitution. The first type of law is virtually always enforced through the use of police officers or agents posing as customers, a practice that comes very close to entrapment. When a man – police officer or civilian – publically advertises himself as desiring the services of a prostitute, and a woman is sent to jail for agreeing to provide that service, the criminal law is obviously acting entirely outside its "prime function": "protecting our persons and our property" (Norris and Hawkins, 1970:2). The enforcement of the antiloitering ordinances often has the effect of punishing women for behavior considered perfectly respectable for men. For example, simply by switching the sex of the object in the following quotation from Seattle's municipal code (Section 12:49), we get a good description of the behavior of many "normal" men when they see an attractive, unattached woman: "such person . . . repeatedly beckons to, stops or attempts to stop, or engages [female] passers-by in conversation. . . ." "normal" behavior for men becomes "deviant," illegal behavior for women, especially for "known prostitutes."

These two laws, as clumsy and discriminatory as they are, can clearly be effective only at keeping prostitution off the streets, not eliminating it. Most other countries have stopped trying to end prostitution and have instead made various less-abusive legal arrangements for its regulation. In West Germany, for example, prostitution is considered a social necessity, and the government supports the building of pimp-free prostitution hostels where prostitutes can live and work in comfortable rooms with access to shopping centers, recreational facilities, and mandatory medical inspections. The Netherlands uses zoning laws to prevent overt street solicitation from offending the general public. A total of 100 member nations of the United Nations have eliminated the crime of prostitution and have abandoned experiments at regulation (United Nations 1951). The criminal laws in those countries seek instead to control public solicitation and to discourage the pimps and procurers who live off the earnings of prostitutes.

We view decriminalization as the least abusive method of dealing with prostitution in the United States. Decriminalization differs from legalization in that, instead of creating more legal involvement, it removes prostitution from the criminal code entirely. An ideal approach would be to put all sexual behavior in private between consenting adults outside the purview of the law, but this ideal must be balanced by the reality of public expediency. Failing the ideal, then, options for controls would depend upon the communities' concern about the overtness of sexual activities, the possible disease problems, business and zoning regulations, and age of consent. Taxation, health, and age requirements can be approached in a number of ways. The least abusive to the individual woman would be a small business license with a health card requirement. Prostitutes would obtain a license much as a masseuse does; her place of business would have to conform with zoning requirements; she would be required to report her income, be of age, and keep her health card current. Violations would mean the revocation of the license and would be handled by a nonpolice agency. Regulations such as the above would, of course, still limit personal freedom in a purely private area. The nonlicensed prostitute could still be prosecuted, although her's would be a civil citation rather than a criminal one. Decriminalization, with some restrictions, is regarded as a provisional solution only while efforts are made to change the more fundamental causes of prostitution. As long as we retain our traditional sex role expectations, we will have prostitution. As long as women are socialized into the traditional female role and see their alternatives limited by that role, prostitution will remain an attractive occupational option.

References

Bell, Robert R., and Balter, Shelli. "Premarital Sexual Experiences of Married Women," *Medical Aspects of Human Sexuality* 7 (1973):110.

Benjamin, Harry, and REL Masters. *Prostitution and Morality*. New York: Julien Press, 1964.

Bryan, James H. "Apprenticeships in Prostitution," in *Sexual Deviance*, edited by John H. Gagnon and William Simon. New York: Harper & Row, 1967, p. 146.

Carns, Donald E. "Talking About Sex: Notes on First Coitus and the Double Sexual Standard," *Journal of Marriage and the Family*, 35 (1973):677-88.

Choisy, Maryse. *Psychoanalysis of the Prostitute*. New York: Philosophical Library, 1961.

Clinard, Marshall. *Sociology of Deviant Behavior*. New York: Rinehart & Co., Inc., 1959.

Davis, Kingsley. "The Sociology of Prostitution," *American Sociological Review*, 2 (1937):744-55.

DeFrancis, Vincent. *Protecting the Child Victim of Sex Crimes by Adults*. Final Report, American Humane Association, Children's Division, Denver, 1969.

Esselstyn, T. C. "Prostitution in the United States," *Annals of the American Academy of Political and Social Sciences* March, 1968. pp. 123-35.

Gray, Diana. "Turning-Out: A Study of Teenage Prostitution," *Urban Life and Culture*, January, 1973, pp. 401-25.

Greenwald, Harold. *The Elegant Prostitute*. New York: Ballantine Books, 1970.

Hollender, Marc H. "Prostitution, the Body, and Human Relatedness," *International Journal of Psychoanalysis*, 42 (1961):404-13.

Jackman, Norman R., O'Toole, Richard and Geis, Gilbert. "The Self-Image of the Prostitute," in *Sexual Deviance*, edited by John H. Gagnon & Wm. Simon. New York: Harper & Row, 1967, pp. 133-46.

James, Jennifer. *A Formal Analysis of Prostitution Final Report, Part I, Basic Statistical Summary*. State of Washington, Department of Social and Health Services, 1971.

_____. Ongoing research includes a sample of 240 female offenders, 120 of whom have been identified as prostitutes. Funded by the National Institute on Drug Abuse, #DA0091801, *Female Criminal Involvement and Narcotic Addiction*, 1974-75.

Kemp, Tage. *Prostitution: An Investigation of its Causes, Especially with Regard to Hereditary Factors*. Copenhagen: Levin & Muskgaard, 1937.

Kinsey, Alfred, Pomeroy, W., Martin, C. & Gebhard, P. *Sexual Behavior in the Human Female*. Philadelphia: Saunders, 1953.

Lombroso, Cesare. *The Female Offender*. New York: D. Appleton & Co., 1898.

Maerov, Arnold S. "Prostitution: a Survey & Review of 20 Cases," *The Pate Report*, 1965, pp. 675-701.

Morris, Norval & Gordon Hawkins. *The Honest Politician's Guide to Crime Control*. Chicago: The University of Chicago Press, 1969.

Pomeroy, Wardell B. "Some Aspects of Prostitution," *Journal of Sex Research*, November, 1965, pp. 177-87.

Rosenblum, Karen E. "Female Deviance and the Female Sex Role: A Preliminary Investigation," *British Journal of Sociology*, 26 (1975):169-85.

Stein, Martha L. *Lovers, Friends, Slaves*. New York: GP Putnam's Sons, 1974.

United Nations. *International Convention for the Suppression of White Slave Traffic.* United Nations Publishing, 1951.

Winick, Charles and Kinsie, Paul M. *The Lively Commerce.* New York: New American Library, 1971.

Table 9A-1
Motivations of Prostitutes

Authors	Economics	Early Life Experience	Occupation	Persuasive Pimp	Latent Homosexuality	Oedipal Fixation	Abuse Parental Neglect	Retardation	Working Conditions	General Psychoanalytic	Adventure
Esselstyn	X	X	X	X							
Jackman, O'Toole & Geis (1963)		X									
Hollender (1964)					X	X					
Lombroso (1920)								X			
Kemp (1936)	X			X	X	X	X	X			X
Glover (1960)					X	X	X	X		X	
Ellis (1937)										X	
Stern (1960)					X	X				X	
Greenwald (1958) (1970)	X				X	X	X		X	X	
Rubin (1961)					X	X				X	X
Segal (1963)										X	
Choisy (1965)						X				X	X
Benjamin & Masters (1964)	X								X		X
Bryan (1966)	X								X		X
Gebhard (1969)	X										
Clinard (1959)		X	X								
Davis (1937)	X										
Hirschi (1962)											
Maerov (1965)		X			X	X	X		X		
Pomeroy (1965)	X								X		X
Stein (1974)	X		X						X		X
Winick & Kinsie (1972)	X									X	
Davis, N. (1971)	X	X		X			X				X
James (1972)	X	X	X	X			X		X		X
James (1976) (Unpublished)	X	X	X	X			X		X		X
Rosenbaum (1975)	X	X					X				
Gray (1973)	X	X					X				X

Table 9A-2
Reason for Starting Prostitution?

	Money-Material Goods	Excitement-Adventure	Influence of Girl Friends	Curiosity	Money for Own Drugs	Money for Man's Drugs	Influence of Man Friend	Attracted to Life-style	Economic Necessity Unrelated to Drugs	Other
Addict-Prostitute (N = 63)	48.4%	3.1%	1.6%	4.7%	18.8%	3.1%	6.3%	3.1%	6.3%	3.1%
Prostitute (N = 68)	62.3%	2.9%	1.4%	2.9%	0.0%	0.0%	14.5%	2.9%	10.1%	1.4%
Total (N = 131)	56.49%	3.05%	1.53%	3.82%	9.16%	1.53%	10.69%	3.05%	8.40%	2.29%
Second Responses Total (N = 68)	20.59%	11.76%	14.71%	7.35%	14.71%	1.47%	10.29%	10.29%	5.88%	2.95%

Appendix 9B
Other Questionnaire and Interview Responses

Chart 1. Have you ever taken a vocational training program? ($N = 135$)

Yes, completed	22.22%
No	42.96
Enrolled but not completed	33.33
Currently enrolled	1.48

Type of vocational program

Business-office work-clerical	46.05%
Nursing, aide, health care	7.89
Beautician, cosmetologist	10.53
Food services (waitress, cook)	3.95
Keypunch, computer	7.89
Other	23.68

Chart 2. Employment at time of first prostitution involvement (of those who were employed)? ($N = 37$)

Sales, cashier	5.41%
Food service (waitress, cook)	16.22
Nursing-medical technician	2.70
Secretarial	27.03
Blue collar (factory)	10.81
Unemployed	2.70
Social services	5.41
Administrative	2.70
Modeling-acting	5.41
Other	21.62

Chart 3. How did you get started in prostitution? ($N = 134$)

Own initiative	37.31%
Pimp recruited	14.18
Pimp's woman recruited	2.99
Madam recruited	4.48
Relative recruited	3.73
Man-boyfried suggested it	13.43
Girl friend suggested it	14.93
In the environment (neighborhood)	2.24
Other	6.72

Chart 4. Why did you leave home?

	1st response ($N = 134$)	2nd response ($N = 52$)
Marriage-living with man	16.42%	13.46%
Institutionalized	2.99	1.92
Family split up (no home maintained)	4.48	1.92

	1st response (N = 134)	2nd response (N = 52)
Working required it (employed elsewhere)	2.99%	0.00%
Education required it (training, college)	6.72	1.92
Desire for independence	29.10	17.31
Dispute with family	27.61	23.08
Never left home	.75	0.00
Physical abuse at home	.75	13.46
Emotional harrassment at home	3.73	15.38
Other	4.48	11.54

Chart 5. What are the advantages of being a prostitute?

	1st response (N = 132)
Easy money-material goods	84.85%
Independence	3.79
Working conditions	.76
Social life	4.55
Being desired by men	.76
To gain power	.76
Other	4.55

	2nd response (N = 83)
Easy money-material goods	8.43%
Independence	18.07
Excitement-adventure	10.84
Working conditions	14.46
Social life	16.87
Being desired by men	2.41
Sexual gratification	1.20
Enhances self-worth	4.82
Maintain relationship with pimp	3.61
Gaining sexual knowledge	4.82
Outlet for hostility toward men	1.20
To gain power	3.61
Other	9.64

Chart 6. Prior to leaving home permanently, did you live with anyone or any place other than with your parents? (N = 133)

No	34.59%
Institution	21.05
Foster home	7.52
Other relatives	18.05
Friends of family	1.50
Husband-boyfriend(s)	3.01
Girl friend(s)	7.52
Self	1.50
Other	5.26

Chart 7. Were either of your natural parents absent from the household while you were growing up? (N = 135)

No	29.63%
Father absent	55.56
Mother absent	10.37
Father absent due to work only	4.44
Mother absent due to work only	0.00

Chart 8. What was your relationship with your general family while growing up? ($N = 135$)

Positive relationship	33.33%
Somewhat positive	17.04
Ambivalent	8.15
Somewhat negative	5.19
Negative	11.11
No relationship	5.19
Some members positive, some negative	20.00

	Additional information ($N = 76$)
Not with family much	23.68%
Too many economic problems	6.58
Physically abused	18.42
Psychologically abused	5.26
Indulged	7.89
Head of household	6.58
Felt isolated	19.74
Other	11.84

Chart 9. From whom did you first learn of prostitution? ($N = 136$)

Read about it	9.56%
Girl friends	23.53
Relatives	18.38
Boyfriends	9.56
School peers	3.68
Through the media	5.15
Neighborhood	13.97
Associates	4.41
Other	11.76

Where did you first come into actual contact with prostitutes?	White ($N = 194$)[a]	Black ($N = 69$)[a]
Friends (of yours were prostitutes)	28.87%	28.99%
Family (member involved in prostitution)	5.67	13.04
School (school mates were prostitutes)	3.61	5.80
Jail	17.01	1.45
Neighborhood (prostitutes worked near where you lived)	9.28	24.64
On the street	19.07	20.29
In a house	2.58	2.90
Mediated through pimp-dealer-hustler	2.58	1.45
Other	11.34	1.45

[a]Includes nonprostitute subjects.

Chart 10. While a juvenile, did your sexual activity ever get you in trouble? (Percentage of
          those who answered yes)[a]

Parents gave difficulty	27.87%
Because of incest	3.28
Because of rape	11.48
Because of pregnancy	31.15
Because of veneral disease	8.20
Needed and abortion	3.28
Recognized as promiscuous	6.56
Recognized as a prostitute	8.20

[a]55.15 percent answered no (N = 75); 44.85 percent answered yes (N = 61).

Chart 11. Frequency of orgasm?

	Bell & Balter	James[a]
Always	6%	33.5%
Usually	22	33.1
Sometimes	31	26.0
Never	41	5.2
Multiple orgasms	–	5.6

[a]excluding customers.

Chart 12. Why do you continue to work?

	1st response (N = 131)	2nd response (N = 65)
Money-material goods	58.78%	16.92%
Excitement-adventure	3.82	7.69
Influence of girl friends	0.76	1.54
Curiosity	0.00	–
Independence	–	7.69
Money for drugs for self	14.50	12.31
Money for drugs for man-boyfriend	0.76	13.85
Influence of man-boyfriend	7.63	4.62
Enjoy life-style	0.76	18.46
Self-abasement	0.00	3.08
Hostility to men	0.00	1.54
Economic necessity	9.92	6.15
Other	3.05	6.15

Chart 13. What are the disadvantages of being a prostitute? (N = 134)

Police-jail-legal expense	32.84%
Danger from customers	16.42
Family reaction	2.24
Society's reaction	2.99
Physical stress-venereal disease	10.45
Emotional Stress	14.93
Control by pimp	2.24
Effect on own children	0.75

Long hours-hard work-working conditions	2.24
Lowered self-esteem	7.46
No future	2.24
Personal vulnerability	0.75
Other	4.48

Chart 14. What do you feel would enable you to stop?

	1st response (N = 130)	2nd response (N = 58)
No desire to stop	10.77%	8.62%
Adequate employment	30.77	12.07
Abstinence from narcotics-drugs	10.00	6.90
Education-training	3.08	10.34
Change in self (self-determination)	14.62	17.24
Change in social environment-life-style	9.23	22.41
Legalization of prostitution	3.08	8.62
Need to be kept busy	0.77	3.45
Increased alternatives-options	3.85	6.90
Other	13.08	17.24
Marry wealthy	0.77	3.45

Chart 15. What do you see as the primary obstacle to your future success?

	1st response (N = 134)	2nd response (N = 50)
Economic need	11.94%	12.00%
Addiction	14.18	4.00
Low self-esteem, depression	17.91	6.00
Lack of alternatives	7.46	16.00
Social environment-friends	2.24	8.00
Husband-man's influence	2.99	14.00
Legal system	15.67	6.00
Lack of education	10.45	24.00
Other	17.16	10.00

10 Hustling for Rights

Marilyn G. Haft

George Bernard Shaw must be smiling down on San Francisco. In the 80 years since he wrote *Mrs. Warren's Profession*, attacking society's hypocrisy toward prostitutes, few voices have been raised in their behalf. Now, San Francisco has provided him with a receptive audience: it has just seen the formation of the first prostitutes' union. Called COYOTE, "a loose woman's organization," its name stands for "Call Off Your Old Tired Ethics" —an acronym inspired by the activities of the most promiscuous creature of the desert. COYOTE's founder, who has appointed herself *chairmadam*, is Margo St. James, a salty, bright, ex-law student, ex-hooker turned unionizer. She has put her town in an uproar with outrageously frank and witty exposes, speeches, articles, and leaflets pointing up the hypocrisy and ignorance surrounding society's and the law's treatment of prostitutes.

The primary goal of St. James and COYOTE is not to legalize prostitution, but to *decriminalize* it; that is, to remove prostitution from any government involvement or control. Merely making prostition legal is abhorrent to COYOTE because it would still enable the government to license and regulate what a woman does with her own body.

St. James has directed her scorn and wrath at her former "johns"—among them, judges, prosecutors, and jailers—who disavow the very women they've patronized once the women have been arrested and find themselves in jail, court, and prison. She has attacked the double sexual standard used in enforcing the prostitution laws: the prostitute is prosecuted, whereas the "respectable" male customer rarely is dragged into court except to testify against her, even though participation in prostitution is illegal for both. And she has disclosed the not-so-funny and often corrupt antics of vice-squad cops in pursuing these "victimless criminals."

Among her momentos is a tape recording of a telephone conversation in which a San Francisco intelligence-squad detective makes a pitch for her to arrange some "girls" for him and his friends. She tells of a recent raid on a fancy bordello in which uniformed vice-squad cops dressed in riot helments complete with chin straps ran from room to room "searching the premises" while the cooler plainclothesmen made off with 60 bottles of liquor from the bar. During a struggle with a police officer over possession of a "little black

Marilyn G. Haft. "Hustling for Rights," *The Civil Liberties Review.* ©1974 by the Civil Liberties Union. Reprinted by permission.

book," the madam leaped or was pushed from a third-story window to the cement courtyard below; she may never walk again. Recently, St. James marshaled prostitutes to picket respectable hotels that regularly supply vice-squad cops with rooms where hookers are ensnared and arrested, sometime before and sometimes after full services are performed.

Since COYOTE's formation on May 1, 1973, a lawsuit has been filed and a preliminary injuction granted prohibiting the administration of mandatory penicillin injections to all women arrested for prostitution in San Francisco. COYOTE has publicized the fact that contrary to popular belief most prostitutes do not have venereal disease; furthermore, the injections can cause manilia (a yeast infection), can breed VD strains resistant to antibiotics, and can even result in death from drug reaction. These and similar exposes have helped to mobilize prostitutes and some of the most influential men and women in San Francisco in COYOTE's campaign to decriminalize prostitution.

Unity among prostitutes has not been limited to the West Coast. Suburban New York's Westchester County witnessed a first show of strength, even before the formation of COYOTE, when a group of prostitutes stormed a feminist meeting that had been called to discuss rehabilitating prostitutes. The feminists were convinced that by performing as paid sex objects prostitutes perpetrate the ultimate insult on themselves and all women. The prostitutes broke up the meeting, announcing they neither needed nor wanted to be rehabilitated. Calling the stunned feminists hypocrites and whores, they asked how many women could honestly say they did not prostitute themselves to men in marriage or other sexual relationships for security and financial support. Women of all classes are taught to "hustle" at an early age in order to sell themselves they declared, and "hustle" men in most sexual relationships. Finally, they called for an end to the ignorance and false piety with which "proper" women and men stigmatize prostitutes.

Prostitutes do not stand alone in their nascent struggle for legal rights and social acceptance. This past year [1974] has seen a sudden groundswell of interest in studying, challenging, and dismantling prostitution laws. The women's movement, legislators, the courts, lawyers, and civil liberties organizations all are beginning to act on some recognition that prostitution must either be decriminalized, or at the very least, the laws must be enforced equally against prostitute and customer. As a result of legal action, an Alaska court found that the state's solicitation law violated the equal protection clause of the Constitution because it made solicitation by females criminal but excluded male prostitutes and male customers from its purview. A Minnesota court struck down an ordinance that violated equal protection because it criminalized prostitution by females only. The District of Columbia Superior Court overturned the D.C. solicitation statute on the grounds of unequal enforcement and invasion of privacy. And in Louisiana a state court declared unconstitutional a statute that punished women but provided no penalties for men involved with prostitutes.

Numerous groups are beginning to press for changes in the law. The ACLU Sexual Privacy Project, for example, is participating in the challenge to Louisiana's prostitution laws and is planning a challenge in Indiana where only prostitution by females is criminal. The new Victimless Crime Project of the Northern California affiliate of the ACLU is concentrating its efforts on decriminalizing sex acts between consenting adults in that state, with a special focus on prostitution. The Minnesota Civil Liberties Union is joining the attack on its state's unequal prostitution laws. In 1972 the American Bar Association's Special Committee on Crime Prevention and Control, headed by Edward Bennett Williams, issued a report, "New Perspectives on Urban Crime," that calls for the decriminalization of prostitution. Recently, the ABA's Committee on Individual Rights and Responsibilities established a special subcommittee under its Equal Protection Committee to study and report on decriminalizing prostitution.

The National Organization of Women recently established a committee on prostitution and is collaborating with the ACLU on a pamphlet calling for decriminalization. And groups of women law students and women attorneys in California are producing a pamphlet advising prostitutes of their rights if arrested, and another urging defense lawyers to raise constitutional challenges when defending their prostitute clients.

On the national level, 3 governmental committees have taken an initial look at the problem of prostitution and have recommended that closer studies be made to determine the advisability of decriminalizing it.[1]

Why now? Why have the members of the oldest profession and their allies suddenly coalesced into America's youngest protest movement? The answer lies essentially in a confluence of events. The rise of the women's movement, expanding notions of the laws of privacy and equal protection, the encouragement of a number of civil rights lawyers, and a new concern about victimless crimes, all have contributed. Most importantly, an increasingly frank, public discussion of sexual mores has helped lift the shroud of secrecy and ignorance enveloping prostitution and has made the time propitious.

The Supreme Court last year handed down decisions on abortion and on sex discrimination in employee benefits that expanded the concepts of sexual privacy and equal protection. These decisions made it obvious to lawyers that the prostitution laws proscribing private sexual activity between consenting adults stand in conflict with the Constitution. Enforcement of those laws unequally against women clearly violates the Court's mandate against sex discrimination under the equal protection clause.

And prostitutes at last are willing to act in concert to assert their rights. This willingness, along with the interest of feminist lawyers on their behalf, certainly is an outgrowth of the activism generated by the women's movement. (Thus far, prostitutes' liberation has been a women's movement because there are comparatively few male prostitutes.) As recently as 1969 it was all but impossible to get a prostitute to be a plaintiff in a legal challenge. That year, responding to the complaints of prostitutes outraged by dragnet arrests in Times Square, the New York Civil Liberties Union prepared to challenge the laws, among other things on the basis of unequal enforcement against women. After the arrests were halted, however, the prostitutes refused to testify.

The court decisions and the rising consciousness of women have created a sudden new interest in taking a good look at the lives of prostitutes and in examining the statutes that set them outside the law.

A History of Ignorance

Those of us setting out to learn "all you wanted to know about prostitution but didn't know whom to ask" have been astounded at the information blackout and consequent ignorance engendered by years of puritanical attitudes. Until recently our society could not countenance publicly the existence of sex outside marriage, so it generated what has become an antiquated, unworkable, and costly apparatus for controlling and hiding prostitution.

Until the Victorian era it was common for American men to marry young. Strict codes of morality in the North tended to assure marital fidelity, so there was little demand for prostitutes. In the South prior to the Civil War, black slave women were available to serve their masters' extramarital sexual predilections. It was not until westward expansion spawned towns peopled by men without women that prostitution began to flourish. It was accepted as necessary and, if not exactly supported by chambers of commerce, at least was largely ignored or restricted to specific areas. Prostitution did not become a "social problem" until around 1900 when hordes of immigrants—confused, poor, and without jobs—provided raw material for exploitation by vice rings operating in virtually every major metropolitan area and in many smaller cities. It was the prevalence of this "white slave" traffic prior to World War I that incensed the Progressive Party and gave rise to campaigns to control crime by virtually banning all but matrimonially-sanctioned sex. That turned out to be about as effective a device for controlling "illicit" sex as would be efforts to control the polluters of our air by placing restrictions on inhaling. But the Progressives were undaunted, concerned as they were with the exploitiveness of the prostitution business. Being straitlaced, they were unhappy also with the low level of public morality then current—as evidenced by the flourishing market for these white slaves and the rising incidence of venereal disease. And they were affected enough by the guilt inherent in human sexuality to want to "reform" the female souls who had gone astray. There is a congruence here with many other contemporary injustices committed in the name of reform, among them incarceration and drug control: What is now a serious infringement of privacy and equality began as an earnest if badly thought out attempt at social rehabilitation.

The immigration laws the Progressives passed (a product as much of xenophobia as of a preoccupation with vice) greatly diminished the number of immigrant girls, particularly from sourthern and eastern Europe, available for prostitution. They also passed the Federal White Slave Act, known as the Mann Act, in 1910, which was intended to curtail the seduction of American girls into prostitution. It was only a matter of time before street solicitation was prohibited and the bordellos and red-light districts shut down. Men now were forced to be more surreptitious—and to feel more guilty—when consorting with prostitutes.

Underlying the Progressive demand for reform were ideals of rehabilitation (however unrealistic), prison improvements, and the amelioration of urban living and working conditions so that women would not need to resort to prostitution. The squalid portrait of the life of the prostitute painted by the Progressives in their muckraking zeal to push through legislation, however, left the public with the worst of images. If only implicitly, all the blame for the spread of venereal disease was placed on the prostitute herself. Progressives might have been trying to save prostitutes, but they only forced them underground, stereotyped them as objects of scorn, and made them the primary victims of the laws designed originally to protect women. White slavery is hardly much of a problem any more, but prostitution laws, as they affect white and black women, are.

The puritanical suppression of prostitution in this century has so removed it as a subject of open public discussion and investigation that not many people are even aware, for example, that the United States is one of the few nations in which prostitution is illegal. When the United Nations passed a resolution in 1958 calling for decriminalization, the American press all but ignored it.[2] The "literature" on prostitution abounds with sensational and pornographic materials. Until recently few had bothered to study the efficacy of the prostitution laws, which have succeeded neither in eliminating prostitution nor in rehabilitating prostitutes. In fact, prostitution laws have become one of the most direct forms of discrimination against women, especially poor and black women. This is just one of the reasons they are unconstitutional.

Prostitution Statutes: Unfair and Unenforceable

Prostitution and prostitution-related activity such as pimping, procuring, and running a house of prostitution are outlawed in various forms in every jurisdiction except Nevada, where local counties may opt for legalization. Thirty-eight states outlaw the act of prostitution by forbidding the performance of sexual acts for payment. Forty-four states and the District of Columbia attempt to suppress prostitution by laws against solicitation that proscribe the preliminary bargaining. In Iowa, Michigan, Missouri, Montana, Nevada, Rhode Island, and the District of Columbia solicitation for the purposes of prostitution is illegal, although prostitution itself is not. The mere *status* of being a prostitute is a crime under state vagrancy laws in Washington, Montana, New Hampshire, Nebraska, Okalahoma, and Texas. In other states the vagrancy and loitering laws commonly are used to harass and arrest people who are suspected of being prostitutes or of participating in prostitution. The most recent addition to the arsenal of anti-prostitution laws are state and municipal statutes aimed at regulating or eliminating massage parlors. In order to deter prostitution, a number of jurisdictions have enacted statutes and ordinances to regulate sexual entertainment in places that have state-authorized liquor permits.

The plethora of laws prohibiting prostitution have had little success. Streetwalkers, bar girls, and call girls ply their trade in every American city. Estimates of the number of full-time prostitutes in this country today range between 250,000 and 500,000.[3] Their primary market consists of white, middle-class men between ages 30 and 60.[4]

The women most penalized by the law are black and poor—racism is as prevalent in the business of prositution as everywhere else in our society. Many bar owners, hotel keepers, and landlords do not allow black prostitutes to use their premises, so black women are forced onto the streets and into blatant solicitation where the risk of arrest is highest. It is 7 times more likely that prostitution arrests will involve black women than women of other races.[11] As might be expected, the largest proportion of arrests of black prostitutes takes place in the inner cities where living standards are low, the level of desperation high, and police prejudice endemic.

In 1968 there were nearly 100,000 arrests for prostitution and related crimes,[5] and the number is rising.[6] Convicted prostitutes account for 30 percent of the population of most women's jails;[7] in some cities, such as New York, they exceed 50 percent.[8] They serve longer sentences than women convicted of most other misdemeanors. Seattle spends about $1 million a year to arrest, prosecute, and jail prostitutes.[9] According to the San Francisco Crime Commission, it cost San Francisco $375,000 in 1971 to arrest and transport more than 2,000 prostitutes to the stationhouse.[10] Most were back working the streets soon after they were released. So despite the staggering outlay of time and money by police, courts, and corrections agencies, prostitution is alive and well. The law seems to be effective only to clear the streets temporarily in response to occasional community pressure. It is as unnecessary a burden on society as it is on the women who are penalized.

Prostitution, a victimless crime, is essentially a private agreement and act between 2 consenting adults. As with all victimless crimes, enforcement of the laws constitutes an increased workload on the police and the entire criminal justice system. Undoubtedly, the personnel and money could be put to better use in preventing white collar and violent crimes.

The prostitution laws are not only a drain on law enforcement, they drain respect for the law. The unsavory methods, bordering on entrapment, used by police to ensnare these "criminals" engender disrespect for the law in the eyes of the criminal and, perhaps even more importantly, in the eyes of the police themselves. In a recent survey, 53 percent of the rank-and-file policemen assigned to the streets in a metropolitan area in the state of Washington favored decriminalizing prostitution.[12] Their supervisors, who don't do the actual arresting, were not quite so willing to see the laws go, possibly because prostitution is well recognized as a lucrative source of police graft. The 1971 report of New York City's Knapp Commission on police corruption is only the latest in a series of official disclosures of high-level police collaboration with houses of prostitution.

One of the primary reasons the laws don't work is that putting a criminal label on prostitutes and locking them up does not eliminate the reasons for prostitution. Dr. Jennifer James, an anthropologist at the University of Washington medical school, spent 3 years in the streets of Seattle gaining the confidence of prostitutes who have hustled in cities throughout the country. She learned that "the life" is similar in most American cities, and that most prostitutes enter the profession for economic reasons, such as the need to escape the degradation of the welfare system, the need to support children, and the need to avoid the discrimination women face in employment.

Like their angry sisters in New York, most of the prostitutes James questioned viewed their work merely as a counterpart of the prostitution that exists in most sexual relationships between men and women, as women marry or live with men in exchange for economic support. Most believed that it is wrong to label a woman criminal or immoral if she has chosen prostitution as a way to survive—and they insisted that condemnation should be directed instead toward the economic system that leads many women to see prostitution as the least repellent mode of life available to them. Most prostitutes do not find their livelihood degrading and therefore do not see any point to being rehabilitated.

Even if rehabilitation were a desirable goal, jails certainly do not rehabilitate prostitutes. Instead, they usually serve to acquaint them with other types of crime. Time and again women in prison explain that their first arrest was for prostitution, and that only in prison did they learn to commit "real crime." Seventy percent of all women in prison today for felonies were first arrested for prostitution.[13] Actually, criminalization can trap women irrevocably into careers of prostitution, because the permanent labeling of these women as "criminals" makes it more difficult for them to obtain a legitimate job if they should wish to stop hustling. Margo St. James has commented that she "never

really did that much hooking. . . . I just wanted to earn some bucks off $20
tricks to help out friends and pay the phone bill." She had a run-in with the
San Francisco vice squad and was arrested for soliciting. "That did it. With
that record I couldn't get any other kind of job." When she was released
from jail she took up "the life."

Bail requirements also work to lock women into prostitution. With no
money and no chance of another job, they have no choice but to turn to pimps
for bail and to hit the streets again. The laws, in effect, help to sever any
normal relationships that prostitutes have with the legitimate world and drive
them into the underworld for protection and friendship where they may become involved in other crime.

As a practical matter, the laws inarguably are counterproductive. This
probably is reason sufficient for eliminating them, except that there is another
even better reason: they are violative of civil liberties. They violate the
constitutional right of privacy because they impose penal sanctions on the
private sexual conduct of consenting adults. Whether a person chooses to
engage in sexual intercourse for pure recreation or in exchange for something
of value is a matter of individual choice, not for governmental interference.
Furthermore, the use of loitering and vagrancy laws to punish prostitutes for
their status, or to arrest them on the basis of reputation and appearance, is
contrary to due process of law; and the discriminatory nature and enforcement
of the laws are certainly a violation of equal protection.

Prostitution and the Constitution

There are 4 basic grounds on which prostitution laws are, and should be found
by the courts to be unconstitutional.

Equal Protection

Prostitution laws clearly discriminate against women. In Indiana, Louisiana,
North Dakota, Wisconsin, and Wyoming, prostitution statutes apply only to
females. According to traditional case law, moreover, a prostitute is by definition a female. The law ignores the fact that male homosexuals can be prostitutes,
and that male customers, without whom prostitution would be impossible, are
accomplices in this so-called criminal act. Judicial opinions are replete with
references to the female prostitute as a "fallen woman" while her (otherwise
respectable) customers are referred to more solicitously.

However, making the language of the law applicable to both female and
male, prostitute and customer, does not eliminate actual discrimination against
women. In many states the statutes are neutral on their face, or there may be

a separate offense for "patronizing a prostitute" (although the penalty for
patronizing is usually less than for being a prostitute). But under criminal
justice systems dominated by male police, prosecutors, and judges, the male
patron is very rarely punished. The New York Code, for instance, makes
patronizing a prostitute a criminal offense, but in 1968 there were only 112
arrests of customers in New York City against 8000 arrests of prostitutes.[14]
Nationally in the same year 78 percent of those arrested for commerce in sex
were female.[15] In the few cases in which a customer is arrested, the charge
often is used as an inducement for him to testify against the prostitute.

   Washington, D.C. has had a history of unequal enforcement typical of the
rest of the country. The D.C. statute, only recently declared unconstitutional,
made it a criminal offense for "any person" to solicit for prostitution. On its
face the law was applicable to either men or women, depending on who
initiated the proceedings. The law was enforced, however, by the use of male
undercover police officers who were trained "to elicit an offer to engage in a
sexual act for a specific price." In an experiment that received nationwide
attention because of a *Newsweek* article called "Flatfoot Floozies," female
police officers were used for a short time in 1970 to enforce the law against
male customers. But the experiment soon ended because of protests from
white middle-class gentlemen from the suburbs. This blatant violation of equal
protection caused the D.C. Superior Court to strike down the District's
"facially neutral" solicitation law.

Privacy

Prostitution laws are an invasion of the individual's right to control his or her
body without unreasonable interference from the state.

   The right of privacy was elevated to a constitutional doctrine by the U.S.
Supreme Court in the *Griswold* case (1965) which struck down a Connecticut
statute prohibiting the prescription and use of contraceptive drugs or devices,
and established that the right of privacy protects married couples in deciding
if their sexual activities are to be procreational. In *Eisenstadt* v. *Baird* (1972)
the Court extended that right to unmarried people by holding unconstitutional
a Massachusetts criminal statute that prohibited the distribution of contraceptives to unmarried people except to prevent the spread of disease. Justice
William Brennan, writing for the majority, noted that "[i] f the right of privacy
means anything, it is the right of the *individual*, married or single, to be free
from unwarranted governmental intrusion. . . ." Last year, in *Roe* v. *Wade*, the
Supreme Court recognized a woman's right of privacy in the decision to term-
inate a pregnancy.

   The private sexual act involved in prostitution is no less a personal right for
being commercial. Therefore, the government should not be able to prohibit

it unless the state can meet the very heavy burden of proof that banning it is beneficial to society.

Cruel and Unusual Punishment

State vagrancy statutes that make the mere status of being a prostitute a crime are direct violations of the Eighth Amendment's prohibition against cruel and unusual punishment. In *Robinson* v. *California* (1962) the Supreme Court held that the status of being a narcotics addict (as distinguished from the act of using drugs) is protected under the Constitution and cannot be punished. The injustice of punishing someone because of what she is rather than what she does is so blatant that one federal court already has held that a vagrancy law making "common prostitutes" criminals violates the Eighth Amendment. I expect that this infringement on the constitutional rights of prostitutes will be one of the easiest to strike down.

Due Process

City loitering ordinances and vagrancy statutes are powerful weapons used by police to arrest women just for standing on the sidewalk if they "look like" prostitutes. Such arrests are often made on the basis of reputation, past record, and presence in an area in which prostitution is practiced. Police frequently make these arrests in bad faith, with no intention of prosecuting, solely to get the women and other "undesirables" off the streets. The Detroit police regularly round up suspected prostitutes as part of a so-called "disorderly persons investigation." Dayton, Ohio, has an ordinance forbidding groups to congregate if they know that a crime is being or has been committed in the area; it is used to disperse people from places where prostitutes often solicit.[16] These practices deprive those arrested of due process of law.

In *Papachristou* v. *City of Jacksonville* (1972) the Supreme Court declared unconstitutional a Florida vagrancy statute that permitted police to arrest people because of their *type* rather than their *acts*. Recognizing that the vagrancy law was being used to prosecute presumed future illegality rather than current criminality, the Court stated that a "vagrancy prosecution may merely be a cloak for a conviction which could not be obtained on the real but undisclosed grounds for arrest." The loitering laws cannot be used to sweep undesirables off the street either. The Constitution protects the "right to be let alone" unless it is necessary to protect the "rights and welfare of others." The courts have said that arbitrary and unfair law enforcement under the vagrancy and loitering statutes is "massively antithetical to traditional concepts of due process, equal protection, and individual liberty."[17]

The Compelling-State-Interest Myth

In law, a compelling state interest often is held to justify otherwise unacceptable legal restraints on personal liberty. There is a myth subscribed to by many Americans, including many civil libertarians, that the state has a compelling interest in outlawing prostitution because it is linked with organized crime and because it is responsible for much ancillary crime and for the increase in, or at least the transmission of, venereal disease. In fact, the grounds for any such compelling state interest do not exist.

Organized Crime

In 1967 the president's Commission on Law Enforcement and the Administration of Justice stated unequivocally that prostitution plays "a small and declining role in organized crime operations." Jennifer James found confirmation of this in her own studies: during 3 years of field research with prostitutes in Seattle, she saw few traces of organized crime. Prostitution is no longer an attractive investment for organized crime. First, it is too difficult to control because of the highly individualized customer-prostitute and pimp-prostitute relationships. Second, organized crime has turned to ventures that are more profitable and less fraught with risk, such as politics, business investment, the stock market, and labor unions.

Venereal Disease

The activities of prostitutes simply do not pose a substantial threat to the health of the community. An international study published more than 10 years ago by the United Nations stated that prostitution is not a major factor in the spread of venereal disease in the United States.[18] A poll of public health advisors on prostitutes and venereal disease shows that almost all believe that most prostitutes are well-educated and are watchful for the signs of venereal disease; they are aware of precautionary techniques, which include the use of prophylactics, checking customers, and seeking medical care. A prostitute's reputation is vitally important to her; a reputation as a VD carrier would cut down the relatively large volume of repeat business on which most prostitutes depend.

Dr. Charles Winick of The City College of New York and the American Social Health Association, notes: "We know from many different studies that the amount of venereal disease attributable to prostitution is remaining fairly constant at a little under 5 percent, which is a negligible proportion compared to the amount of venereal disease that we now have." The general consensus seems to be that the increase in venereal disease is the result of changes in the sexual mores of young people, unaccompanied by an improvement in their health education. In recent studies the highest rate—up to 84 percent of all reported venereal disease—is in the 15-to-30-year-old age group. Men in this age group rarely go to prostitutes (the average age of prostitutes' customers is well over 30).

Admittedly, even a 5 percent rate is a public problem. But keeping prostitutes jailed for days while awaiting results of a health inspection, or injecting them with penicillin whether they are infected or not, is meaningless. Inspection is ineffective in controlling the disease because a prostitute can acquire VD immediately after inspection and can infect numerous men before she is inspected again.

Perhaps if prostitution were not outlawed, prostitutes with venereal disease would be encouraged to seek treatment without fear of reprisal. In recognition of the fact that prostitution is not the major source of VD, 40 jurisdictions have already repealed or at least relaxed the administrative regulations requiring medical testing and treatment of prostitutes.

Ancillary Crime

In the minds of most people, larceny, robbery, assault, and narcotics are commonly associated with prostitution. And it is undeniable that some amount of such crime is indeed linked to prostitution. It is often suggested, therefore, that prostitution itself must remain illegal in order to reduce or control concomitant crime.

This contention really is more an argument for decriminalization than a justification for penal sanctions, however. If prostitution were not a crime, then those who consort with prostitutes and then become the victims of robberies and assaults might be more likely to report these crimes. But the fact is that the *prostitute* is the most frequent victim of so-called "related crimes." She is an easy target for her customer because as a criminal herself she is outside the protection of the law. Of 76 prostitutes interviewed by Jennifer James, 64 percent reported they had been injured by customers but did not seek police protection because they feared criminal sanctions.[19]

It is rare that a customer is assaulted by a prostitute or her accomplice. Such a situation is more likely to be a set-up with no intent of prostitution, or a clear case of robbery. Strict enforcement of the robbery and assault statutes is probably the most effective way to deal with that problem.

Many heroin addicts turn to prostitution to support their habits because it is one of the few easily available sources of fast money for women. Other prostitutes, however, look down on and disassociate themselves from the "hypes." The addicts are caught in a double bind, engaging in the criminal activity of prostitution to support the criminal activity of using drugs. The involvement of addicted prostitutes in drug dealing is limited, though; they rarely sell drugs, although by necessity they are associated with dealers or may be supporting addicted pimps who deal. Heroin addicts who are prostitutes pose the same problem for society as do other addicts. Keeping prostitution illegal only exacerbates the situation by making the prostitute a double fugitive from the law. Decriminalization certainly cannot worsen this dilemma.

The problem of minors and prostitution is not as knotty as the drug problem. Minors should be allowed to patronize prostitutes if they wish; that right is consistent with the present trend to extend to minors the right to obtain contraceptives and have abortions, as well as other rights of sexual privacy. There are laws in most states that proscribe sexual relations between adults and minors, so it is unnecessary to pass separate prostitution laws to prevent prostitution by minors. The effect of such laws would not be to protect minors but to stamp them as criminals and trap them in a life of crime at a very early age.

It has been argued that to decriminalize prostitution is to abandon the prostitutes to the pimps: if they no longer need fear police interference, pimps will be able to exert more powerful control over their prostitutes. The pimp menace, however, is overrated. Most prostitutes do not object to their pimps; indeed, most of those interviewed say they are in love with them: the pimp represents status much the same as a boyfriend or husband represents status and love for a woman in legitimate society. The dependence of prostitutes on pimps for love and for managing their finances probably will not change until women and men alter their roles generally.

Nevertheless, legalizing prostitution does not require eliminating laws against procuring or against assault if pimps do brutalize their women. If they were beaten, prostitutes no longer would be outside the law and could report violence to the police. But prostitutes presently fear violence from their clients and police more than from pimps. Decriminalization can in fact *loosen* any grip pimps have on prostitutes. It can foster the independence of a prostitute from her pimp if she so desires, by eliminating the need for bail, lawyers, and someone to look after her children and affairs while she is in jail.

Legislating Morality

Perhaps the greatest fear underlying all the arguments against decriminalization is that prostitution strikes at the moral fiber of this country, that it is immoral and therefore should remain outlawed. This argument cannot be dealt with lightly by those of us who fail to see sex-as-business as a step down the road to Gomorrah. It is the one point of view held by many judges, legislators, and opinion makers that is most difficult to change because its roots lie more in emotion than in reason.

However, to assert that prostitution should be decriminalized is not to assert that prostitution is moral or immoral; it is simply a judgment about the proper use of the criminal law, which is intended to protect people and property and not to legislate an individual's moral conduct. The Wolfenden Report, the well-known British study of homosexual offenses and prostitution, denounced government regulation of public morals as being beyond the scope of the law:

> Unless a deliberate attempt is made by society, acting through the agency of the law, to equate the sphere of crime with that of sin, there must remain a realm of private morality and immorality which is, in brief and crude terms, not the law's business.[20]

To legislate morality probably violates the establishment clause of the First Amendment. To attempt to enforce morality by means that often are demeaning or even illegal undermines the very rule of law.

Prostitution Yes, Solicitation No?

If the state has no compelling interest in prohibiting prostitution, does it at least have an interest in keeping prostitutes off the streets? Is it not in the interest of the state to protect the public from annoying and offensive solicitation and to ensure orderly streets and the free flow of pedestrian traffic?

I would like to be able to argue that solicitation laws are an unconstitutional violation of free speech. This claim has little chance of being upheld, however, because prostitution is essentially a commercial enterprise. But to legalize prostitution while prohibiting solicitation mades as much sense as encouraging free elections but prohibiting compaigning. Solicitation should be decriminalized for the very same reasons that laws against prostitution should be eliminated. Prostitutes are arrested for solicitation more than for the actual act of prostitution. Even if prostitution were legal, the prostitute who went out to solicit business would still be labeled a criminal. The result would have the same detrimental and counterproductive consequences as do other anti-prostitution laws.

The question is whether men are really offended by prostitutes' solicitations. Probably not; there is little evidence that they are. Furthermore, prostitutes usually solicit in areas and at times of the night when they are most likely to find willing customers.

Women have traditionally been the object of "pick-up" attempts and off-color remarks by men on the streets, yet there is no outcry to criminalize those solicitations, although they are highly offensive to women. In line with notions of fair play and equal protection, both forms of solicitation should be outlawed or neither form should be. And it is unlikely that male solicitation of females will be outlawed.

Britain made prostitution legal, but its Street Offences Act of 1959 made soliciting a punishable deed. Although British streets are relatively clear of prostitutes, many protection rackets involving graft and coercion have developed because of the criminal statutes barring solicitation. It would seem the Street Offences Act has brought a net loss in morality.

Many people fear that if the prostitution laws go, prostitutes will invade respectable neighborhoods. Zoning, a practice used to prevent other undesir-ables—such as blacks—from "ruining the neighborhood," appeals to some as an expedient solution. Under this scheme, the government would treat prostitution as any other business and issue zoning ordinances to restrict prostitutes to cer-tain areas. Civil citations would be issued to violations. But the transience of the parties to solicitation, the likelihood that prostitutes would not comply if they were segregated to unlucrative areas, and the fact that it is likely most neighborhoods would try to zone out prostitution, point to enforcement prob-lems and probable failure.

A civil citation system may not be completely impracticable, though. It is being tested in part in Eugene, Oregon, where civil, rather than criminal, cita-tions are being issued for public solicitation. To date everyone has shown up to pay the tickets. But it is not clear if the system has discouraged blatant solicitation.

Some may have visions of prostitutes lined up 10-deep, hustling at hotel doorways and subway entrances once the criminal solicitation laws are repealed. But criminal laws protecting citizens against assault should discourage unwanted physical contact from a prostitute soliciting on the street, while very narrowly drawn *civil* regulations could keep abusive hawking of wares down to a minimum.

The solicitation question is a complex one, and any claim to having all the answers would be foolhardy. Decriminalizing commercial sex and solicitation is the first and necessary step. If complete government disassociation is un-workable, in time some accommodation—through civil regulation—may have to be made.

Licensing

The thought of prostitution flourishing unfettered in America troubles some civil libertarians who, though they readily agree that our present laws are oppressive, lean toward licensing or other types of civil regulation as a reasonable alternative to criminal laws. But the experience of other countries teaches that it is not really a workable alternative to complete decriminalization.

The main reason usually given for licensing prostitution is that government would then have an opportunity to require health inspections of licensed prostitutes so as to protect customers from the hazard of venereal disease. But the VD argument for control of prostitution, as I hope I have already shown, is spurious. Other concerns that people may think call for government regulation, such as protecting consumers against prostitutes who defraud them by not performing, can be managed under the criminal law. And after all, in most industries, word of an unscrupulous merchant usually gets around pretty quickly.

A system of licensing would stigmatize those who hold licenses as prostitutes. Because of our society's current attitudes toward prostitution, it probably would prevent prostitutes who later wished to obtain other types of employment from doing so. Actually, a license system might further encourage prostitution because a prostitute's license could become a condition of employment for such jobs as dancer or cocktail waitress—which is just fine if the government's overriding interest is in augmenting the available supply of prostitutes.

Prostitution is legal in most places in the world. Countries in the Middle East, the Far East, the Caribbean, and South America regulate it by requiring brothels to be licensed and by subjecting prostitutes to health inspections. Some countries that formerly regulated prostitution through licensing did so in an attempt to stem rampant disease by concentrating prostitutes in specified districts where their health could be monitored. They found, however, that it was impossible to regulate prostitutes because a majority would not register and would not be herded into licensed brothels. They also learned that inspecting prostitutes did not prevent venereal disease from spreading.

The nations that decriminalized prostitution and that completely disentangled themselves from regulations usually arrived at their position after experiencing the failure of licensing. France, Britain, Italy, Japan, Germany, and a total of 100 members of the United Nations, with UN endorsement, have eliminated the crime of prostitution and have abandoned experiments at regulation. The criminal laws in those countries seek instead to control public solicitation and to discourage the pimps and procurers who live off the earnings of prostitutes.

West Germany has become the most open-minded of countries in its treatment of prostitution. There, prostitution is considered a social necessity, and the government actively supports the building of pimp-free prostitution hostels where prostitutes can live and work in comfortable rooms with access to shopping centers, bowling and tennis, and mandatory medical inspection.

It is fashionable in Germany to consider the hostels as the solution to prostitution; but even in Germany most prostitutes live outside these hostels, and a number of the hostel residents see their pimps "on the side."

The newest commercial innovation is a public offering of limited partnership interests in new hostel operations in a number of western European countries. This is thought to be the first time capital has been raised publicly for such an enterprise; 120 investors have already bought $1.5 million worth of these partnerships.[21]

The notion of prostitution as a legitimate business is on the horizon. Some have suggested that if the profession is to be recognized then government ought to have the right to exercise some regulation over it as a retail service industry for purposes of consumer protection. Although the idea may be laudable in certain respects, the fact is that government control of prostitution has never worked before, and there is no reason to believe it can be feasible now.

Unions, public stock offerings, and laissez-faire proposals are all a far cry from America's ubiquitous policed puritanism. But virtually anything that indicates some movement away from know-nothingism and toward affording prostitutes the equality and privacy to which they (and their customers) have a right, is laudable. It is a pity that prostitution has been swept under the moral rug all these years, for our ignorance about it has encouraged the myths that have stood in the way of rational behavior. It is time for us to acknowledge that the American way of sex has been hypocritical, ineffective, and inequitable in its treatment of prostitutes and prostitution, and that we must begin to explore some of the (admittedly complex) options that are available. One of these may be that not everything in our society can or should be regulated by law because to do so is not realistic, constitutional, or just.

A Note on Sources

The most comprehensive, serious book on prostitution to date is Charles Winick's and Paul Kinsie's, *The Lively Commerce* (1971) which is valuable for its compilation and presentation of otherwise uncollected reports and studies on prostitution.

Charles Rosenbleet's and Barbara J. Pariente's, "The Prostitution of the Criminal Law," 11 *American Criminal Law Review*, 373 (1973) has a fine analysis of the constitutionality of the prostitution laws. The prostitution statutes of all states and the District of Columbia and a number of cities are collected and summarized as an appendix to the article.

An unpublished paper prepared by Judge Charles W. Halleck, "Legal Regulation of Commercial Sex: A Survey," for the SIECUS Conference in October 1973 surveys and discusses the constitutionality of all types of laws regulating commercial sex in this country including prostitution, soliciting, procuring, massage parlors, and liquor licensing.

Vern Bullough's *The History of Prostitution* (1964) is an interesting and well-documented history of prostitution in this country. Other good published works on the history of prostitution are W. O'Neill's, *Everyone Was Brave* (1969) and T. C. Esseltyn's, "Prostitution in the United States," 376 Annals of the American Academy of Political and Social Sciences 123 (March, 1968).

The history of prostitution and licensing in foreign countries is discussed in A. Flexner's, *Prostitution in Europe* (1914); Winick's and Kinsie's, *The Lively Commerce*, (1971); and "An International Dilemma: A Comparative Study of Foreign and Domestic Prostitution," (1972) an unpublished paper by law student William B. Stadiem on file with me.

N. Morris's and G. Hawkins's, *The Honest Politician's Guide to Crime Control* (1970) and H. L. Packer's, *The Limits of the Criminal Sanction* (1968) should be consulted for comprehensive and thoughtful discussions of victimless crimes and their relation to morality, law enforcement, and the criminal justice system.

I relied very heavily on the innovative thinking of Jennifer James in my treatment of the myths surrounding prostitution, including the involvement of organized crime, ancillary crime, pimps, and venereal disease. Some of her works include *A Formal Analysis of Prostitution in Seattle* (1972), a doctoral thesis based on 3 years of research in the streets, of police files, health reports and surveys, statistical analyses, and interviews; Burnstin and James, "Prostitution in Seattle," *Washington State Bar News* (August-September 1971); and "The Law and Commercialized Sex," an unpublished paper presented at a SIECUS Conference, October 26, 1973. She and I are collaborating on a pamphlet to be published shortly by NOW advocating the decriminalization of prostitution.

The article, "Legal, Medical and Psychiatric Considerations in the Control of Prostitution," by B. J. George, 60 *Michigan Law Review,* 717 (1962), and the works of Jennifer James look at the psychological reasons that women turn to prostitution.

Most of the stories about and by Margo St. James and COYOTE are reported in the *Seattle Post-Intelligencer,* August 19, 1973, p. A 18.

Statistics and studies on venereal disease may be found in the following: "Prostitution and Venereal Disease," (report on UN survey) 13 *International Review of Criminal Policy,* 67 (October 1958); Burnstin & James, "Prostitution in Seattle," *Washington State Bar News,* 29 No. 1 (survey of public health advisors); Winick, C., "Should Prostitution Be Legalized?" *Sexual Behavior,* 72 (January 1972); Wilcox, R. R., "Prostitution and Venereal Disease," 38 *British Journal of Venereal Disease,* 37-42 (1962); Rosenthal, T. and Vandow, J., "Prevalence of Venereal Disease in Prostitutes," 34 *British Journal of Venereal Disease,* 94-99 (1959); Winick & Kinsie, *The Lively Commerce, supra* (all corroborate the 5 percent figure for VD in prostitutes); VD Fact Sheet, "Basic Statistics on Venereal Disease Problems in the United States," Department of HEW Center for Disease Control, Atlanta, Georgia (1971) (says 84 percent of VD is found in people 15-30 years of age); Winick & Kinsie, *The Lively Commerce, supra,* 66-67 (dangerous effects of overuse of penicillin to treat VD); George, B. J., "Legal, Medical and Psychological Considerations in the Control of Prostitution," *supra*, 740 (40 jurisdictions repealed or relaxed mandatory treatment or examination of prostitutes for VD).

A special note of thanks goes to Dee Pridgen, third-year student at New York University School at Law, for her legal research on the constitutionality of the prostitution laws.

Cases Discussed

Prostitution

State v. *Fields*, Crim. No. 72-4788 (3d Jud. Dist. Ct., Alaska, June 27, 1973). Opinion excerpted in 13 Cr. L. R. 2376. Case was reversed and remanded for evidence of unequal enforcement by the Alaska Superior Court, Case No. 73-416 Cr. (Nov. 26, 1973).

State v. *Woods*, No. 443072 (Minneapolis, Minn., Mun. Ct. Dec. 21, 1971).

City of Portland v. *Sherrill*, No. M-47623 (Multnumah County, Oregon Cir. Ct. Jan. 10, 1067).

United States v. *Moses*, Superior Court of the District of Columbia, Crim. No. 17778-72 (Nov. 3, 1972). An excerpted version of the opinion is published in 41 U.S.L.W. 2298.

Griggs v. *Scott*, Civ. No. 669690 (San Francisco Superior Court filed Jan. 9, 1974). A temporary injunction issued against VD examination and treatment. Attys: ACLU of Northern California.

Fletcher v. *Giarrusso*, Civ. No. 73-1939-G (E.D.La., 1973). Three-judge court convened to challenge Louisiana prostitution laws.

State v. *Devall*, No. 12-73-7806, 19th Judicial District Ct. (Feb. 8, 1974). Louisiana prostitution statute unconstitutional.

Kirkwood v. *Loeb*, 323 F. Supp. 611 (W.D. Tenn. 1971). The mere status of being a "common prostitute" is not punishable under criminal law.

In re Carey, 57 Cal. App. 297 (1922). Prostitute as "fallen woman."

People v. *Anonymous*, 161 Misc. 379, 292 N.Y.S. 282 (1936). Prostitutes' customer respectable.

Ladweg v. *Arlington Hotel*, 286 S.W.2d 853 (Ark. 1956); *People ex. rel. Anderson* v. *Chicago*, 312 Ill. App. 187, 37 N.E. 2d 929 (1941); *New York State Society of Medical Masseurs, Inc.* v. *City of New York*, 345 N.Y.S. 2nd 866 (1973). Massage parlor cases.

California v. *LaRue*, 409 U.S. 109 (1972); *Cherbounie* v. *Kergler*, 359 F. Supp. 252 (D. New Jersey 1973). Liquor licensing and sex shows.

Equal Protection

Frontiero v. *Richardson,* 411 U.S. 677 (1973). Plurality of Supreme Court found discrimination on basis of sex a suspect classification under equal protection clause.
Roe v. *Wade,* 410 U.S. 113 (1973). Abortion decision.
Prostitution cases: *State* v. *Fields, supra; State* v. *Woods, supra; U.S.* v. *Moses, supra; State* v. *Devall, supra.*

Right of Privacy

Roe v. *Wade,* 410 U.S. 113 (1973).
Griswold v. *Connecticut,* 381 U.S. 479 (1965).
Eisenstadt v. *Baird,* 405 S. 438 (1972).

Cruel and Unusual Punishment

Robinson v. *California,* 370 U.S. 660 (1962).
Kirkwood v. *Loeb,* 323 F. Supp. 611 (W.D. Tenn. 1971), *supra.*

Due Process

Papachristou v. *City of Jacksonville,* 405 U.S. 156 (1972).
Reno v. *Second Judicial District Court,* 83 Nev. 427 P. 2d 4 (1967). Struck down the law criminalizing "persons of evil reputation."
Fenster v. *Leary,* 20 N.Y. 2d 309, 282 N.Y.S. 2d 739, 229 N.E. 2d 426 (1967). New York City vagrancy law struck down.
Decker v. *Fillis,* 306 F. Supp. 613 (D. Utah, 1969). Found that status crimes are abused by police as a means of getting "undesirables" off the streets.
Seattle v. *Drew,* 70 Wash. 2d 405, 423 P. 2d (1967). Loitering laws cannot interfere with "the right to be let alone" unless necessary to protect "the rights and welfare of others."

First Amendment (Solicitation)

Valentine v. *Christensen,* 316 U.S. 52 (1942).
New York Times v. *Sullivan,* 376 U.S. 254 (1964).

Pittsburgh Press Co. v. *Pittsburgh Commission on Human Rights,* _____ U.S.
_____, 93 S. Ct. 2553 (1973).

Notes

1. *Task Force Report on Law and Law Enforcement to the National Com-
mission on the Causes and Prevention of Violence* (1970); National Advisory
Commission on Criminal Justice Standards and Goals, *A National Strategy to
Reduce Crime* (1973); Report of the Select Committee on Crime of the House
of Representatives, *Street Crime Reduction Through Positive Criminal Justice
Responses* (1973).

2. The official UN position has been set forth in a report, *Study in Traffic
in Persons and Prostitution.* The report was adopted as a resolution, U.N. Gen.
Ass. Re. IV, on Dec. 2, 1949, effective July 25, 1951.

3. C. Winick and P. Kinsie, *The Lively Commerce, Prostitution in the
United States,* 5 (1971).

4. C. Winick, "Clients' Perceptions of Prostitutes and of Themselves."
International Journal of Social Psychiatry, Vol. 8 (1961-1962); Harry Benjamin
and R. E. L. Masters, *Prostitution and Morality* (1964); Jennifer James, *A Formal
Analysis of Prostitution in Seattle* (1972); Kinsey, Pomeroy, Martin, and Gebhard.
Sexual Behavior in the Human Male, 597 (1948).

5. *Uniform Crime Reports in the United States,* FBI (1968). Winick and
Kinsey supra, at 4 agree with the figure of 95,550 arrests for 1966.

6. *The New York Times* August 14, 1967, at 1; August 21, 1967, at 16;
January 27, 1969, at 20; September 30, 1969, at 11; San Francisco Committee
on Crime, *Report on Non-Victim Crime in San Francisco* (1971).

7. James, Jennifer, *A Formal Analysis of Prostitution, Final Report to the
Division of Research, Part I—Basic Statistical Analysis,* University of Washington,
1971.

8. FBI *Uniform Crime Reports* (1969). In D. C. the figure is 40 percent.
D. C. Department of Corrections Research Report No. 39, *Movement and
Characteristics of Women's Detention Center* (1969).

9. Burnstin, J. and James, J., "Prostitution in Seattle," *Washington State
Bar News,* 29 No. 31 (August-September 1971).

10. San Francisco Committee on Crime, *Report on Non-Victim Crime in
San Francisco* (1971).

11. FBI *Uniform Crime Reports* (1969-1971); D. C. Department of Corrections Research Report No. 43 (1971).

12. *Second Mile,* program and publication sponsored by the Puget Sound
Coalition through the resources of the Law and Justice Planning Office, Olympia,
Washington, 1973.

13. *Id.*

14. *The New York Times,* January 27, 1969, at 1.

15. FBI *Uniform Crime Reports,* 116 (1968).

16. W. LaFave, *Arrest, the Decision to Take a Suspect into Custody,* 450-456 (1965).

17. *United States* v. *Moses,* Superior Court of the District of Columbia, Crim. No. 17778-72, at 21 (November 3, 1972).

18. "Prostitution and Venereal Disease," 13 *International Review of Crim. Policy* 67, 69 (October 1958).

19. James, J., *A Formal Analysis of Prostitution, op. cit.*

20. *Wolfenden Report: Committee on Homosexual Offenses and Prostitution Reports,* 247, (1951).

21. *Wall Street Journal,* December 31, 1971, at 1.

About the Contributors

Karen Blumenthal earned the MSW from Columbia University. She served as consultant on the Children's Defense Fund study of the children of women prisoners, and is currently special assistant to the Assistant Commissioner of the New York City Department of Social Services.

Jennifer James received the PhD. in anthropology from the University of Washington where she is now assistant professor. She spent several years gaining the confidence of prostitutes in Seattle for work on her dissertation and has since become a leading advocate for decriminalization of prostitution.

Marilyn G. Haft received the J.D. from New York University and is now with the American Civil Liberties Union as head of its National Project on Sexual Privacy. As a member of the American Bar Association, she continues to promote endorsement by that organization and the legal profession for the decriminalization of prostitution. She chairs an ABA subcommittee on prostitution and one on victimless crimes.

Dorie Klein is a doctoral candidate at the School of Criminology, University of California, Berkeley. She is currently engaged in research on methadone and is on the Editorial Board of *Crime and Social Justice,* a journal of radical criminology.

Brenda G. McGowan earned her Doctorate in Social Work at Columbia University where she is now an assistant professor. Her dissertation research "Case Advocacy: A Study of the Interventive Process in Child Advocacy" led the way to her role as the lead researcher on the Children's Defense Fund study of the children of female offenders.

Rosemary Sarri received the PhD. in social work and sociology from the University of Michigan. For several years she was head of the doctoral program in social work and social sciences at that university and is now co-director of the National Assessment of Juvenile Corrections.

Elaine Selo is a doctoral candidate in sociology at the University of Michigan. She currently doubles as an instructor in the School of Social Work at the university and a research associate on the National Assessment of Juvenile Corrections.

Patsy Sims has been a staff reporter with the San Francisco *Chronicle,* New Orleans *States-Item,* and Philadelphia *Inquirer.* Both her *States-Item* series on sugar cane workers and on black-white relations in New Orleans won investigative reporting awards in the Louisiana-Mississippi Associated Press Awards competition.

Carolyn Temin received the J.D. from the University of Pennsylvania Law School. After several years as a private attorney in criminal law, she is now assistant district attorney in Philadelphia. Ms. Temin was counsel for appellants in *Commonwealth* v. *Daniel* and *Commonwealth* v. *Douglas,* the Pennsylvania cases which she discusses in her article.

About the Editor

Laura Crites received her MS in Administration of Justice from American University. She is recipient of a "distinguished alumni award" from that institution for her contribution to the field of criminal justice. She is former director of the American Bar Association's National Resource Center on Women Offenders.

0

Please remember that this is a library book,
and that it belongs only temporarily to each
person who uses it. Be considerate. Do
not write in this, or any, library book.